W9-CXW-658

PERGAMON GENERAL PSYCHOLOGY SERIES

Editors: Arnold P. Goldstein, *Syracuse University*
Leonard Krasner, *SUNY, Stony Brook*

Psych City: A Simulated Community
(An Integrated Learning Experience in the Psychology
of Community Participation)

PGPS-35

Psych City:

A Simulated Community

(An Integrated Learning Experience in the Psychology
of Community Participation)

⌐ROBERT COHEN, JOHN McMANUS,
DAVID FOX, and CONNIE KASTELNIK ⌐
Institute for Community Development
Syracuse, N.Y.

PERGAMON PRESS INC.

New York · Toronto · Oxford · Sydney · Braunschweig

PERGAMON PRESS INC.
Maxwell House, Fairview Park, Elmsford, N.Y. 10523

PERGAMON OF CANADA LTD.
207 Queen's Quay West, Toronto 117, Ontario

PERGAMON PRESS LTD.
Headington Hill Hall, Oxford

PERGAMON PRESS (AUST.) PTY. LTD.
Rushcutters Bay, Sydney, N.S.W.

VIEWEG & SOHN GmbH
Burgplatz 1, Braunschweig

Library of Congress Cataloging in Publication Data
Main entry under title:

Psych City, a simulated community.

(Pergamon general psychology series, 35)
"Readings and exercises": p.
Includes bibliographical references.
1.   Community life--Simulation methods.
2.   Social participation.   I.   Cohen, Robert, 1941–
HM131.P734   1973   301.34'01'84   72-11593
ISBN 0-08-017082-X
ISBN 0-08-017083-8 (pbk)

Printed in the United States of America

For Nancy, Eli, Terry, Charles, and Josephine

Contents

List of Tables

ABOUT THE AUTHORS

Robert Cohen (Ph.D. Syracuse University) is the Director of the Institute for Community Development, an independent, not-for-profit organization concerned with the application of social science knowledge and methods toward the resolution of community problems. He also holds adjunct teaching appointments at Syracuse University and Upstate Medical Center. He was formerly Head of the Institute for Community Psychology at Syracuse University. He and William Claiborn co-edited *School Intervention* (Behavioral Publications)—a book for mental health practitioners interested in working with school officials.

John McManus (M.A. Syracuse University) is Senior Research Psychologist for the North Central Philadelphia Community Mental Health Center, a community controlled mental health facility. His current research projects include an investigation into the role of work in the social performance of schizophrenics, developmental studies in drug and alcohol abuse, treatment modalities for these disorders and a cognitive-developmentally based program for the prevention of alcoholism. He is currently working on his Ph.D. in Social Psychology.

David Fox (Ph.D. Syracuse University) is currently a counselor at the Jewish Family and Children's Bureau in Miami, Florida. He also teaches courses at some of the local colleges. He was formerly a Research Associate at the Institute for Community Psychology. His primary interests are counseling and Community Psychology.

Connie Kastelnik (B.A. Syracuse University) is a coordinator of training and education at the Institute for Community Development. She has worked as a counselor for children with emotional difficulties, has assisted in the construction of attitude surveys, and in the development of a project which assesses community attitudes concerning issues in the public domain, has participated in community human relations projects, and has also trained groups responsible for setting up preventive drug abuse programs in the areas of communication, problem solving, group cohesion, and self-awareness.

Acknowledgments

Our primary expression of gratitude is for the students of the undergraduate community psychology course at Syracuse University, whose spirited involvement first brought Psych City to life. Their words and actions, as participants, transformed the Psych City simulation from an abstract two-dimensional manuscript into a viable learning experience.

We are also grateful to many other individuals who provided us with spiritual, intellectual, and physical assistance. Arnold P. Goldstein and Leonard Krasner gave us editorial encouragement. Steven Apter, Sidney Oglesby, and Robert P. Sprafkin, fellow workers at the Institute for Community Development, offered us continuous support. Dennis Angelini, William Claiborn, and Rosanne Orenstein contributed directly to the book by writing special selections. Assistance in the actual preparation of the manuscript was provided by Jean Allen, Trish Benton, Kenneth Bobis, Carole Fallon, Joan Early, William Ferraldo, Stuart Franklin, Linda Garnets, Linda Hassan, Lorraine Mason, John May, JoAnn Schmidt, Greg Webb, Karen Whipple, and Kathy Young. To all these people we offer our thanks.

Finally, we wish to acknowledge the support and patience of our families and close friends, who shared our frustrations and moments of joy with us.

Introduction

This book has evolved in response to our desire to create a learning experience which would help people make sense of the complex and often confusing events and patterns of life found in our contemporary communities. We wanted to enable individuals to examine the political, psychological, and social systems which influence the behavior of all members of any neighborhood, town, city, state, country, or world community. From this study, we hoped that students would be able to further develop their perspective for understanding the causes of social problems and conflict, and to appreciate the factors and forces which are involved in reducing these problems. In short, we wanted to assist people in raising their level of awareness concerning the dynamics of community behavior.

The task of developing this learning experience proved to be as awesome and challenging as it first appeared. We quickly discarded the notion that this experience could be unidimensional. Academic work by itself was too sterile; community-based experience was helpful, but did not provide enough resources for conceptual integrations and generalization; and gamelike simulations were interesting, but not very lifelike. We chose to approach the situation in a multi-method manner. Believing that significant learning involves knowledge, attitudes, emotions, and behavior, we set out to design an experience which would relate to all of these facets, individually and in relation to each other. Our aim was to reach the whole person. Realizing that any single experience can only have limited impact, we proceeded to articulate our objectives for this learning experience. We finally agreed on the following objectives:

1. To provide an opportunity for each participant to learn how another person might think, feel, and behave by role playing the part of a particular character in a simulated community situation.

2. To encourage participants to increase their awareness of how and why decisions are made and actions are taken in community settings by having participants:

(a) serve as participant observers in the simulation,
(b) attend actual community meetings,
(c) read relevant fiction and nonfiction material,
(d) engage in prescribed exercises,
(e) discuss all of these experiences.

3. To assist participants in learning to relate psychological concepts and research to community behavior by presenting experiential and academic alternatives in an integrated manner.

4. To provide participants an opportunity to assess various methods of learning about community behavior by having them experience these alternatives and presenting them with material which describes methods for assessing their experience.

NATURE AND ORGANIZATION OF BOOK

The *Psych City* book is intended to serve as a guideline for working toward these objectives. There are several components to this book. First, there is the simulated community exercise, which is structured as a town meeting, in which participants play prescribed roles in order to deal with a common problem which confronts the community in which the characters live. A second component of the book consists of a series of fiction and nonfiction readings which are organized into topics which relate to the simulation and community dynamics. These readings include theoretical articles, research reports, illustrative excerpts from literature, and essays which may facilitate the actual implementation and assessment of the simulation. Finally, there are a series of exercises which may be used as aids for clarifying and elaborating issues raised by the simulation and readings.

While the book is written so that all parts of the book form a complete and unified experience, it is possible to use only selected sections of the book. For instance, the simulation may be used without the readings in certain nonacademic settings. Or, particular exercises may be omitted and new exercises may be created by each group utilizing *Psych City*.

The book is organized into two sections: (1) the simulation exercises and (2) the accompanying readings and exercises.

Section I contains all the information needed for planning and implementing the Psych City simulation. Procedures are explained, background information about the community is given, problems and tasks are defined, and characters are described.

Section II is divided into chapters which are organized according to psychological issues or topics which relate to community behavior. Each chapter consists of commentary, readings, and exercises. At the beginning of each chapter there is an overview description of the issue written by the authors of the book. This is followed by several short readings related to the issue being discussed. Some of these readings have been selected from the large body of social scientific knowledge, while others come from the fields of essay and fictional writing. At the end of each chapter are exercises and discussion guides (References and Suggested Readings for each chapter in Section II may be found on page 321). These may serve to stimulate individual thinking and group discussion.

The chapters in Section II are presented in sequential order, which we believe corresponds with the chronological pattern of experiences which are likely to occur within the simulation. Thus, the chapter on role expectation has been placed at the beginning of the second section because we felt that participants would be dealing with what to expect from their own and other people's roles in the initial phases of the simulation. Likewise, group decision making would probably occur more frequently toward the latter part of the simulation, so we decided to place this chapter toward the end of the section.

Before proceeding to the main body of the book, there is one further observation we wish to convey. We view this book as a tool for creating an integrated learning experience. The product which the tool forges is determined by those who use the tool. In this case, both the supervisors and participants are in control of the tool. While we can supply the material needed and shape this material into the form of a tool, the success of the instrument is ultimately determined by those who use it. For this reason, we offer our suggested use of the book as a tentative guideline, rather than a rigid set of prescribed rules. Each group which engages in the Psych City experience is unique. Interests, needs, and goals vary from group to group. It is our belief that each group is in the best position to determine *its own* priorities and consequently to choose *its own* mode of operation. If a group decides that a particular method of utilizing the material in this book is more appropriate than our suggested plan, we would encourage that group to follow *their* inclination. We feel that the probability that *Psych City* will stimulate a significant learning experience will be greater if its use can be adapted to the particular needs of the individuals and groups which use it.

Section I   Psych City Simulation

CHAPTER 1

What is Psych City?

Psych City is a simulated community which may be used to assist you in learning about the dynamics of community behavior. The simulation operates as a hypothetical community with its own people, resources, and problems. You will be asked to play a role in this community. It is through your activities in this role, in interaction with the role behaviors of the other members of your group, which will transform Psych City from an abstract set of descriptions into a complex, animate community.

The community is designed so that it may be used as described or adapted to the interests of your particular group. For example, the population and financial statistics presented are based on a city of approximately 100,000 people. However, percentage equivalents are given for these statistics so they may be converted to numbers appropriate for a community of 10,000 or 1,000,000, or whatever size you desire.

The basic activity medium in the simulation is the *Town Meeting*. It is in this meeting that you will come together with other group members, in your assigned roles, for the purpose of solving the problem which has been presented to your community. The solution of this problem (see Chapter 3 for description of problems) will be achieved when 75% of the community agrees upon a single plan of action regarding the problem. The Town Meeting may be used by community members for presentation of ideas, facts, and plans; persuasion, debate, and negotiations; establishing procedures and laws for the community; and voting on issues and plans.

While much activity takes place within the Town Meetings, it is also possible to break up into subgroups which meet in caucus to discuss and act upon the issues which concern the community.

3

The major key to the success of the Psych City simulation is the ability of the participants to effectively understand and enact the characters they are asked to play. You will be given some information to assist you learning your role (see Chapter 5). It is hoped that you will be able to learn enough about your role so that you will play your character as a real, complex individual, with specific interests, thoughts, and feelings, rather than as a superficial, stereotyped caricature. To accomplish this, you should attempt to meet and talk with someone who fits the description of your role.

In your simulation it will be necessary to have a *moderator*. Preferably this should be an instructor or group leader. This person will be responsible for (1) assigning roles; (2) organizing the initial Town Meeting; (3) providing necessary materials (e.g. name cards); (4) introducing information and decisions which are outside of the capabilities of the community (i.e. rulings of the governor or Supreme Court); and (5) moderating the post-simulation discussion. The moderator should *not* play an active role while the simulation is in progress (consider the moderator to be a non-participant observor); neither should the moderator attempt to steer the direction of the simulation with the exception of situations where there is an unnatural and unrealistic distribution of influence developing. The simulation is most effective when it evolves through the assumed behaviors of the role-playing participants. When this evolution is allowed to occur you may experience the early stages of the simulation as "awkward" and "slow," but momentum will increase as the participants become more familiar with their roles and less inhibited about displaying them publicly. Artificially directing the simulation from "outside" may alleviate the immediate tedium or stalemate, but will impede the potential development of the simulation into an almost-real experience.

USE OF THE BOOK

Psych City may be used by groups of people ranging in size from 1 to 50, the optimal size is 20 to 35. Preferably there should be someone such as a teacher or group leader who serves as coordinator and supervisor.

The entire experience (for one problem) may vary from 1 to 15 weeks, with our experience indicating that 6 to 8 weeks is ideal. The suggested number of hours of meeting time for the simulation is between 15 and 20 hours, with an equivalent amount of time devoted to doing exercises, and discussing the simulation and issues which emerge from it. This estimate does not include time required for reading. The total number of sessions should be predetermined so that everyone knows when the simulation ends. Each simulation session may last from 1 to 3 hours. Our suggestion is that the simulation sessions be conducted 2 or 3 times per week, for a period of 1 to $1\frac{1}{2}$ hours, allowing about 10 minutes at the end for group assessment of the session which has just been conducted. Discussion about whether people were "in character" and why people reacted in the manner they did, are examples of what might be dealt with at this time. In addition, one or two group discussion sessions of 1 to $1\frac{1}{2}$ hours should be held each week in order to work on the exercises, discuss the readings and simulation, and to integrate the various components of the experience. These discussions may be held immediately after the simulation sessions, but because people usually need time to disengage themselves from their roles, it is advisable to allow some time between the simulation and discussion sessions. Each chapter can usually be adequately covered in the course of one or two discussion sessions.

After the deadline for terminating the simulations has been reached, a number of discussion sessions should be planned. The purpose of these sessions are threefold: (1) participants will need time to analyze and assess the dynamics of what happened in the course of their simulation (e.g. what forces facilitated or impeded the solution of the problem with which they were confronted); (2) participants may wish to explore other behaviors and strategies which may have been utilized in solving the problem (e.g. how might a *real* community deal with this problem?); (3) because of the often intense personal involvement of participants in the simulation, it is important to allow people to differentiate between their responses to other members of the group as characters in the simulation and as the actual persons they are. This "de-briefing" phase is especially important when simulations have produced strong conflicts among members of the group.

CHAPTER 2

The Community

The following description of the community of Psych City can be used as it is presented (population 107,000) or can be adapted to the size of your own community. We have left blank columns next to the figures for Psych City for you to fill in the numbers corresponding to the percentages given for your own city or town. Not all relevant information is included. We recommend you do outside research in relating Psych City to your community.

You can choose to have either one or two minority groups represented in the simulation. The statistics for both are given in the tables presented below.

GEOGRAPHICAL DESCRIPTION

Your community is the size of a small city. At its widest points, Psych City is 5 miles from east to west, and 4 miles from north to south (see Fig 1). Psych City is divided geographically by railroad tracks and the major business district. The quarry and a federal housing project are located on the west side. In the east lies the business district, factories, and Psych City State College. The city is bordered on the south by Psych City Municipal Park and Psych Lake.

POPULATION

The total population of Psych City is 107,000. Whites make up the majority, constituting 65% of the population. However, Psych City has a

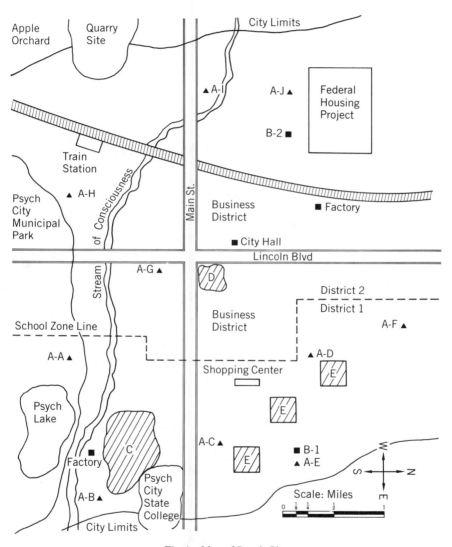

Fig. 1   Map of Psych City.

A-A to A-J: Elementary Schools   D: Downtown Land (Problem 6)
B-1 to B-2: High Schools   E: Low Income Housing (Problem 7)
C: Vacant Land (Problem 2)

sizeable minority group of 37,450 people or 35% of the total population. Table 1 breaks down the population according to sectors of the city. Table 2 shows population breakdown according to age and race.

ECONOMIC STRUCTURE

Mainly an industrial city, Psych City manufacturers employ 65% of the total working force. Of this 65%, most are employed by two factories: Ego Incorporated, located near the business district, and Id Manufacturing Company, situated near Psych City State College. The majority of white family incomes (65%) range from $6,000 to $10,000; 80% of minority group family incomes lie in the $3,000 to $6,000 bracket. The quarry and mines in the south-western area of the city are the major employers of the minority groups (80%).

There is a large local labor union in Psych City, composed mainly of those people who work in the factories, quarry, and mines.

HOUSING

Psych City has a white majority, but a sizeable minority group. As with most racially mixed cities of this size, the distribution of population by race results in areas of Psych City being either predominantly white, or predominantly minority group. The west side of the city is composed mainly of minority group and those whites of lower economic status; the east side is populated largely by middle-class whites. The more affluent citizens of Psych City also live on the east side.

Psych City's west side is typical of many city ghetto areas. The population is highly transitory, with 40% of the people having lived in the area less than 5 years. There are few homeowners; most people rent apartments or houses. In terms of education, almost half (45%) of these residents have not completed 12 years of formal schooling. There are few businesses owned and operated by the local populace.

GOVERNMENT

The city is divided into four council districts. Psych City has a mayor-council form of government. The mayor is elected every four years. Three of the seven members of City Council are elected for four-year terms at that time, with the other four councilmen being elected two years later. Three of the councilmen are elected at-large (entire city votes) and

Table 1 Population breakdown by sector.

	East Side	% of total	Your own community	West Side	% of total	Your own community	Central City	% of total	Your own community	Total	%	Your own community
White	51,467	74		16,692	24		1,391	2		69,550	100	
One minority group	4,494	12	—	32,582	87	—	374	1	—	37,450	100	—
TOTAL	55,961			49,274			1,765			107,000		
*Two minority groups												
Group 1	2,696	7.2		19,549	52.2		224	0.6		22,470	60	
Group 2	1,798	4.8		13,033	34.8		150	0.4		14,980	40	

East Side: Defined as that section of the city east of the School Zone Line,
West Side: Defined as that section of the city west of the railroad tracks,
Central City: Defined as that section of the city between the School Zone Line and the railroad tracks.
*If you prefer to use two minority groups rather than one.

9

Table 2 Population structure.

Age group	Total	%	Your own community	White	% of total	Your own community	One minority group	%	Your own community
0–14	29,000	27.1		18,000	62.0		11,000	38.0	
15–20	17,450	16.1		11,800	67.7		5,650	32.3	
21–34	14,400	13.3		8,900	61.8		5,500	38.2	
35–54	27,250	25.5		16,950	62.2		10,300	37.8	
55+	18,900	18.0		13,900	73.6		5,000	26.4	
TOTAL	107,000	100.0	—	69,550	65.0	—	37,450	35.0	—

*Optional Two Minority Group

Age group	Group 1	%	Your own community	Group 2	%	Your own community
0–14	6,600	22.8		4,400	15.2	
15–20	3,390	19.4		2,260	12.9	
21–34	3,300	22.9		2,200	15.3	
35–54	6,180	22.7		4,120	15.1	
55+	3,000	15.8		2,000	10.6	
TOTAL	22,470	21.0	—	14,980	14.0	—

*If you prefer to use two minority groups rather than one.

Table 3 Economic structure.

	Total	%	Your own community	White	% of total	Your own community	One minority group	% of total	Your own community
Agriculture	1,080	2.0		1,026	95.0		54	5.0	
Manufacturing, durable goods									
operatives	18,900	60.0		11,340	60.0		7,560	40.0	
management	2,700	5.0		2,511	93.0		189	7.0	
Quarries, mining	3,780	7.0		756	20.0		3,024	80.0	
Wholesale-retail, secretaries, clerks, small store owners	9,720	18.0		8,748	90.0		972	10.0	
Professional, doctors, lawyers, nurses, etc.	4,330	8.0		3,234	98.0		86	2.0	
Public Administration, police, teachers, civil servants, etc.	2,700	5.0		2,295	85.0		405	15.0	
Transportation	4,860	9.0		4,374	90.0		486	10.0	
Entertainment	540	1.0		513	95.0		27	5.0	
Service, minimum wage, laundry, hospital, restaurant, domestic, dishwasher, etc.	2,700	5.0		540	20.0		2,160	80.0	
Construction	2,700	5.0		2,565	95.0		135	5.0	
TOTAL	54,000	100.0		38,902	72.0		15,098	28.0	

Table 3 (*Continued*)   *Optional Two Minority Group

	Group 1	% of total	Your own community	Group 2	% of total	Your own community
Agriculture	33	3.0		21	2.0	
Manufacturing, durable goods operatives	4,536	24.0		3,024	16.0	
management	113	4.2		76	2.8	
Quarries, mining	1,814	48.0		1,210	32.0	
Wholesale-retail, secretaries, clerks, small store owners	583	6.0		389	4.0	
Professional, doctors, lawyers, nurses, etc.	52	1.2		34	0.8	
Public Administration, police, teachers, civil servants, etc.	243	9.0		162	6.0	
Transportation	291	6.0		195	4.0	
Entertainment	16	3.0		11	2.0	
Service, minimum wage, laundry, hospital, restaurant, domestic, etc.	1,296	48.0		864	32.0	
Construction	81	3.0		54	2.0	
TOTAL	9,058	16.8	—	6,040	11.2	—

*If you prefer to use two minority groups rather than one.

Table 4 Income Distribution (Family income).

	White	One minority group	*Optional two minority group	
			Group 1	Group 2
$ 0–$3,000	1.0%	3.0%	1.8%	1.2%
3,000– 6,000	9.0	80.0	48.0	32.0
6,000–10,000	65.0	15.0	9.0	6.0
10,000–20,000	23.0	2.0	1.2	0.8
20,000+	2.0	—	—	—

*If you prefer to use two minority groups rather than one.

the remaining four are elected from their districts only. This year is an election year, with the mayor, one councilman-at-large and two district councilmen running for reelection. Directors, commissioners, and chiefs of various departments in the city (police, urban development, fire, etc.) are appointed by the mayor with the approval of City Council.

Psych City has two major political parties; the Repressives and the Impulsives. The Repressive party is largely business-oriented; most of the money contributed to the party for campaigns comes from large corporations and businesses in the city. The labor force and unions are the main concern of the Impulsive party; it gains much political support and most of its campaign funds from the local labor union which, in Psych City, has a large membership. Below is a diagram (Fig. 2) of Psych City's government structure.

Psych City is located in the State of Mind. State aid is granted to Psych City for the City School district, Urban Aid to Cities, and eight other programs and projects. State funds amount to almost 30% of the total budget. In many of the problems, state aid is contingent upon the community reaching certain decisions in compliance with the guidelines set down by the legislature of the State of Mind. Sometimes the federal government (Union of Self-Actualization) offers grants and bonus money to Psych City, to elicit the city's cooperation in certain matters. The community *must* come to decisions on these matters if Psych City is to continue to receive state aid. Moreover, any bill sent to the state legislature must be passed by 75% or more of the Psych City community. The section on finances contains the city budget, tax, bond, and grant information.

EDUCATION

There are two public high schools, ten elementary schools, and one college in Psych City. Psych City State College is located in the south-

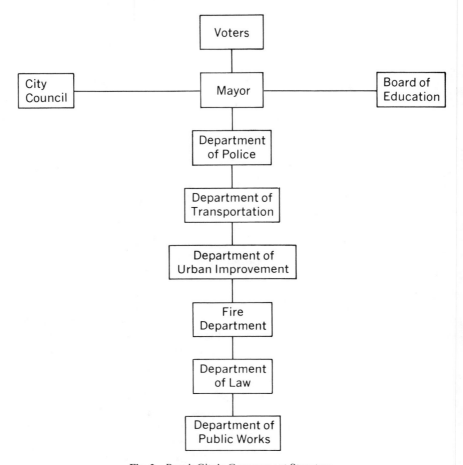

Fig. 2   Psych City's Government Structure.

east corner of the city. The two high schools are located on opposite sides of the city, a considerable distance apart. One of the schools is in a middle-class neighborhood on the city's east side, with 58% of Psych City high school students attending. The other school is located in a lower-class neighborhood, on the west side, near the Federal Housing Project; the remaining 42% of the students attend this school. Six of the city's elementary schools are in the east side area and four are on the west side.

One of the city government functions is the maintenance of an adequate

Table 5 School structure.

	Total	%	Your own community	White	%	Your own community	One minority group	%	Your own community
Eligible for high school (15–18)	7,850	45.0		5,310	45.0		2,540	45.0	
Actually in high school	6,280	80.0		4,520	85.0		1,760	69.0	
TOTAL	6,280	100.0	—	4,520	72.0	—	1,760	28.0	—

*Optional Two Minority Group

	Group 1	%	Your own community	Group 2	%	Your own community
Eligible for high school (15–18)	1,524	27.0		1,016	18.0	
Actually in high school	1,056	41.4		704	27.6	
TOTAL	1,056	16.8	—	704	11.2	—

*If you prefer to use two minority groups rather than one.

Explanation:
- 45% of those between 15 and 20 years of age are eligible for high school, 15–18.
- 80% of those eligible for high school are actually in high school.
- 85% of whites eligible for high school are actually in high school.
- 69% of minority group eligible for high school are actually in high school.
- 72% of those actually in high school are white: i.e. whites make up 72% of the high school population.
- 28% of those actually in high school are minority group; i.e. minority groups make up 28% of the high school population.

15

Table 6 Population distribution in Psych City high schools.

	Total	%	Your own community	White	% of total	Your own community	One minority group	% of total	Your own community
High School 1: white	3,640	58.0		3,460	95.0		180	5.0	
High School 2: minority group	2,640	42.0	——	1,060	40.0	——	1,580	60.0	——
TOTAL	6,280	100.0		4,520	72.0		1,760	28.0	

*Optional Two Minority Group

	Group 1	% of total	Your own community	Group 2	% of total	Your own community
High School 1: white	108	3.0		72	2.0	
High School 2: minority group	948	36.0	——	632	24.0	——
TOTAL	1,056	16.8		704	11.2	

*If you prefer to use two minority groups rather than one.

Explanation: High School 1 houses 58% of all the students; 95% of the students are white; 5% of the students are minority group.

High School 2 houses 42% of all the students; 40% of the students are white; 60% of the students are minority group.

Table 7   Student population breakdown by school.

	White	Minority group	Number of students	Direct aid
High School 1	3,460	180	3,640	$1,892,000
High School 2	1,060	1,580	2,640	1,188,000
Elementary School A	1,486	214	1,700	935,000
Elementary School B	1,506	194	1,700	935,000
Elementary School C	1,478	202	1,680	924,000
Elementary School D	1,330	170	1,500	825,000
Elementary School E	1,310	190	1,500	825,000
Elementary School F	1,408	192	1,600	880,000
Elementary School G	400	1,200	1,600	720,000
Elementary School H	375	1,125	1,500	675,000
Elementary School I	350	1,050	1,400	630,000
Elementary School J	385	1,125	1,510	681,750
TOTAL	14,548	7,422	21,970	$11,110,750

system of public education. The superintendent of schools, who is appointed by the mayor with the approval of City Council, is responsible for the operation of this system. Any matter which concerns public education in the city must be dealt with through the superintendent administratively, or the mayor and City Council politically. The finance section contains the city school district budget, and other pertinent information.

FINANCES

The tables presented in this section contain the necessary financial information you will need for the simulation. Is there enough money for a new school? If not, where will the money come from? Would the community agree to raise taxes? What about "floating" a bond? The city and school district breakdowns and taxing structure are included to assist you as a community in making realistic financial decisions. We suggest you do your own research on taxes, city budgeting, and other related topics to fill out the fiscal summaries which are given below.

Taxes

Revenue from the property tax is the major source of income for local governments. Each year a property tax is levied on the citizens of Psych City. The revenue from this tax goes to the city, county and state, school

Table 8 1973 Budget – Where the money came from.

		%	Your own community
STATE AID:	City School District	$6,500,000	
	Urban Aid to Cities	1,420,000	
	Per Capita Assistance	1,070,000	
	Highway, Traffic & Transportation Control	112,500	
	Mortgage Tax	100,000	
	State Highway Maintenance	17,500	
	Youth Projects	16,500	
	Aid-in-lieu of Railroad Taxes	15,000	
	Neighborhood Detached Worker Program	9,000	
	Program for the Aging	3,500	
		$9,264,000	29.95
School Tax Levy		7,670,000	24.64
City Tax Levy		5,205,000	16.72
3% County Sales Tax		4,700,000	15.10
Bureau of Water		1,300,000	4.18
Surpluses and Unexpended Balances		657,000	2.11
Department of Aviation		600,000	1.93
Delinquent Taxes and Fees		325,000	1.05
City School District (other revenues)		270,000	0.88
City Court (Civil, Criminal, Traffic Violations)		253,000	0.82
Department of Transportation (parking garages, meters, lots)		210,000	0.67
1% Utilities Tax		200,000	0.64
Licenses (City Clerk – License Commission)		70,000	0.22
Special Lighting Tax		37,500	0.12
Miscellaneous		302,000	0.97
TOTAL INCOME		$31,063,500	100.00

18

district and county water district. The particular levy is determined by the amount of money raised by other means (sales tax, state aid) to account for the budget in each of these four areas. For the city, county and state budgets, property tax accounts for a part of the total budget; for the school district and county water district budgets, property tax accounts for all of the budget.

The tax rate is dependent on the amount of money needed in each of the categories and on the total taxable assessed valuation on real estate. Each year all of the property in Psych City is assessed for value and a total arrived at. This total is then divided into the levy for each of the above categories and a tax rate for that category is set. The tax rates for all four categories are summed and the total is the tax rate that each taxpayer pays for that year.

The tax rate this year in Psych City has been computed to be $91.40 per $1,000 of assessed valuation. Property is not taxed on 100% valuation; taxes are computed on some percentage (44% in Psych City) of the assessed valuation.

Below is an example of what the tax rate means to Mr. and Mrs. Jones, residents of Psych City.

Mr. and Mrs. Jones both work. Their combined salary is $11,000 per year. They own their own home. They payed $18,500 for it and have invested another $3,500 in it (another room added, landscaping, plumbing). Their home has been assessed at $23,000. The property tax that they will pay this year is determined by the formula:

$$\$91.40 \text{ per } \$1,000 \text{ on } 44\% \text{ assessed valuation}$$

That is, for the Jones's, $91.40 on $10,120 (44% of 23,000) or approximately $914.

Many decisions in Psych City will revolve around how the residents use available money. Some solutions to problems could be the rejection of state or federal money, in which case the community must raise money by other means, one of which could be a tax increase.

For example, if the decision by the Town Meeting in the housing problem is to raise taxes and build a new school, what does this mean taxwise? Assuming the cost of a new building to be $2 million, the tax levy for the school district would be increased by $2 million. The tax rate would then increase by $9.30 per $1,000; in terms of the Jones's, that would mean $1,007 per year in property tax.

Table 9 1973 BUDGET – How the money was used.

		%	Your Own Community
Education			
City School District, including debt service and capital appropriation	$14,709,000	47.25	
Capital Appropriation and Debt Service – City			
Capital appropriation	$ 315,000	1.01	
Principal and interest on bonds and notes other than school and water	1,754,000	5.64	
TOTAL CAPITAL AND DEBT SERVICE	2,069,000	6.65	
Operation and Maintenance			
Fire	2,409,000	7.74	
Police	2,450,000	7.87	
Pensions, social security, and health insurance other than City School District	2,133,500	6.85	
Public works	1,843,500	5.92	
Parks and recreation	1,034,600	3.32	
Water (including debt service; excluding pensions, social security, and health insurance)	940,000	3.03	

Transportation	849,000	2.73
Public library	365,000	1.17
Tax deficiencies	325,000	1.04
Courts and law	290,900	0.94
Aviation (excluding pensions, social security, and health insurance)	247,000	0.96
Finance and assessment	225,700	0.72
Engineering	287,700	0.96
Audit and purchase	151,000	0.49
Executive	72,500	0.23
Elections and primaries	65,100	0.21
City Clerk and Common Council	57,000	0.18
Urban improvement	104,000	0.34
License Commission	11,700	0.04
All other appropriations	423,300	1.36
TOTAL OPERATION AND MAINTENANCE	$14,297,000	46.10
TOTAL APPROPRIATIONS	$31,063,500	100.00

21

Table 10   Psych City School District — 1973 general fund revenues.

		Your own community
Surplus Balances of Prior Years	$ 207,239.00	
Other Revenues	274,560.00	
Day school tuition, individuals		
Summer school tuition		
Interests on investments		
Miscellaneous revenues		
State Aid	6,500,000.00	
TOTAL REVENUES	6,981,799.00	
Computation of Tax Levy		
Total appropriations	14,709,000.00	
Less: Revenues	6,981,799.00	
Tax budget	7,727,201.00	
One % added pursuant to law	77,272.00	
TOTAL — SCHOOL TAX LEVY	$ 7,804,473.00	

Bonds and Federal Grants

Debt limits are placed on local governments by the city charter. Usually, a low dollar amount is set; this is the maximum amount of money the city can borrow each year. This limit typically cannot exceed some percentage of the local property tax base. The constitutional debt limit in Psych City is stated as "9% of average full valuation of taxable property for the current and four (4) preceding years." Expressed in dollars, the debt limit is $43,853,240. Psych City is already in debt for a total of $14,290,000. This leaves a total debt margin of $29,563,240 which the city can legally borrow.

If the city needs money for certain purposes, bonds can be a means of getting this money. These bonds are backed by the revenue of a specific project, rather than the general tax revenue of the city. There are generally two types of bonds: temporary and permanent. Temporary bonds mature in five years or less, and are bought by banks at a low (3%) rate of interest. Permanent bonds take a longer time to mature, and are bought on the open market at a higher rate of interest.

If residents of Psych City decide to float a bond, they must be sure that they are familiar with the types of bonds and what this method of financing a project will mean to the entire community.

Table 11 Psych City School District – Summary of budget by budget division.

		%	Your own community
Board of Education			
District clerk	$ 3,458		
Professional services	4,000		
Census	3,862		
Conferences	6,250		
TOTAL – BOARD OF EDUCATION	$ 17,570	0.12	
Central Administration			
Chief school administrator	34,600		
Curriculum development	36,070		
Occupational and continuing education	12,944		
Business administration	58,317		
Research	34,594		
Personnel	58,624		
Pupil services	12,495		
School community relations	9,200		
TOTAL – CENTRAL ADMINISTRATION	256,844	1.76	

Table 11 *(Continued)*

		%	Your own community
Instruction Regular Day Schools			
Supervision, principals	$ 655,035		
Supervision, others	120,462		
Teaching	6,526,471		
Special education, handicapped	457,672		
Driver education	25,325		
Helping teachers	19,100		
Physical education	239,555		
Instructional resources	109,869		
Interscholastic athletics	43,767		
Guidance	203,680		
Psychological services	29,960		
Attendance services	32,745		
Health services	171,163		
Visiting teachers	99,510		
Special projects	112,186		
TOTAL – INSTRUCTION REGULAR DAY SCHOOLS	$8,846,500	60.47	——
Instruction Special Schools			
Adult education	104,492		
Summer school	61,720		
Americanization league	10,786		
School of practical nursing	31,205		
TOTAL – INSTRUCTION SPECIAL SCHOOLS	208,203	1.72	
Transportation			
TOTAL – TRANSPORTATION	398,775	2.21	
Operation and Maintenance of Plant			
TOTAL – OPERATION AND MAINTENANCE OF PLANT	1,459,773	9.97	

Undistributed Service Units

Data processing unit	55,050	
Employee benefits	2,243,180	
Insurance	50,550	
Unclassified	25,000	
TOTAL—UNDISTRIBUTED SERVICE UNITS	2,373,780	16.22

Debt Service (Bonds):

Principal	480,000	
Interest	90,683	
TOTAL—DEBT SERVICE	570,683	3.90

Inter Fund Transfers

TOTAL—INTER FUND TRANSFERS	576,872	3.94
GRAND TOTAL	$14,709,000	100.00

Summary of Budget by Object of Expenditure

Personal services	$ 9,909,000	67.72
Materials and supplies	196,206	1.34
Other expenses	1,024,392	6.48
Service from other districts	2,000	0.01
Undistributed expenses	2,429,847	16.61
Debt service	570,683	3.90
Transfers	576,872	3.94
GRAND TOTAL	$14,709,000	100.00

Table 12   Budgets and tax levies.

		Your own community
City Budget for 1973		
Total appropriations	$31,063,500.00	
Total estimated revenues	25,858,500.00	
Total city tax levy	5,205,000.00	
County and State Budget for 1973		
Total appropriations	$ 6,958,000.00	
Total estimated revenues (city collection fee)	68,000.00	
Total county and state tax levy	6,890,000.00	
City School District Budget for 1973		
Total appropriations	$14,709,000.00	
Total estimated revenues	6,981,799.00	
Total school tax levy	7,727,201.00	
County Water District Budget for 1973		
Total appropriations	$ 317,000.00	
Total estimated revenues	—	
Total water district tax levy	317,000.00	
TOTAL TAX LEVY	$20,139,201.00	

The federal government offers grants to local and state governments in compliance with certain standards that the government stipulates. Revenue for these grants comes from all residents in the country, usually from personal income taxes. Hence it is in the state's best interest to accept these grants; in effect, the federal government is returning tax dollars to the state or city. Sometimes, a grant offer means that the federal

Table 13   Assessed valuation on real estate 1973.

		Your own community
Real estate	$198,806,700.00	
Less: Over 65 exemption	2,072,700.00	
Total real estate	196,734,000.00	
Special franchises	11,729,250.00	
For city, state and county tax purposes	$208,463,250.00	
Veterans' pension exemptions	5,622,000.00	
Add: Over 65 exemption taxable for school	18,250.00	
For school tax purposes	$214,103,500.00	
All other exemptions	73,194,000.00	
For county water district tax purposes	$287,297,500.00	

Table 14 Tax rate 1973.

		Your own community
Total tax levy	$20,139,201.00	
City tax rate per $1,000	24.00	
State and county tax rate per $1,000	33.65	
Total	57.65	
School tax rate per $1,000	32.70	
County water district tax rate per $1,000	1.05	
TOTAL RATE	91.40	

Table 15 Debt statement as of September 1, 1973.

			Your own community
Constitutional debt limit:	9% of average full valuation of taxable property for the current and four (4) preceding years	$43,853,240.00	
Gross Indebtedness			
Bonds — City	$ 3,696,500		
Bonds — School	3,595,000		
Bond anticipation notes — City	6,832,500		
Bond anticipation notes for assessable improvements	290,725		
TOTAL GROSS INDEBTEDNESS	$14,414,725		
Exclusions:			
Water bonds	$ 124,000		
TOTAL EXCLUSIONS		$124,000	
NET INDEBTEDNESS		$14,290,000.00	
Constitutional Debt Margin		$29,563,240.00	

government will pay 90% of costs of a certain project for the first year, with local or state government paying the remaining 10%; the second year the federal government will pay 80% with local or state government paying 20%, etc. The federal–state matching percentages can be adjusted and bonus money can be attached to these grants in order to entice the state or city into cooperating with federal guidelines.

CHAPTER 3

The Problems

You as a community will have to find viable solutions to certain problems regarding education, housing, employment, etc. In this chapter, problems related to these issues are presented. Each series of simulation sessions (e.g. eight Town Meetings) constitute one formal simulation. For each formal simulation, it is recommended that you select only one of these problems.

Most of the background information you will need is presented with each problem. Other information (taxes, population statistics) is provided in Chapter 2. You might want to do outside research, particularly if you are adapting Psych City to your own community. How does your city government work? What are the taxes levied? You can find the answers to these and other relevant questions by doing some reading, and talking to the people in your community.

The problems in this section deal with specific issues. If you find that these problems, as they are presented, do not fit your own interests and needs, you can modify them. Or, you can develop your own problems.

During the simulation, questions often arise about the "outside" world. Is there a precedent for establishing a black school district? Would it be legal to "float" a bond to raise money for a new school? Will the State of Mind legislature accept a certain solution voted on by the town meeting? One option is to have the moderator act as the governor of the State of Mind. He would be a nonparticipant observer, but would be the source of information concerning the legality of solutions to problems, decisions of the Supreme Court, and other relevant information.

In all of the problems there is a deadline date. This is the day when a specific plan or program must be approved by 75% of the residents of Psych City. You should set this deadline one week before the formal simulation ends. If there is any question about the legality or acceptability of the decision of the town meeting, the moderator can "rule" on the decision, and send it back to the Town Meeting for necessary modifications. In this way, the community can still meet the deadline date by using the last week of formal simulation, if necessary, for revisions of programs, plans, etc. Leave a few weeks open after the simulation sessions end for discussion of the simulation. There are exercises and discussion topics in the second part of the book that will help you integrate and summarize your experience in the Psych City community.

It may be helpful to remember that while your stated objective is to solve these problems, the most important goal is to learn about how a community functions. Therefore, your success should not be judged by how quickly or effectively you arrive at a solution. The problems are deliberately designed in a difficult manner, so that solutions are hard to achieve. In fact, many groups never reach a solution. This does not mean that the group has not functioned effectively, since these are problems which in reality are complex and frustrating.

1   SCHOOL INTEGRATION

Introduction

Recently the Education Committee of the State of Mind legislature passed a bill to eliminate racial imbalance in schools. All school districts in the state must have a plan for racial balance of their schools by _____ (next to last week of formal simulation). If no plan is chosen by this date, all state financial aid to education will be withdrawn from that school district immediately.

Residents of Psych City that oppose this bill claim that busing children across town is not the answer. Others argue that almost half of the city school district's budget comes from the state; if Psych City does not come up with a plan for integration of the schools, this money will be forfeited. Some minority group teachers and parents are concerned about the quality of the education their children are getting; perhaps the implementation of an integration plan will alleviate this situation.

The residents of Psych City must decide by _____ (next to last week of formal simulation) on a plan for racial balance of city schools. If no decision is reached, all state aid to education will be withdrawn immediately. The plan must be approved by 75% of the residents of Psych City.

Problem

Education Committee of the State Legislature
State of Mind
Office of the Chairman

I. *Article*

Be it known that a condition of racial imbalance currently exists in the public schools of this state.

II. *Resolution*

A. All school districts or systems in this state must either effect or have a plan for the effect of racial balance of their schools by _____.
B. If any school system or district has not effected or proposed a plan for the effect of racial balance of their schools by the above date, state financial aid for education will be withdrawn from that school system or district immediately.
C. Racial balance in the schools shall apply to both student body and faculty.

III. *Article*

A. Racial balance, as defined by this committee, is roughly equivalent to a representation in the schools of any one particular racial group's proportional representation in any one particular community.

  1. If minority group members make up fifty percent (50%) of the population of a community any single school in that community shall be composed of a student body that is no less than forty-three percent (43%) and no more than fifty-seven percent (57%) minority group. Seven percent (7%) = accepted spread for racial imbalance.
  2. The racial distribution of teachers in any school district should be proportional to the racial distribution of students in that district. That is, if a school has forty percent (40%) of a district's minority group students, it should have approximately forty percent (40%) of its minority group teachers.

2 VACANT LAND USAGE

Introduction

The following article appeared recently in *The Psych City Clarion:*

Ednick Zawicki, a life-long resident of Psych City and former owner of Ego Incorporated, died today after a long illness. Mr. Zawicki has willed a 100-acre tract of unspoiled, undeveloped land in the southeast corner of Psych City near Psych City State College and Psych Lake, to the residents of Psych City to be developed for one specific purpose. Four alternatives, mentioned in his will, have been discussed in previous Town Meetings. (1) The land could be used as a site for new industries. Id Manufacturing Company has been searching for an area to expand; new jobs would be created, but Id Manufacturing Company has been known in the past to pour great amounts of pollutants into the air and the Stream of Consciousness. (2) A game preserve and land conservation area outside the city is another alternative; this donated land would be an ideal spot, being next to Psych Lake, for ecological purposes and recreational facilities. (3) Psych City has no stadium (City Council has repeatedly voted down proposals for a stadium due to a lack of a suitable site). A place for athletic events would be a welcome and profitable addition. (4) Since it is adjacent to Psych City State College, the tract of land could be used for the expansion of the college. The State of Mind has stipulated that if the college is expanded, its status would change from present two-year status to a four-year university. If the land is not developed for one purpose, it will be returned to the estate of Mr. Zawicki and his relatives, who live outside the city.

It is in the best interests of the residents of Psych City to decide how they will use this land. The alternative selected must be passed by 75% of the Town Meeting. If no decision is reached by _____ (next to last week of formal simulation) the land will be returned to Mr. Zawicki's relatives.

Below is an exerpt from Mr. Zawicki's will:

I, Ednick T. Zawicki, hereby bequeath a 100-acre tract of land, bounded by Psych City Municipal Park on the south, School District 1 zone line on the west, Psych City State College on the north, and the city limits on the east. to the citizens of Psych City. This land must be developed for only one purpose. Some suggested uses of the land are: (1) a site for new industries, (2) a game preserve and ecological conservation area, (3) a stadium, or (4) expansion of Psych City State College. The residents of Psych City must choose one alternative. The four purposes mentioned above are only suggestions. The Town Meeting may decide on *any* use of the land. The proposed alternative must be passed by 75% of the residents of Psych City by _____ (next to last week of formal simulation), at which time, if no decision is reached, the land will return to my estate, to be used as my heirs determine.

3   WELFARE PLAN

Introduction

Several months ago, in response to a growing concern about the increased problems with our welfare system, the federal government of the Union of Self-Actualization (USA) appointed a blue-ribbon panel to investigate the welfare situation and to make recommendations for modifications of our present system. Last week, this panel released a report of its findings and recommendations. Below is an excerpt from the summary of the welfare panel's report:

1. The federal panel on review and modifications of the welfare system has verified the government's express concern about the scope and intensity of problems with our current welfare system. Not only are there increasing numbers of persons joining the welfare roles, but people are remaining on welfare for indeterminate lengths of time, standards about who should receive welfare are inconsistent and arbitrary, the social problems which welfare supposedly is directed toward seem to be increasing, and all sectors of our society seem dissatisfied with the current system.
2. The welfare panel recognizes that centrally-imposed solutions are usually not effective when applied to local municipalities, recommends that each city or county be held responsible for developing a plan which will improve the welfare system as it applies to their district.
3. The welfare panel recognizes that long-term changes which ultimately prove to be more efficient are often expensive to develop initially. Therefore, the panel recommends that the federal government allot $1 million to local municipalities which develop welfare reform programs so that these municipalities may implement the most effective plans.

Shortly after release of this report, the U.S.A. Welfare Commission declared that all local municipalities must develop their own plans for improving the welfare system which exists in their district. These plans, which must be approved by 75% of the city must be submitted to the office of the Welfare Commission on _____ (next to last week of formal simulation). Those cities which comply with this declaration will continue to receive the federal subsidy. In the case of Psych City, this subsidy amounts to $8 million. Fifty-one percent (51%) of this comes from the federal government. Those cities which do not comply with this declaration will lose their federal subsidy, but will be required, under law, to continue to pay welfare at the rate they are currently paying.

In discussions about welfare reform, several possible approaches have been described by various sectors of the community. Some of these possibilities are: (1) making welfare requirements stricter, and therefore cutting down the number of people enrolled in welfare; (2) developing educational, job training, and other programs which will enable people to help themselves; (3) requiring that all people enrolled in welfare must actively seek employment, and if employment is not reached within six months, these persons will be removed from the welfare rolls, unless they can present convincing reasons why they should be allowed to remain; (4) giving money to local neighborhoods and allowing them to choose how they will improve social conditions; and (5) providing a guaranteed annual income to all persons. These and other proposals which may be suggested by the community might be considered possible solutions. It should be remembered that some people see it as being to their advantage to have the community not come up with a plan and therefore lose the federal subsidy.

Problem

Office of Welfare Commission
Union of Self-Actualization (USA)

I. Be it known that the current system of welfare is inadequate.

II. A. Each city or county will be responsible for the development of a plan which will improve the welfare system as it applies to their district.
   B. The federal government will provide a $1 million grant to those local municipalities that come up with a feasible plan to improve the welfare system. This plan will include how the money will be used, and who will administer the program.
   C. Those cities which do not comply with the above declaration will lose their federal subsidy for welfare.

III. A plan for improvement of welfare services must be approved by 75% of the local community by _____ (next to last week of formal simulation). If a plan is not submitted to the Commission by this date, the federal government will withdraw the federal welfare subsidy of that city.

4   CITIZEN PROTECTION PROBLEM

Introduction

The State of Mind legislature has announced that those five cities in the state that submit their completed budget on or before _____ (next to last week of formal simulation) will be granted $100,000 for repair and maintenance of roads and other physical improvements. Psych City has worked out and approved all items of the budget, except $80,000 which is allocated for Citizen Protection. To complete approval of the budget, by the deadline set by the state, residents in the Town Meeting must choose between using these funds for better police protection or for the establishment of a Consumer Protection Bureau. Increased police protection could mean policemen salary increases, buying of equipment, more policemen trained, provisions for police to take social science courses at Psych City State College. The Consumer Protection Bureau could involve the hiring of staff (director, lawyers, researchers), money for court cases, and provision of office space and equipment and supplies. The Town Meeting must decide on one allocation of funds, either for police protection or consumer safeguards. The plan must be passed by 75% of the Town Meeting; the completed budget must be submitted to the state legislature on or before _____ (next to last week of formal simulation). If the budget is not sent in at this time, Psych City will lose the state bonus money for physical improvements of the city.

Problem

Office of the Commissioner of Finance
State Legislature
State of Mind

I. Those five cities in the State of Mind that submit their budgets on or before _____ (next to last week of formal simulation) will receive a $100,000 grant from the State of Mind.

II. Above grant can be used for highway maintenance, road repairs, or other physical improvements of the recipient city.

III. A. The city must send its completed budget, approved by 75% of residents, by the deadline date.
   B. If the city fails to send its completed and approved budget to the state legislature by _____ (next to last week of formal simulation), the State of Mind will withdraw its grant offer.

5 DRUG PROBLEM

Introduction

Four weeks ago, a 17-year-old honor student at one of Psych City's high schools was hospitalized due to an overdose of drugs. This incident, the first of its kind in Psych City, prompted the Board of Education, in cooperation with a research center at Psych City State College, to undertake a survey to determine the nature and extent of the drug problem in Psych City schools. Each of the students in elementary, junior and senior high schools, and all private schools in the area were asked to anonymously complete a questionnaire aimed at assessing the degree of drug usage in Psych City. When the results of this study were published in *The Psych City Clarion* (see below), several parents who confronted their children with the drug issue were surprised and dismayed to learn that their children were among those who had used and were using drugs. Following are the published results of that survey:

	High School	Junior High	Elementary School
Soft Drugs (i.e. marijuana)	%	%	%
Never used	38	46	90
Experimented only	34	42	8.5
Infrequent use	18	8	1
Frequent use	10	4	0.5
Hallucinogenic Drugs (i.e. LSD, THC, mescaline)			
Never used	45	56	92
Experimented only	40	31	7
Infrequent use	9	9	1
Frequent use	6	4	0
Mood Drugs (i.e. amphetamines, barbiturates)			
Never used	42	51	92
Experimented only	47	38	8
Infrequent use	9	11	0
Frequent use	2	0	0
Hard Drugs (i.e. heroin, cocaine)			
Never used	97	98	99
Experimented only	2.5	1.5	1
Infrequent use	0	0	0
Frequent use	0.5	0.5	0

Shortly after the publication of the drug survey, the legislature of the State of Mind passed a bill proposing that all cities with a population of

100,000 or more must institute a drug program for the students in their school districts. The nature of the program, and decisions involving who would administer the program, would be left up to each individual city. The objective of this plan is to decrease the number of young people who presently are using illegal drugs (heroin, amphetamines, marijuana, etc.).

The residents of Psych City must decide on the particular type of program. Some people believe that a preventive program is best. This would involve drug education in the schools. Others feel that those youths convicted of dealing or using illegal drugs should be offered extensive counseling. Another solution which has been discussed is stepped-up police activities dealing with drug offenders. Some parents in recent Town Meetings seem to feel that if you give kids something to do, they will not have time to experiment with drugs. People of this view believe that the money could be used most effectively in the building of more youth and recreation centers. Psych City must decide who will oversee the administration of the drug program (students, in cooperation with the Board of Education, City Council, special commission, etc.). The state will appropriate $100,000 for this drug program and attach it to the state's aid to education. Psych City must decide how these funds will be spent and who will administer the program by _____ (next to last week of formal simulation), or the State of Mind will withdraw state aid to education.

Problem

Education Committee of the State Legislature
State of Mind
Office of the Chairman

   I. Be it known that a serious drug problem exists in the large cities of the State of Mind.

 II. A. All cities with a population of 100,000 or more residents must institute a drug program; its objective to be the decrease in the number of adolescents who use illegal drugs.

      B. Each city must decide what the focus of the drug program will be. Any plan which will accomplish the stated objective will be accepted by the state.

      C. Each city must decide how the program will be administered.

      D. The State of Mind will provide $100,000 for the drug program.

III. A. Each city must decide on the type of drug program and the administrators of that program by _____ (next to last week of formal simulation).

B. If the plan for a drug program is not submitted to the state legislature by _____ (next to last week of formal simulation), all state aid for education will be withdrawn from that school system or district immediately.

6 USE OF DOWNTOWN LAND

Introduction

There is a four-acre tract of vacant land, located near the downtown business area, which the city owns. Recently, local businessmen have been clamoring for more parking facilities for shoppers. This land could be used for a multi-level parking building. Environmentalists have also been eying the land; they would like to see it developed into a pedestrian mall and improve public transportation facilities for shoppers and consumers. Senior citizens of Psych City have advocated using the land for housing for senior citizens. The city has agreed to provide money (maximum of $15 million) from the Urban Renewal Agency and use these funds for whatever one purpose the residents decide the land should be used. If no decision is reached by _____ (next to last week of formal simulation), the land will be used by the city for a warehouse, storing equipment for the Department of Public Works, etc. Citizens must approve of a plan for the land by _____ (next to last week of formal simulation); if no decision is reached at this time, the city will use the land for its own purposes. The plan must be approved by 75% of the residents of Psych City.

Problem

Office of the Commissioner
Department of Urban Improvement
Psych City

I. Psych City owns a four-acre tract of land north of Main Street and east of Lincoln Boulevard.

II. If the residents of Psych City decide on one purpose for this land, the city will make available up to $15 million in funds from the Urban Renewal Agency for the use of the land.

III. A. If no decision is reached by _____ (next to last week of formal simulation), the city will use the land as a warehouse and storage center.
   B. An alternative use of the land must be approved by 75% of the residents of Psych City.

7 LOW-INCOME HOUSING

Introduction

The Commissioner of Urban Renewal has announced that the federal government will provide funds to build a civic center near the downtown business district. The proposed civic center could include a shopping mall, attracting outside business interests to Psych City, a theater and other facilities for cultural events, a complex of dental and medical offices, a museum and office buildings. The federal government has agreed to appropriate funds for the civic center on one condition: low-income housing must be built in selected pockets on the east side of the city. Many of the most influential people, who live on the east side, are opposed to this low-income housing.

Total estimated cost of the housing is $5 million. Urban Renewal will provide 85% of the $5 million; the city must match the remaining 15%. The Town Meeting must reach a decision, agreed upon by 75% of the residents, by _____ (next to last week of formal simulation) or the federal government will withdraw the funds for the proposed civic center.

Problem

Office of the Commissioner
Urban Renewal Agency
Psych City

I. Be it known that there is a demonstrated need for low-income housing in Psych City.

II. A. The federal government, through the Urban Renewal Agency of Psych City, will provide funds for the development of a civic center in downtown Psych City.

B. Proposed funds for the civic center will be appropriated only if low-income housing is developed in selected areas east of Lincoln Boulevard and north of Main Street. These areas will be selected by the Urban Renewal Agency.

C. The federal government will match 85% of local monies for the construction of low-income housing.

III. A. Psych City must approve the above plan by _____ (next to last week of formal simulation). The plan must be approved by 75% of the residents of Psych City and submitted to the Urban Renewal Agency.

B. If above plan is not approved by _____ (next to last week of formal simulation), the federal government will withdraw funds for the proposed civic center.

8   HIGH SCHOOL DISRUPTION

Introduction

Last week, a sophomore at one of Psych City's high schools was hospitalized due to injuries received in a fight at school. This incident, the first of its kind in Psych City, provoked many angry parents to speak up at the local Town Meeting. The incident involved both white and minority group students.

Many residents in Psych City believe this incident was caused by the relaxed discipline in the schools. Some parents think that teachers should supervise the students in lunchrooms, and hallways so that fights will be prevented. Others have been blaming the minority group militants in the school for the disruption. Minority group students have recently been asking for changes in the curriculum to fit their needs. Teachers in the Psych City Teachers Association have said they cannot both teach and be policemen at the same time. They would like to see more teacher aides hired. A few residents see this incident as a prime example of the lack of law and order in the country. They would like to see the students involved in these disruptions punished, and security around the schools increased. Other people believe that the lack of communication sparked this incident. They would advocate more human relations training for students of all races, faculty, parents, and school administrators.

Since these disruptions have been occurring all over the state, the State of Mind legislature has declared that each city must establish a program to eliminate disruptions in the high schools. If the city does not propose a plan by _____ (next to last week of formal simulation), the state will withdraw all state aid to education. The plan must be approved by 75% of the residents of Psych City.

Problem

Education Committee of the State Legislature
State of Mind
Office of the Chairman

I. Because of the recent disruptions in high schools around the state, each city in the state must plan and implement a program designed to eliminate these disruptions.

II. A. Each city must decide what the focus of the program will be. Any plan which will accomplish the above stated objective will be accepted by the state.

   B. Each city must decide how the program will be administered.

III. A. The State of Mind will provide $90,000 for the proposed program.

   B. If the plan for a program is not submitted to the state legislature by _____ (next to last week of formal simulation), all state aid for education will be withdrawn from that school system or district immediately.

   C. The proposed plan must be approved by 75% of the residents of the community.

9   EQUAL EMPLOYMENT FOR WOMEN

Introduction

The legislature of the Union of Self-Actualization (USA) has just passed a bill aimed at eliminating job discrimination against women after a report, issued by the Commission on Equal Job Opportunities, revealed that women were underrepresented in jobs at most levels of employment. Following are some statistics the Commission has released:

Major Occupation Group	Women as Percentage of Total Employed
Professional, technical	36.8
Managers, officials, proprietors	13.9
Clerical workers	71.7
Sales workers	44.8
Craftsmen, foremen	3.9
Operatives	28.6
Farmers, farm managers	5.9

In effect, all federal contracts to Psych City and federally-funded agencies in Psych City will be renewed only if women are placed in a certain percentage of government jobs and jobs in those federally-funded agencies. In Psych City women make up 53% of the population. Many people in Psych City are opposing this bill. Women will be displacing many men already employed. Also, those women who fill the jobs do not necessarily have to have the qualifications that were required of the men hired. The local labor union is known to be against this compensatory program; the chapter president claims that the bill violates many rights of his union's members, among these being seniority privileges. Supporters of the bill warn that if the city does not go along with the plan, it will lose close to $20 million in federal contracts. They cite the following figures:

Contracts to:	Amount
Federally-funded agencies	$11.5 million
School District	5.2 million
Department of Public Works	2.3 million
Department of Parks and Recreation	1.0 million

A local women's organization states that the bill is long overdue; it is about time women can be executives and administrators as well as clerks and secretaries. The community must decide by _____ (next to last week of formal simulation) if the government plan is to be approved. If no decision is reached, or if the Town Meeting decides against the bill, all federal contracts to Psych City and federally-funded agencies will be revoked.

Problem

Commission on Equal Job Opportunities
Union of Self-Actualization (USA)

I. *Article*

Be it known that a condition of job discrimination against women currently exists.

II. *Resolution*

A. All cities in the USA must have a certain percentage of women employed in all city government departments and federally-funded agencies.
B. If any city does not effect or propose a plan for equal employment of women by _____ (next to last week of formal simulation), all contracts to that city and its federally-funded agencies will be revoked.
C. Plan must be approved by 75% of the residents of the community.

III. *Article*

A. Equal employment for women is roughly equivalent to a representation in jobs of the proportional representation of women in any one particular community. If women make up fifty percent (50%) of the population of a community, any single department shall be composed of no less than forty-three percent (43%) and no more than fifty-seven percent (57%) women employees. Seven percent (7%) = accepted spread for equal employment of women.

10   SEX EDUCATION

Introduction

The Board of Education is considering putting sex education into the curriculum of both elementary and high schools in Psych City. This would include courses in biology, instruction in the cultural aspects of sex, and, for the high school students, referral by the school nurse to family planning centers.

After reading about the proposed actions of the Board of Education, parents have shown their opposition by speaking at the Town Meetings. Some parents have even threatened to take their children out of the public schools. One woman has even decided to start her own school, at her home, and has received support from other mothers. The Psych City curricula of all school districts must be handed in by _____ (next to last week of formal simulation) or the state will withdraw 30% of the state aid to education. In Psych City this amounts to close to $2 million. The city must reach a decision; 75% of the residents must approve of the plan.

Problem

Education Committee
State of Mind

  I. All school systems and districts must have their curricula submitted to the state legislature by _____ (next to last week of formal simulation).

 II. If the curricula are not submitted by _____ (next to last week of formal simulation) thirty percent (30%) of that school district's state aid to education will be withdrawn.

III. The curricula must have the approval of 75% of the residents.

11   YOUR OWN PROBLEM

12   YOUR OWN PROBLEM

CHAPTER 4

The People

You will each be assigned a role. Your task will be to play that role and, to the best of your ability, to become that person.

The roles have been created to consist of three aspects. First is the individual aspect. Each person is separate and unique, has his own interests, values, goals, and needs. Second, there is the subgroup aspect. Each person belongs to a subgroup (e.g. school administrators, white parents) and each subgroup has its own interests, values, goals, and needs. Finally, there is the total group aspect. As a total group, a common goal exists.

The roles were written to encompass a constant state of imbalance. That is, there will be conflict within the subgroups and between subgroups; sometimes within and between individuals. Part of the task is the resolution of these conflicts without totally compromising and undermining the values and objectives of the individuals and the subgroup to which you belong. Along with between-group conflict and differences, the roles have been structured so that there may be an alliance between subgroups (i.e. those with similar objectives) and between individuals in different subgroups (i.e. those with similar personal objectives). These may be taken advantage of, but at the same time, keeping in mind your subgroup and total group goals.

The people whom you represent by the roles you are assigned to play constitute a reasonable sampling of the people who might be found in a small city. Thus, there is a mayor running for reelection, a superintendent of schools who is a well-intentioned bureaucrat, a minority group teacher in a predominantly white school, a white parent who thinks that what this country needs is more law and order, a Young Americans for Freedom representative, a college professor, an ecology advocate, and a middle-class frustrated housewife.

Certain information has been provided with each of the roles. While some of this information is specific, it is, for the most part, ambiguous. The facts that you are provided with will help to give you a general feel for the person you are to play, in terms of his values, beliefs, lifestyle, etc. How you interpret this information will determine the kind of role you will play and the things you will do. Reading about a particular type of character and personal contact with a person fitting the description of your role will help in filling out your character's description.

For each problem, the roles should constitute a representative sampling of people (e.g. mayor, teacher, parent, student, professional, blue-collar worker, etc.) as well as a heterogeneous pool of opinions on the issue. If you decide to do the busing problem, some examples of appropriate roles would be a minority group militant, a white parent opposed to busing, a black teacher who wants a separate black-run school district, and a conservative laborer.

Roles may be selected either randomly or on a dissimilarity basis (choosing a role that is different from you). The types of roles chosen will be determined by the problem you decide to do and the size of your class.

Appropriate roles can be added for each problem. Before the simulation begins, the moderator could choose (and add) the roles to be used.

The moderator could also supply name cards or signs for each participant. People should use their own names during the simulation, and decide which sex they will be. On these name tags should be the person's name, his role (black parent, superintendent of schools), and a brief description of his role (works in a factory, lives on the east side, etc.).

ROLES IN PSYCH CITY

Government Officials

1. Mayor
   (a) White, married with two children in elementary school.
   (b) Believes in and promised as a part of his campaign "a good education for every child in the city."
   (c) Active in trying to get as much state money back into the cities as possible.

    (d) Has proposed an increase in the budget for education.

    (e) Up for reelection in the fall.

2. Corporation Counsel

    (a) White, married with two children in elementary school.

    (b) Handles legal matters for the city.

    (c) Graduated high in his law school class at prestigious college in east.

    (d) Views his job as "running a tight ship"; is hard-working, expects his employees to be that way; believes in social change through legal system.

    (e) Wants to help the mayor to do a good job.

    (f) Has political ambitions.

3. Councilman

    (a) Minority group, married with three children in city schools.

    (b) Active in minority group community.

    (c) Believes in total equal rights for minority group members – as integrated in the white community.

    (d) Believes education the way to change the occupational and social stigma of the minority group member.

    (e) Is opposed to low-income housing on East Side.

4. Councilman-at-large

    (a) White, no children.

    (b) Conservative point of view.

    (c) Believes in equal education for all.

    (d) "Law and order" proponent.

    (e) Aspiring to higher position in city government.

    (f) Believes women's place is at home.

5. Councilman

    (a) White, married with two children in high school.

    (b) Represents part of east side of city.

    (c) Is interested in keeping his constituents happy.

    (d) Received campaign contributions from some influential people in the city.

    (e) World War II veteran.

    (f) Compromise on some issues; shares his constituents' concern about minority groups moving into neighborhood.

6. Police Chief

    (a) White, married with three children in elementary and high school.

    (b) Feels major function of police is to maintain law and order.

    (c) Wants to better the popular image of the police.

   (d) Sees the way to accomplishing this is through behavior and action.
   (e) Sympathetic to all groups in that he tries to understand all groups.
   (f) Wants the cop on the beat to strive for objective understanding before making decisions.
   (g) Open to social reform via the Establishment; social change should not be drastic but continual.
 7. Commissioner of Parks and Recreation
   (a) White, three elementary school age children.
   (b) Has college degree in city planning.
   (c) Worked his way through college.
   (d) Wants his children to have everything he did not have.
   (e) Wife is head of League of Women Voters.
   (f) Sees his job as key to success for himself and his family.
 8. Commissioner of Urban Renewal
   (a) White, married with four elementary and high school age children.
   (b) Comes from lower middle-class neighborhood.
   (c) Believes that neighborhoods should have a say in what urban renewal does in their area.
   (d) Has political pressure on him to do what government wants.
   (e) Would like to leave government job someday and open a small store — be his own boss.
 9. Human Rights Commissioner
   (a) Minority group, married with five elementary school age children.
   (b) Has recently purchased a home on East Side.
   (c) Believes in nonviolent pursuit of civil rights.
   (d) Would fight for higher quality education for minority group.
   (e) Sees his job as one of the most important in the city.
 10. Assistant Director of Social Services
   (a) White, single.
   (b) Comes from wealthy family involved in politics.
   (c) Thinks his department needs a lot more money than it receives.
   (d) Believes it is a person's privilege not to work.
   (e) Would like to see marijuana legalized.

School Administrators

 1. Superintendent of Schools
   (a) White, married, one child in high school, one in college.
   (b) Well-intentioned bureaucrat.

    (c) Main goal is state aid to education.

    (d) A moderate innovator, but won't rock the boat too much.

    (e) Somewhat removed from the reality of the schools — little contact with teachers and students.

    (f) Is concerned about public image of his schools; is upset about publicity about drugs, etc.

2. Assistant Superintendent of Schools

    (a) White, young, married with one child in elementary school.

    (b) Graduated from progressive educational school.

    (c) Wants to make sweeping changes in school system.

    (d) Is eager to do a good job.

    (e) Has extensive contact with principals and teachers.

3. Board of Education Member

    (a) White, married with one child in high school.

    (b) Ran for the board as an intermediate step to a higher position in city government.

    (c) Moderately successful professional — lawyer.

    (d) Will take the popular side of issues.

    (e) Wants things to go smoothly so that he can run in the next election with no aggravation.

    (f) Holds stock in Id Manufacturing Company.

4. Board of Education Member

    (a) White, widower, no children.

    (b) A dedicated educator.

    (c) Sees integration as a necessary evil — get it over with, with as little trouble as possible.

    (d) Doesn't understand what the country is coming to — thinks people are worried about the wrong things — it's *what kind* of an education the kids will get, not in *what school.*

    (e) Takes no position on any other issue other than education and the value of it.

5. Principal

    (a) White, married with three children in high school.

    (b) Principal in predominantly minority group school.

    (c) Is there by choice — turned down a suburban school.

    (d) Innovative — always willing to try new things.

    (e) Likes to "keep in touch" with issues and people in the school.

    (f) Believes in what he is doing.

6. Principal

    (a) White, married with one son in college.

(b) Principal in predominantly white school.
(c) Wants his school to run smoothly.
(d) Wants *his* students and teachers to be happy.
(e) Been principal in this school for several years.
(f) Talks about the good old days, when there was no problem with drugs in his school.

School Personnel

1. Teacher
   (a) Minority group, single.
   (b) Teaching in predominantly minority group school.
   (c) Teaching in this school because that is where he (she) was assigned — believes this is where he (she) should be.
   (d) Little contact with white people other than those in the school.
   (e) Some fear of white people.
   (f) Graduated from a minority group college.
   (g) First in his (her) family to get to college and proud of it.
2. Teacher
   (a) White, single.
   (b) Teaching in predominantly minority group school.
   (c) Believes in total assimilation of minority groups into white world.
   (d) Teaching in this school because that is where he (she) was assigned.
   (e) Wants to be effective, but not sure he (she) is.
   (f) Comes from a working-class background — father a construction worker.
3. Teacher
   (a) Minority group, married with one child.
   (b) Has assimilated white middle-class values.
   (c) Teaching in a predominantly white school.
   (d) Graduated several years ago from a traditional college.
   (e) Recently moved to East Side.
4. Teacher
   (a) White, married with one child in elementary school.
   (b) Teaching in a predominantly white school.
   (c) Has had little contact with minority groups.
   (d) Major concern is with teaching.
   (e) Believes he (she) is not prejudiced.

5. Teacher
   (a) Minority group, single.
   (b) Teaching in predominantly minority group school.
   (c) Militant type.
   (d) Graduated four years ago from a high prestige college.
   (e) Wants more money for minority group education.
6. Teacher
   (a) White, three children.
   (b) Teaching in a predominantly white school.
   (c) Does not understand youth of today — on the "over 30" side of generation gap.
   (d) Frightened by the recent riots in the country — wondering what it is all coming to.
   (e) Has three children in the school system — main concern is for them and the quality of their education.
   (f) Sees kids as needing more discipline.
7. Teacher
   (a) Minority group, married, no children.
   (b) Moved to Psych City after teaching in urban ghetto.
   (c) Teaches in predominantly minority group school.
   (d) Is active in Psych City's Teachers Association.
   (e) Thinks teachers are grossly underpaid.
   (f) Is concerned about the environment.
   (g) Volunteers as a counselor for underprivileged children.
8. Counselor
   (a) White
   (b) Counseling in a predominantly white school.
   (c) Believes in social innovation and reform.
   (d) Coming up for tenure so he (she) does not want to rock the boat too much.
   (e) Believes the way to change is through the Establishment.
9. Counselor
   (a) White, single.
   (b) Counseling in a predominantly white school.
   (c) Sees role as getting kids into college.
   (d) Has not taken a course since he (she) got his Master's 15 years ago.
   (e) Member of the PTA.
10. Counselor
    (a) Minority group, married with two preschool age children.

(b) Works in predominantly minority group high school.
(c) Believes education is best way for minority group members.
(d) Honor student in college.
(e) Thinks people can pull themselves "up" no matter what their race.

Civic Leaders

1. President – Chamber of Commerce
    (a) White, Anglo-Saxon Protestant, all children are married.
    (b) Prominent businessman from a family that has resided in Psych City many years.
    (c) Went to Ivy League school; very interested in culture.
    (d) Genuinely concerned about improvement of city.
    (e) Business is first interest; but concerned about plight of all peoples.
    (f) Believes in free enterprise, aware that social problems are result of complex series of factors.
2. President – Junior Chamber of Commerce
    (a) White, young, married with two children, one in elementary school, one preschooler.
    (b) Ambitious junior executive.
    (c) Political aspirations.
    (d) Comes from middle-class background; is fast surpassing that.
    (e) Against government control.
    (f) Firm believer in keeping cultural traditions of ethnic groups.
    (g) Believes in progress (technology) but thinks social change takes longer.
3. President – Parents Teachers Association
    (a) White, married with three children, two in high school.
    (b) Had strict Catholic education.
    (c) Believes parents should have more say in what goes on in the schools.
    (d) Feels that schools should stick to academics.
    (e) Is anxious about her (his) son's drug usage.
4. Vice-President – Parents Teachers Association
    (a) Minority group, single.
    (b) Was token minority group member at small college.
    (c) Believes schools should be improved.
    (d) Thinks teachers should be given more authority to discipline students.

(e) Wants human relations training programs in school.
5. Treasurer — Parents Teachers Association
   (a) White, married with three children, one in high school, two in elementary school.
   (b) Went to private girls' school in South.
   (c) Considers small things she does as very important.
   (d) Often runs bake sales and other fund-raising activities for new facilities for schools.
   (e) Believes teachers must set moral example for their students.
6. Director of Community Chest
   (a) Minority group, married, no children.
   (b) Comes from lower middle-class family.
   (c) Social work background; often uneasy around people.
   (d) Relies on contributions from wealthy people and business; has to be sensitive to contributor's needs.
   (e) Believes in progressive, innovative ways of social reform.
7. Representative — Council of Churches
   (a) White, married with three children, all married.
   (b) Known as quiet, nice guy when training for ministry.
   (c) Believes in reason as tool in solving problems.
   (d) Committed to social reform, but will be an arbitrator in conflicts.
8. Rabbi
   (a) White, married with three daughters, one in college, two married.
   (b) Escaped persecution during World War II by emigrating to U.S.A.
   (c) Is very aware of prejudice.
   (d) Participates in interdenominational group.
   (e) Is strict father.
   (f) Concerned about daughters' liberal attitude toward religion.
9. Priest
   (a) White, former athlete in high school.
   (b) Has been reprimanded by superiors for his modernization ideas.
   (c) Sees himself as a crusader for social reform.
   (d) Realizes he cannot afford to alienate older members of community by his actions.
10. President — Police Benevolence Association
    (a) White, married with two children, one in high school, one in elementary school.
    (b) Lower middle-class background.
    (c) Wants less restrictions on policeman's authority.

      (d) Thinks of a policeman as a professional.
      (e) Will "do favors" for certain people.
11. President – Firefighters Association
      (a) White, married with four children, two in elementary school, one in high school, one in college.
      (b) Middle-class.
      (c) Thinks the "old ways" are the best.
      (d) Is proud to be in the silent majority.
      (e) Wants increased salaries for his firemen.
12. President – Local Labor Union
      (a) White, married with two children in high school, one in elementary school.
      (b) High school education – average student.
      (c) Though he is strong physically, is aware that "quick mind" is how you succeed.
      (d) Wants to underplay his intelligence.
      (e) Thinks that working man should stop paying taxes for "loafer" (i.e. welfare recipients).
13. Head of League of Women Voters
      (a) White, married with three elementary children in school district.
      (b) Has a degree in sociology from big university.
      (c) Believes in the democratic system.
      (d) Tries to stay impartial in local politics.
      (e) Wants citizens to get involved.
      (f) Thinks she should be doing more – not sure what.
14. President – Junior League
      (a) White, married with two children in elementary school.
      (b) Comes from established wealthy family in Psych City.
      (c) Sees herself as helping others.
      (d) Tries to bring into the league the wives of young successful men in city.
      (e) Wants a better home, new car every year, etc.
15. Women's Club Representative
      (a) White, married with two children in elementary school.
      (b) Went to college, met her husband there and married shortly afterward.
      (c) Organizes teas and other social gatherings.
      (d) Would like to work when children are older.
      (e) Believes she is naïve about politics – will agree with her husband on most issues.

Political and Social Activists

1. Peace and Freedom Party Representative
   (a) Believes in minority group pride.
   (b) Favors integration but not at the cost of minority group identity.
   (c) Believes in equal rights for all.
   (d) Participated in first voter registration in the South.
2. Young Repressives Representative
   (a) White, married with one preschool age child.
   (b) Went to business college.
   (c) In management-trainee position.
   (d) Likes to please everyone.
   (e) Thinks low-income housing in his neighborhood would economically hurt everyone involved.
3. Chairman — Impulsive Party
   (a) White, married with two married children.
   (b) High school graduate, takes an occasional course at Psych City State College.
   (e) Believes machine politics can still work.
   (d) Wants young people to get involved in party.
   (e) Has political ambitions for eldest son.
4. NAACP Representative
   (a) Believes in a better life for minority group members.
   (b) Believes education is the way.
   (c) Assimilation of the minority group into the white world is desirable.
   (d) Integration as a means to assimilation.
   (e) He has assimilated.
5. Black Panther Representative
   (a) Fighting assimilation of blacks into the white world.
   (b) Black nationalist, believing in separate black political, social, and economic structure.
   (c) Wants good education for the blacks, but in *black* schools.
   (d) Anti-busing.
6. Socialists Representative
   (a) White, single.
   (b) Dropped out after two years of college.
   (c) Feels compelled to change Establishment.
   (d) Is active in community affairs, in government.

  (e) Is aware that there is enough money in this country for all people; problems arise in bureaucracy.
 7. American Legion Representative
  (a) White, married with two children; one in high school and one in elementary school.
  (b) World War II veteran.
  (c) Believes in Protestant ethic.
  (d) Thinks no one should be spoon-fed.
 8. Young Americans for Freedom Representative
  (a) Believes in individual choice without government intervention.
  (b) Not opposed to integration if it is chosen by the community.
  (c) "You cannot legislate morality."
  (d) White, graduated from college recently, upper-class family, with long-term residence in Psych City.
  (e) Opposed to demonstrations involving civil disobedience.
 9. Women's Liberation Group Representative
  (a) White, single, about 28 years old.
  (b) Has a doctorate in political science.
  (c) Taught at Psych City State College; contract was not renewed.
  (d) Will fight for rights of all oppressed groups.

Citizens

 1. Citizen
  (a) Minority group.
  (b) Skilled laborer — tool and dye maker.
  (c) Concerned over the rise in taxes.
  (d) Wants best education for his three kids — does not care if schools are integrated or not but wants the best for his children.
 2. Citizen
  (a) Minority group.
  (b) Thinks something should have been done before now and that it is about time that something is being done about the school situation.
  (c) Has militant leanings.
  (d) Never went to college but wants his kids to.
  (e) Angered over the seeming better quality of education (teachers and curriculum) in the white schools.
  (f) Mistrustful of whites.

3. Citizen
   (a) White, married with four children in city schools.
   (b) Small ethnic group background — Irish descent.
   (c) Middle-aged.
   (d) Semiprofessional — bookkeeper for large company.
   (e) Believes in law and order, drafting of war protesters, and disgusted by the trouble on college campuses.
   (f) Does not understand all the fuss — he came from a minority group and made it, why can't these people?
4. Citizen
   (a) White, married with one teenage son.
   (b) Believes what's happening is right (i.e. integration).
   (c) Active in community affairs.
   (d) On the "over 30" side of generation gap, but believes in kids.
   (e) Well-informed on current issues — does not agree with all that is happening but tries to understand.
   (f) Wants everyone to have an equal chance to make a "good life."
   (g) Anglo-Saxon ancestry; runs small business.
5. Citizen
   (a) Minority group; two kids.
   (b) Middle-class, assimilated.
   (c) Does not really understand the ghetto black.
   (d) Main concern is with retaining his own position and not being identified with the ghetto black.
   (e) Believes in law and order.
6. Citizen
   (a) White.
   (b) Working man — blue-collar job.
   (c) On PTA.
   (d) Fears for safety of his children in an integrated system — does not want them bused.
   (e) Believes kids of today spoiled.
   (f) Of the opinion that the disorder on college campuses a result of parents that were too permissive with their children.
7. Citizen
   (a) White.
   (b) Cop with some limited experience in the ghetto.
   (c) Does not trust minority group members — or Jews, or Catholics, or Italians, or Irish.

    (d) Sees his kids as getting the raw end of the stick.

    (e) Believes that what the country needs is more law and order.

8. Citizen
   (a) Minority group, two kids in high school, one in elementary school, one preschool.
   (b) Leery of integration — afraid his (her) kids will wind up worse off than they are now.
   (c) Cannot see integration as ever working.
   (d) Holds clerk position — earns enough to support his (her) family; afraid that if there is too much noise he (she) is apt to lose that job.
   (e) In conflict with his (her) children who lean toward militancy.

9. Citizen
   (a) Minority group.
   (b) Migrant worker from the South.
   (c) 5th grade education.
   (d) Wants an equitable standard of living, economically and educationally.
   (e) Two children in the minority group school.
   (f) Straining under poor living conditions, low wages, and poor education for children.

10. Citizen
    (a) Minority group.
    (b) Farm owner.
    (c) Lives on East Side.
    (d) High school graduate.
    (e) Struggled hard to make it through hard work and saving.
    (f) Anti-busing — does not want the education of his children to become inferior in any way.
    (g) Struggle with farmers — does not want to raise wages.

11. Citizen
    (a) White, married with two kids.
    (b) Owns factory in Psych City.
    (c) Inherited wealth — has been of a wealthy family.
    (d) Belongs to John Birch Society.
    (e) Fighting to keep taxes from rising.

12. Citizen
    (a) Minority group.
    (b) Lower-class.
    (c) Born and raised on the west side of Psych City.

(d) Factory worker with regular attendance and good work record.
(e) Prides self on being a family man.
(f) Does considerable work for the community, not for any personal gain or for any social cause, but because the community needs improvement.
(g) Currently enrolled in night school to complete high school education.

13. Citizen
    (a) White, four kids.
    (b) Construction worker.
    (c) Member of labor union.
    (d) Served in Korea and member of reserves — Captain's rank.
    (e) Law and order proponent.
    (f) On local censorship committee.

14. Citizen
    (a) White.
    (b) Bill collector on West Side.
    (c) Authoritarian — maintains rigid control over his family.
    (d) Worked for Conservative party as a volunteer in last election.

15. Citizen
    (a) White, three children, two in college, one out of school.
    (b) Middle-class.
    (c) Branch manager of bank.
    (d) Two years of college; dropped out to help family during rough period and never managed to finish school.
    (e) Started as teller and worked way up to branch manager.
    (f) Upwardly mobile; aspiring to climbing the social ladder and opposed to anything that will get in the way.

16. Citizen
    (a) Minority group.
    (b) Lives on West Side even though can afford to move out.
    (c) Appears to be fighting for equality.
    (d) Aspiring to public office.

17. Citizen
    (a) Doctor, white, married, three kids; two in elementary school, one in high school.
    (b) Large private practice on East Side.
    (c) Believes people can be successful if they try hard.
    (d) Concerned about deterioration of urban areas.

(e) Thinks parents need to be firm but loving.
18. Citizen
    (a) White, married with two kids; one in elementary school, one pre-school.
    (b) Recent graduate of dental school.
    (c) Likes working with children.
    (d) Does volunteer work in inner city clinic one day a week.
    (e) Does not condone drugs, but does not condemn them.
19. Citizen
    (a) White, married with five kids.
    (b) Born in "old country" — emigrated at age 18.
    (c) Has small store in downtown business area.
    (d) Naïve in political matters.
    (e) Wants to protect his store, his family.
20. Citizen
    (a) White, married with two kids; one in college, one married.
    (b) College administrator at Psych City State College.
    (c) Wants more money in state colleges.
    (d) Impersonal, businesslike.
    (e) Is an efficiency expert.
21. Citizen
    (a) White, married, one kid in Ivy League College.
    (b) Professor of social psychology at Psych City State College.
    (c) Is open-minded to students' ideas.
    (d) Enjoys intellectual discussions.
    (e) Was on presidential committee to study welfare.
22. Citizen
    (a) White, married with two elementary school kids.
    (b) Doctorate in electrical engineering from good engineering college.
    (c) Tries to be very logical and rational, often becoming impersonal.
    (d) Senses a feeling of community obligation, but does not know what to do.
    (e) Plagued by a status-seeking wife.
23. Citizen
    (a) White, married with one preschool age child.
    (b) Was drafted into army; went to night school for accounting.
    (c) Has nine-to-five accountant job.
    (d) Always wanted to be a musician.
24. Citizen
    (a) White, about 45 years old, married with two sons, one daughter.

    (b) High school, owns a construction firm.

    (c) Had connections in labor union.

    (d) Does not believe in welfare.

    (e) Hopes son will take over business.

    (f) Likes to have friendly relationship with employees.

25. Citizen

    (a) Minority group, married with three kids.

    (b) Dropped out of high school.

    (c) Is on welfare, has left family.

    (d) Talks a lot at Town Meeting, but is not too informed.

26. Citizen

    (a) Minority group, married with three kids in elementary school.

    (b) High school education; owns store and lives on West Side.

    (c) Wants to keep store for his "people."

    (d) Is plagued by robberies.

    (e) Believes his children get an okay education at school.

27. Citizen

    (a) White.

    (b) Unemployed; in local union, was carpenter.

    (c) Would like to see money used to build things.

    (d) Does odd jobs for many people in city.

    (e) Hates to see natural resources butchered.

28. Citizen

    (a) White, married, no kids.

    (b) Went to college for three years.

    (c) Cannot find job – trained in psychology.

    (d) Will not do "menial" labor.

    (e) Uses soft drugs occasionally.

29. Citizen

    (a) White, widower, about 65.

    (b) Worked in a factory for 40 years.

    (c) Completed elementary school.

    (d) Is at a loss now that spouse is dead.

    (e) Has fears of being useless.

30. Citizen

    (a) Minority group, retired.

    (b) Had two years of high school.

    (c) Did all types of jobs.

    (d) Wants to take it easy, now that he has retired.

    (e) Feels community must take care of him now.

31. Citizen
    (a) White, married with four kids; two in elementary school, one in high school.
    (b) Fireman.
    (c) Wanted to go to college, but parents did not have money.
    (d) Is angered by living conditions in parts of West Side.
    (e) Active in Firefighters Association.
    (f) Wants kids to go to college.
32. Citizen
    (a) Minority group, married with three kids in elementary school.
    (b) Takes some courses at Psych City State College.
    (c) Is one of few minority group members on police force.
    (d) Lives on East Side.
    (e) Thinks police force in general is prejudiced against minority group.
33. Citizen
    (a) White.
    (b) Married right after high school; two children in white high school.
    (c) Does news show on local TV station.
    (d) Tries hard to be objective about reporting news.
    (e) Sees his job as making public aware of social problems.
34. Citizen
    (a) Minority group, married with one preschool child.
    (b) Door-to-door salesman.
    (c) Dropped out of high school.
    (d) Is assimilated into white community.
    (e) Would like to move to East Side but cannot afford to do so.
35. Citizen
    (a) White, young (25), married, no children.
    (b) Went to two-year college.
    (c) Father is professional.
    (d) Runs a small leather store with help of spouse.
    (e) Believes people should "live and let live."
36. Citizen
    (a) White, married to minority group person, no children.
    (b) Parents planned big career in politics — were against marriage.
    (c) Works in an office downtown.
    (d) Lives on East Side.
37. Newspaper Editor
    (a) Participant observer.

(b) There to cover what happens for his newspaper.

(c) Has personal feelings about what is happening.

(d) Believes in maintaining state and federal aid to education.

(e) Supports the president's foreign and domestic policies.

(f) Did internship in a Southern city where he had a good deal of contact with minority group members.

38. University Professor

(a) Main interest is in group processes, procedures, and dynamics.

(b) A specialist in group processes — worked at National Training Labs.

(c) Has no vested interest in the problem at hand.

(d) Nonparticipating — there to observe the group process and to observe what goes on.

Students

1. Student

(a) White.

(b) Attending a predominantly white school in the school system under consideration.

(c) First generation American — parents immigrated from Poland.

(d) Both parents work to support large family.

(e) Works after school to meet as many of his (her) own needs as possible — wants to earn things for him (her) self rather than having them given to him (her).

2. Student

(a) Minority group.

(b) Star basketball player.

(c) Was offered a scholarship to college because of sports ability.

(d) Is somewhat militant.

(e) Wants to try drugs.

3. Student

(a) White.

(b) Attending a predominantly white school in the school system under consideration.

(c) Has some negative feelings about busing — especially if he (she) is one of those to be bused.

(d) Little contact with minority group kids.

(e) Working-class background — father a construction worker.

(f) Of Italian descent.

4. Student
    (a) White.
    (b) Attending predominantly white school in the school system under consideration.
    (c) Middle-class background — father a pharmacist.
    (d) Has not yet formed his (her) own opinions but has rather adopted those of his (her) parents.
    (e) Aware of what is going on in the world but it has little effect on him (her).
5. Student
    (a) Minority group.
    (b) Attending a predominantly minority group school in the school system under consideration.
    (c) Wants good education for minority groups but not sold on integration.
    (d) Little contact with whites.
    (e) Fear of prejudice — fear of going to school with whites.
    (f) Wants respect and acceptance as a person, not because of his (her) race.
    (g) Both parents work to support family of six — father a mailman and mother a supermarket cashier.
6. Student
    (a) Minority group.
    (b) Attending a predominantly white school in the school system under consideration.
    (c) Middle-class background — father holds civil service job.
    (d) Conflict — has adopted white middle-class values but fears rejection by both groups if integration occurs.
    (e) Active in school activities.
7. Student
    (a) White.
    (b) Attending predominantly white school in school system under consideration.
    (c) Believes minority group kids deserve as good an education as others.
    (d) Wants to do what is right.
    (e) Class officer.
    (f) Believes in change, but not radical in coming; rather slow.
8. Student
    (a) White.

(b) Attending a predominantly white school in school system under consideration.

(c) Active in school activities.

(d) Believes a good high school education important for getting into a "good" college.

(e) Concerned about the implications of having attended an integrated school — will it hinder his (her) education and therefore his (her) chances of getting into a "good" college.

9. Student
   (a) Minority group.
   (b) Attending a predominantly minority group school in the school system under consideration.
   (c) No father in the home — family on welfare.
   (d) Hesitant about busing — especially if he (she) has to be bused.
   (e) Not sure about integration as a concept — whether it is necessary at all.
   (f) Some bad experience with prejudice and discrimination.

10. Student
    (a) White.
    (b) Uses drugs but parents do not know.
    (c) Friend of student that overdosed.
    (d) Above average grades, planning on attending Ivy League College.

11. Student
    (a) Minority group.
    (b) Uses drugs infrequently.
    (c) Has had arguments with parents over it.
    (d) Above average student.

12. Student
    (a) Minority group.
    (b) Does not use drugs nor do friends.
    (c) Has had minor difficulty with law.
    (d) Average student.

13. Student
    (a) White.
    (b) President of Student Government at predominantly white high school.
    (c) Father is a doctor.
    (d) Feels students should be more active.

14. Student
    (a) Minority group.

    (b) Attending a predominantly minority group school in the school system under consideration.

    (c) Militant leanings.

    (d) Conflict with parents who want him (her) to assimilate — he (she) feels it would be compromising his (her) integrity.

    (e) Feels he (she) is doing the right thing and wants to do the right thing.

    (f) A student leader — on the student council.

15. Student (graduate)

    (a) Interested in group procedures, processes, and dynamics.

    (b) Some experiences in group procedures.

    (c) No vested interest in the issue at hand.

    (d) Nonparticipant — there to observe the group process and to observe what goes on.

CHAPTER 5

The Town Meeting

The Town Meeting is a meeting of all the representatives of the community interest groups (i.e. all the participants in Psych City). All individuals present at the Town Meeting are there in the form of the roles assigned to them. Words, actions, and viewpoints expressed in the meeting will be only those which reflect the role which you are playing. The function of the Town Meeting is to serve as a forum for the opinions of interest groups and individuals as well as a setting where decisions concerning the community-at-large can be made.

Each session of Psych City will convene in the form of a Town Meeting. This format will give structure to the session and inform members as to the state of the community. It is not necessary that every session meet in the form of a Town Meeting for its entirety. Each session must, however, both begin and end in the Town Meeting format. The actual working time for a session of Psych City should be from 1 to 1½ hours. Approximately 15 minutes should be reserved at the end of the session to discuss procedural questions, improvement of role-playing techniques, and to receive the observations of the instructor and other observers.

Participants might feel awkward about the role playing for the first three or four sessions of the Town Meeting; however, this initial feeling will disappear after the first few sessions.

Your group should set some attendance requirements before the first Town Meeting. Attendance at Town Meetings by all participants is important; every person's performance will affect the others in the simulation (e.g. who will chair the meeting in the mayor's absence?).

There is no formal record-keeping of the simulation. Each participant might want to keep a journal of his experience during Town Meetings. Thoughts on your own role, ideas which pertain to Psych City and other communities, and whatever other learning experiences the simulation initiates could go into your journal.

PROCEDURE

Each session of the Town Meeting will be chaired by the mayor. The mayor will summarize the general situation in Psych City and inform citizens of some changes that may have taken place since the previous meeting. When the mayor is not in attendance, a replacement will chair the meeting. This replacement should be selected from among the members of the community at an early session of the Town Meeting. A Town Meeting may be called at any time by any individual who is able to persuade the mayor that a meeting is needed. These meetings may be adjourned for caucus at any time desired if a majority present agrees to it. In addition, a subgroup may hold an informal caucus while the meeting is in session if they feel that this is necessary. Subgroup plans for solving community problems may be presented, discussed, and voted on in the Town Meeting.

THE INITIAL MEETING

Among the issues you should deal with at the initial meeting are:

(1) How decisions will be arrived at. There are many ways of coming to a community decision (i.e. equal votes per person — majority rule, etc.), and one of your tasks is to decide which method you want to use.

(2) How voting procedures will proceed — straw vote, secret ballot, etc.

(3) How structured or flexible you want the decision process to be. You may want the same procedure for all community decisions or you may want procedures to depend on the situation at hand. You are to decide upon procedures that will best suit your individual and community goals.

(4) What kind of power hierarchy you desire for subsequent meetings. An example — the mayor may be absent from some sessions. Who will chair or call Town Meetings? Who makes community decisions in the mayor's absence, etc.?

The initial Town Meeting should establish the rules by which subsequent meetings are run. It will be your responsibility, as a community, to see that Town Meetings are convened, run, and adjourned each week. It is through these meetings that decisions may be made concerning the community, where issues can be discussed with the group as a whole, and where public officials and other interest groups can be persuaded to your point of view. If any problems arise during the duration of Psych City they should be brought before the Town Meeting so that decisions may be reached. The moderator should *not* be consulted during the meeting. Questions about the prescribed limitations of the community should be asked *after* the meeting. All other decisions should be made by *you*.

SUBGROUPS

Certain groups have, to this point, been delineated for you such as the parent group, school administrators, students, etc. (see Roles in Chapter 4). In addition to these groups, there are others that should develop in the natural course of events. Such groups may be a pro-integration, an anti-integration group, an ecology group, a low-income housing group, a minority youth group, a white-parent group, or even a pro-integration, anti low-income housing group. As you develop your role, you, as an individual in this community, are going to see a way or ways to accomplish the task and at the same time satisfy your own needs. You will need the support of other people like yourself (i.e. like you are as you play your role) and try to work together. As such, you will have to cross the delineated group lines.

These groups may come together naturally or may be called together at any time by any person or persons. There will be times, however, when two or more groups in which you have an interest (i.e. teacher group and anti-integration group) are meeting simultaneously. Obviously you cannot attend both meetings. The choice of which meeting you will attend will be left up to you at all times. These choices should be made thoughtfully so that alternatives and consequences are considered. What would the person you are playing do in that situation?

After each subgroup meets, there may or may not be information or decisions or whatever that the group may want to relate to the total group. If there is something that is to be presented to the whole group, the manner of presentation will be left up to the subgroup to decide. For example, your subgroup is anti-integration and has decided to take a firm stance. As a group you have decided (by majority vote, consensus?) to sacrifice state and federal aid to maintain the status quo. As a group, you want the whole group to know this. A chairman has been elected to report this decision for the whole group. Or, as a group of minority group parents who are anti-busing, you have decided that it would be best for your children to have better teachers, equipment, and facilities in your school and keep the imbalance in color. Realizing you will lose aid this way, you propose to fund your own school. Each member speaks as he sees fit when this notion is presented to the total group. In summary, what you decide, how you go about making the decision and relating it to the whole group is up to you as a group.

THE CAUCUS

As previously mentioned, a subgroup may want to get together for a meeting (caucus). There are a number of reasons why a group would meet. For example, the minority group anti-integration parent group has met and proposed to the community a plan to keep the schools segregated but supply the minority group school children with better teachers, equipment, and facilities. Realizing the loss in aid, they propose that the community fund its own school so that keeping the schools apart can be accomplished. This has been presented to the larger group. Your particular subgroup may meet to do one of the following:

(1) Accept, reject, or modify the proposal.
(2) Discuss the proposal and arrive at a position regarding the proposal.
(3) Come up with an alternative proposal.
(4) Come up with a new and different and perhaps antagonistic proposal.
(5) Block the original proposal.
(6) Come up with a compromise proposal.

These caucuses may constitute the bulk of most sessions. Initially, they may convene for the purpose of arriving at a group position on an issue. Most likely the formal groups will meet and attempt to work out their own conflicts and arrive at a decision or position. As these decisions and positions are arrived at, some people will not be satisfied. It is at this time that alliances are formed among individuals, across groups, and new interest groups are formed. How, when, and what these groups will be, should develop out of the initial meetings and what transpires in these meetings. The procedures for coming together and reporting have been discussed under the topic *Subgroups*.

OUTSIDE FEEDBACK

The Psych City Clarion Newspaper

Information about changes in the nature of Psych City, important events taking place in that community, and the relative status of various subgroups will be made available to members of the community. The purpose of this information is to provide feedback about the groups' performance in the simulation. In addition, it may become necessary to change the structure of the situation from time to time in order to maintain activity. The positions of other groups within the community will be made available to you so that you are better able to make decisions within your own subgroups.

The major formal channel of communication within the community will be the Psych City newspaper. This paper will carry information about important changes outside of Psych City which will have effects within the community. This information will be provided by the moderator. The opinions of observers concerning the activities of some groups within the community will also be published in the paper. Subgroups within Psych City may make their opinions known to the community-at-large by having the paper's editor publish their position statements and activities. The paper's editor may provide editorial comments concerning various happenings of the community in his capacity as a participant observer. *The Psych City Clarion*, then, functions as a feedback system to tell you what is happening in Psych City and the world around it, as well as a barometer of how various groups are performing. The news items found in the paper are to be considered as reflections of reality. Changes in the situation, as related by the paper, should be interpreted as changes in the environment with which you will have to deal. This information should affect your responses to the problems at hand.

The *Clarion* should be published at least once a week. The editor will be responsible for collecting news articles and letters-to-the-editor. The moderator will be responsible for printing and distributing the newspaper. The most efficient method of printing the *Clarion* is through the use of a ditto or mimeograph machine. Figure 1 contains a sample of *The Psych City Clarion*.

Post-Meeting Feedback

After each Town Meeting, the participants should discuss their reactions to the meeting, under the supervision of the moderator. Questions

THE PSYCH CITY CLARION

... with a view of what's new   April 9, 1970

DEADLINE PUSHED AHEAD

Psych City—Due to the recent mail strike, Freedom Fight Foundation has moved the deadline date for proposals up. Those organizations concerned will now have until noon today to submit their proposals to the local board. It is still expected that the decision of the board will still be announced on or before April 22.

EDITORIALS

A Time for Alternatives

Time is running out, and what definite proposals for racially balancing the Psych City Schools do the citizens have before them? As far as this editor can see, the only proposal that has been openly discussed to any degree is that of busing the students from one school to another. Whether there is a satisfactory alternative or not is not the point here. What *is* important is that other possibilities be brought to the attention of the community very soon. Some groups in the city may have such proposals in mind, but how can the other residents think pro or con on an issue about which they are uninformed? Either by way of town meetings, through the Psych City *Clarion* or by printed handouts, these alternatives must come to the surface and be judged by the people.

LETTERS TO THE EDITOR

The announcement in last week's *Clarion* that the unemployment rate has risen to 8.2% at the factory should be of grave concern to those who still consider noncompliance with the State Education Bill a viable alternative. Noncompliance would result in a cutting of all federal and state funds, making a high increase in local taxes inevitable. With higher taxes new industry would be hesitant to move into Psych City and present industry might move out or at least be forced to lay off additional workers. Psych City *must* comply with the state bill; there is no other alternative.   A Taxpayer

The subject of busing has finally come up in the town meeting. Busing, bah, humbug!!! In my opinion, the money that is to go to busing should, instead, go to alternative programs to build up the black community. This is the only way black children can get a quality education. Busing them to the white school won't do it. After getting an inferior education for years these kids will not be able to compete with the white children. If you want to bus, why not consider starting with kindergarten only and then the next year with kindergarten and first grade, etc. In the meantime, these funds from the government should be used in the community and the black school to repair classrooms and clean up the garbage in the yards, get new equipment and better teachers. Only then can the quality of black education rise to meet that of white. Busing is not the answer.
A Parent

Fig. 1   The Psych City Clarion.

may be raised about the validity of participants' interpretation of their roles. Would that character *really* respond that way? Is the information she gave accurate? Is he responding to the stereotype, rather than to the whole person? Is she role playing her character or merely acting out her own feelings? Is the lack of active participation "in character" or are people reluctant to speak out in their roles because of their own self-consciousness?

While these discussions should be directed by the moderator, you should also raise questions or give your own reactions to these issues. It is in these post-meeting sessions that inaccuracies and unrealistic performances are corrected and for this reason it is important that you be open and honest in your comments and reactions.

The following article was written especially for this book. It will help you to fill out, and play, your role in Psych City.

ROLE PLAYING IN PSYCH CITY*

Rosanne Orenstein

Components of Role Playing

Role playing is a technique used to promote experientially based understanding. It may be compared with other techniques used in teaching like lecture methods and discussion groups in that it is a vehicle through which learning may take place. Sarbin (1964, p. 177) sees role playing as the performance of patterned behaviors by an individual who has been assigned a position in a given social structure. For instance, enacting the role of student includes the patterned behaviors of attending classes, doing homework, and taking tests. Playing the role of parent may include changing diapers, reading bedtime stories, and preparing meals. Taking the role of foreman in an industrial plant may consist of checking on schedules, assigning individuals to jobs, and hiring new employees. As Sarbin's definition indicates, each of these patterned behaviors, or roles, is enacted in the context of a particular social structure; in the above examples they are a college, a family, and a factory. We will be chiefly concerned in this course, with enacting the roles that each class member has been assigned in the context of a community called Psych City.

At first, it may seem like a formidable task to enact a role with which one has little or no familiarity. However, knowing what the general

*Prepared especially for this book.

components of role enactment are and seeing how they might be applied to a particular role may be helpful. Sarbin (1964) describes four main components to role playing—cognitive, motoric, empathic, and specificity. Each of these elements is an essential part of any given role.

The cognitive element, Sarbin says, is made up of role expectations deriving from stereotypes. Let us say we are attempting to portray the role of teacher. There are ideas or cognitions that are generally attributed to teachers which are inferred from common knowledge. For example, it is likely that as a teacher one believes that education is important, is aware of problems facing both students with their parents and parents with their children, and has values in common with others in the service professions. That is, beliefs like these which are widely held by teachers make up the cognitive component of the teacher role. In preparing for the role you are to play in Psych City, you can learn about the cognitive aspects of your role by reading about people who enact your assigned role in their real life and seeing how these individuals are regarded by society.

According to Sarbin, motoric and gestural components consist of the use of bodily movement and gestures associated with a given role. In addition to how a person uses his body to enact his role, the motoric component includes the spoken language he uses and the effect he displays. In some cases, we would expect these components to vary from role to role, e.g. from Black Panther to white middle-class schoolteacher. Body carriage and gesturing and the use of role appropriate jargon are important in creating convincing characters. Watching television, listening to the radio, and talking with people who live the role are good ways of getting acquainted with these physical elements of role enactment.

The empathic component that Sarbin describes is the understanding of, and insights into, a role that go beyond cognitive generalities. You may acquire these by talking to specific people you know in that role about their thoughts and feelings concerning their situation, by thinking about the role you are portraying, or indeed, from the role playing itself. The empathic component makes a significant contribution toward establishing depth personalities versus stereotypic facades. It is the most difficult aspect of role playing to master.

Sarbin's specificity component refers to particular skills or knowledge that is part of a given role. Policemen know how to use guns, teachers know how to write lesson plans and housewives know about the price of food. It is important to acquaint yourself with the skills you, as the character you are playing, possess.

As we move on to examine how these various components of role enactment are developed and applied, we should keep in mind that role playing consists not only of *en*acting, but also of *re*acting. That is, not only must you assert yourself within the cognitive, motoric, empathic, and specificity framework, but you must respond to others while bringing these elements to bear on your response. You are a teacher, mayor, policeman, or parent in Psych City not only when you are speaking to others but also as you attend to others. Role playing requires that you be active at all times, whether you are a spokesman or a listener.

So far, we have looked at role playing as portraying the role of teacher *or* parent *or* political activist. In reality, however, it is a fact that most people enact multiple roles. A single person may be a teacher *and* a parent *and* a political activist. That is, each of us performs particular roles or patterned behaviors at particular times. It is the collection of these behavior patterns that adds up to the unique person each of us is. You may now be enacting the role of a student in attending this class, at other times the role of daughter, of friend, or of fraternity member. Each of us enacts many roles during the course of a single day and from this perspective we can view people as being made up of many roles, these various roles contributing to complex human behavior. As well as enacting multiple roles, our behavior changes with changing circumstances. The social structure in which you as a student find yourself may vary from a two-person group to a lecture class. "Rapping" with a friend about a book and making a comment on that book in your lecture class may carry with it concomitant changes in behavior. That is, the social structure, as well as the role may influence behavior.

Each of you in this class has been assigned a particular role in the social structure of Psych City which we can now see consists of a multiplicity of roles. For example, the NAACP representative's brief role description (see p. 55) can be used to illustrate the many facets of a given role assignment. Let us say that calling him an NAACP representative implies that his primary group identification—his primary reference group is the NAACP. The concept of what a reference group is may help to put a role label in better perspective. Reference group identification often is the key to understanding a person's behavior in terms of the social structure in which he operates. A reference group is "any group with which an individual identifies himself such that he tends to use the group as a standard for self-evaluation and as a source of his personal values and goals. The reference groups of the individual may include both membership groups and groups to which he aspires to belong." (Kretch, Crutchfield, and Ballachey, 1962, p. 102.) A person's reference groups are only partially known by knowing his role label. Again, let us look at the NAACP representative. His primary reference group is the NAACP, that is, that he identifies with this organization in that he uses this group as a standard for self-evaluation and as a source of his personal values and goals. However, there are other reference groups called secondary reference groups and knowing more about the NAACP representative's life will tell us more about aspects of his life other than those derived from his NAACP affiliation. For example, his role description says he thinks that "education is the way." Knowing how he got to this belief may be helpful in finding out more about his other reference groups. He may be a teacher in an integrated school, blue-collar worker who has worked hard to send his children to college, or a corporation president who sees integration and education from the viewpoint of the economic advantages it offers. Each of these different situations would provide him with different secondary reference groups, other groups whose values and attitudes have an important influence on his own. This picture of the complexity of a "role" is presented so that the reader may appreciate that although there will be differences between the NAACP representative with say, the Black Panther representative (e.g. on the use of violence), there is the possibility that these two men may have more in common regarding secondary reference groups like the church, their families and job associates than one NAACP representative has with another NAACP representative.

Most role assignments, besides telling us something about a person's reference group identification, reflect what Parson and Shils (1951) call universalistic values. Universalistic values apply to situations in which the mode of interaction is defined culturally by the person's position in the social structure and is independent of his personal relationship. That is, a position in society be it teacher, judge, politician, or policeman carries with it behaviors separate from the personal feelings of the people in those roles. These personal thoughts, feelings, and attitudes are what Parsons and Shils call "particularistic" values. There are times when universalistic and particularistic values may come into conflict. A policeman may give a traffic ticket to a traffic violator who is also his friend. Here, the role of policeman and the universalistic values associated with the role may conflict with the personal friendship relationship of the policeman. Particularistic differences may also account for differences between two people cast in the same primary role (e.g. two policemen), leading one to be emotional, outspoken in his beliefs and articulate, while another is rational, soft-spoken, and less articulate.

Summing up, people generally enact many roles in life. In role playing it is not feasible for any person to represent every aspect of a role. Especially in a simulated community where there is only one NAACP representative or one policeman, it is likely that at Town Meetings the universalistic aspect of his role will dominate. That is, he does indeed represent behaviors, values, and attitudes that the NAACP or the police force stands for, and it is likely that his primary reference group identification and universalistic values will determine much of his behavior. However, it is important if role playing is to be more than the acting out of caricatures of people, and is to reflect complex human beings interacting, that each person fashion his role not only from his assignment, or primary reference group affiliation and universalistic values, but from the entire range of roles, group memberships, and particularistic attributes of which people are made up. It is also important to bear in mind that conflicts can arise not only between two people of different primary roles and beliefs, but also between two people of the same primary role and also between the various roles played by any one person.

The Techniques of Role Playing

Role playing is a skill that can be learned like any other skill and improved upon. Just as in acquiring other abilities, some people are initially more adept at role playing than others. However, with practice, most people can develop proficiency in using the tool of role playing and have fun doing it as well.

The Role Play Leader   At the outset of creating Psych City, one- or two-hour sessions should be devoted to teaching and practicing role-playing skills. One person should conduct these introductory sessions, either the teacher, or someone who has had experience with role playing. The leadership responsibilities include providing direction and in an assured and fairly assertive manner, fulfilling the following role requirements: the leader should be warm, friendly, and accepting of the anxiety that class members may feel in embarking on the new venture of role playing. He should have confidence that role playing is an effective learning tool and operate under the assumption that the class will enjoy and benefit from role playing once they get up and try it. He must help guide the directing of the scenes while remaining group centered so that the problem situations to be enacted are elicited from the group. It is also the leader's job to insure that the classroom is a safe place to try on different roles. Often new role players get very involved in their roles, especially the more dramatic, aggressive aspects of them. The best way to assure physical safety is to be prepared to step in the moment anyone is in danger of being hit or pushed. Most often this assurance is directed more at the participant observers than the actors, since they are less sure about what the players are doing than those engaged in the acting.

Procedures in Role Playing   Here are steps (see Klein (1956) for a more detailed description) that the leader and the members of Psych City should follow together in the introductory role-playing sessions:

1. Create a readiness for role playing by using a "warm-up."
2. Establish a situation and cast the characters.
3. Set the scene for role enactment and play it out.
4. Involve the entire class.
5. Evaluate and discuss the role-playing situation.

A more detailed look at these steps may be helpful in conveying the techniques of role playing.

The Warm-Up   The warm-up is the very first thing that follows a brief introduction to role playing. Since role playing is an experiential, action method of teaching we encourage trying it out rather than talking about it, as soon as possible. Warm-ups are most successful if everyone in the group can be involved. The warm-up should, therefore, (1) be done quickly and (2) involve everyone. Here is an example of a warm-up technique:

> After roles in Psych City have been assigned, choose an issue (e.g. busing) and have each person state his opinion on that issue from the viewpoint of the role he has been assigned.

This exercise begins the process of each person's looking at the cognitive component of his role, as well as getting everyone involved. The warm-up serves to break the ice. Here is another example of a warm-up technique:

> Using the assigned roles, have each person mention two specialized abilities they have.

This exercise highlights the specificity component of role playing. It is best in this activity to stay in these cognitive realms, dealing with how the person being enacted would think versus how he would feel. This approach is generally more comfortable and initial participation can be somewhat anxiety arousing.

Establishing the Situation   The situation may be established in the following ways:

1. The leader can suggest a plausible situation in Psych City and cast the characters.
2. The class can establish the situation and volunteers can cast themselves.

Sometimes ideas expressed in a warm-up provide ready-made situations. For example, if, in giving their brief view of busing in the warm-up two people's opinions were in direct opposition, they may wish to come up to the front of the room and engage in a dialogue.

Setting the Scene   Two steps should be followed in setting the scene:

1. Real or imaginary setting and props should be described by the participants.
2. The leader interviews each of the participants.

The rationale behind step 1 is to make the enactment as realistic as possible. The purpose of step 2, the interviewing, is to have the role player and the class see, *in vivo*, how a role is established. Some questions that can be asked in the interview are as follows:

What is your name? What kind of work do you do? How large a family do you have? Do you belong to a church? What is your opinion about the city government? What is your opinion about the issue of school integration? etc.

The first few questions necessitate that the role player construct a real person, one with a name and a situation in the community. The other questions are geared toward understanding the person's opinions and ideas. Questions should be aimed at eliciting information about both primary as well as secondary reference groups and particularistic as well as universalistic characteristics.

Playing the Scene   Once the participants have been interviewed, they begin to enact the scene. There are several ways that understanding the roles of the Psych City community can be helped along while also allowing for *Audience Involvement and Evaluation of Role Playing*. They are as follows:

1. The acting can be stopped at several points, e.g. when a problem becomes clear or when an impasse has been reached. At these points the class can discuss the situation.

2. The role players can reverse roles. That is, two participants trade roles and continue to enact the scene. This 180° switch is helpful in highlighting the conflict not only for the class, but in the player's own mind, now being forced to see both sides of the issue from the "inside," and is helpful in developing the empathic aspect of role playing.

3. Different members of the audience can step in and out of a role quickly, to show alternatives to how it was enacted.

4. The audience looks for particular things in the role playing. For example, each participant observer looks for who, in the scene being enacted, he feels the most kinship with in terms of his own role. The participant observer's task need not be complex because watching the role play efforts of one's classmates is engrossing enough.

By repeating this process of creating new scenes, casting the characters, enacting the situations, and discussing, evaluating, and providing alternatives to the way the scene was enacted, members of Psych City will become familiar with the basic techniques of role playing. After one or two sessions in which the preceding procedure is followed, Psych City will come into being as a credible laboratory for understanding the workings of a community.

Pro's and Con's of Role Playing

Every technique has its special advantages, and its limitations, and role playing is no exception. On the plus side, role playing provides maximum flexibility in tailoring situations to suit the needs at hand. The scope of ideas and feelings that can be investigated through role playing is limited by little more than one's imagination. A second, but related advantage is that these ideas can be tried out while the enactor is not "playing for keeps" (Klein, 1956). In role playing, what is done, *can* be undone and what fails one way can be tried in a multitude of other ways. In this way the role-playing method allows human life to be studied in laboratory situations, like Psych City, where action and reaction can be played out, discussed, criticized, analyzed and reanalyzed with minimal risk.

Role playing also sensitizes the participants to new areas of their environment. When a teacher, say in his own role, goes into a public school to teach a class, he may attend to student attitudes, classroom routine, and decorations on the bulletin boards. In role playing, if that teacher is cast in the role of fire inspector, mayor of the city, or NAACP representative and "visits" that school, he may find himself attending to very different things. Sarbin (1964, p. 181) calls this a change in one's "search of the ecology for inputs" that is facilitated by and is a major benefit of role playing. Finally, role playing is, perhaps because it allows for all of the above to take place, a major vehicle for attitude change. Studies (see Goldstein, 1972 for a review of attitude change studies using role playing) point to role playing as a highly effective way to modify opinions and attitudes of the participants.

There are some sacrifices made by using role playing exclusively as a means to learn. Chief among these is the price, in time it takes to become involved in the role and to experience the potential benefits of role playing. Utilizing class time in this way also means paying less attention to some of the cognitive complexities of the subject matter that might be covered more fully by lecture. Finally, in order to be most effective, role playing necessitates the sharing of the experiences and personal feelings and insights which accrue during role enactment. Some students may be reluctant to do this and would not at all need to talk about themselves if they were in a class in which similar material was being surveyed by more traditional methods.

Above all, the price to be paid for learning through role playing is involvement. Role playing is an experiential teaching method that offers an opportunity to the participants for the discovery and rediscovery of community problems in a highly personal and meaningful way.

References and Suggested Readings

Corsini, R. J., and Cardone, S. *Role playing in psychotherapy: a manual.* Chicago: Aldine Publishing Company, 1966.

Deutsch, M., and Krauss, R. M. *Theories in social psychology.* New York: Basic Books, Inc., 1965, pp. 173–211.

Goldstein, A. P. *Structured learning therapy: A psychotherapy for the lower-class patient.* New York: Academic Press, 1972.

Klein, A. F. *Role playing in leadership training and group problem solving.* New York: Association Press, 1956.

Kretch, D., Crutchfield, R. S., and Ballachey, E. L. *Individual in society.* New York: McGraw-Hill Book Co., Inc., 1962.

Parsons, T., and E. A. Shils (Eds.) *Toward a general theory of action.* Cambridge, Mass.: Harvard University Press, 1951.

Sarbin, T. R. Role theoretical interpretation of psychological change. In P. Worchel and D. Byrne (Eds.) *Personality change.* New York: John Wiley & Sons, Inc., 1964.

Section II   Readings and Exercises

CHAPTER 6

Role Expectancies

Your role in Psych City can be defined in terms of the relationships you have with other participants in the simulation. The relationships which develop between you and participants who have similar goals in the simulation are likely to be different from those which develop between you and people whose goals are in conflict with yours. These relationships or social roles are based upon anticipations concerning the behavior of people occupying other role positions (Secord and Backman, 1964). We are able to function smoothly in social situations partially because we are able to predict or anticipate the behavior of other people in these situations. Most people are able to function more smoothly and feel more comfortable in familiar situations, among people they know than in unfamiliar situations or among people they do not know. To a large extent this is because you know what to expect from your friends or in situations where you have had some experience. Knowledge of a person's past behavior, personality, or attitudes facilitates interaction because you are able to anticipate how he will react to a wide variety of behavior. The information upon which these anticipations are based is minimal in an unfamiliar situation. If you or your family has ever moved, you may remember that making new friends or joining new groups at school seemed more difficult or less comfortable than interacting with old friends at your former school. The new experience contained fewer cues about how you were expected to act and how other people would behave than did your earlier situation.

The role a person fills in any social grouping provides some of the cues to behavior that were contained in familiar situations. By knowing what role a person fills we can reduce the probable variability in his expected behavior. Assume that you have just met someone for the first time. The knowledge that he is a policeman reduces uncertainty about what you might expect his behavior and attitudes to be. It is likely that he will be against the use of drugs, probable that he is politically conservative, and almost certain that he will take a dim view of your desire to hold up the corner drugstore. A person's occupation alone tells a great deal about him, such as his probable economic level, the kind of neighborhood in which he is most likely to live, and many of his attitudes. Organizations to which he belongs give more specific information about him. The impression you have of a member of the Students for a Democratic Society is usually different from that indicated by membership in the Young Americans for Freedom. In general, information about an individual's social role helps determine how you interact with him and your actions in turn influence how he interacts with you.

Initially, Psych City should contain many of the elements of an unfamiliar situation. The participants in the simulation, if they are adequately filling their roles, will be strangers to you, even if you have known them previously. The roles of the other participants will provide the major cues from which you can anticipate their behavior. The longer you are in the simulation, the more cues you will have available based upon their past behavior in the exercise. They in turn will be anticipating your behavior in terms of the role you play and the goals and interests implicit in that role. Both your expectations and theirs will influence the kind of relationships that you will have with the other participants.

In order to effectively comprehend the character you are playing and the behavior you observe within the simulated community, it is necessary to be aware of what motivates the behavior of the various persons being portrayed in the simulation. One guideline which may be used for making sense of people's behavior involves analyzing the interests and goals which are important to a person.

These interests and goals may be roughly categorized into three classes: (1) personal, (2) subgroup, and (3) community. Using a female white middle-class teacher, one might see the following examples of interests and goals. A strong personal interest of the teacher might be teaching. A related personal goal would be to effectively teach students the subject matter which she has been trained in. Looking at it from another direction, a personal interest of hers might be personal security and a related goal would be to avoid either personal physical harm or the possibility of losing her job. This teacher belongs to a number of subgroups. Some of these subgroups would include teachers, females, families, middle-class, whites, etc. An example of a goal of her middle-class subgroups would be to achieve the Protestant ethic (i.e. to work in a productive manner). Perhaps the most obvious example of a community goal would be the achievement of equal education opportunity for all members of the community.

Once you have understood what the various interests and goals of the people and subgroups in the community are, you may begin to grasp why a person acts in a particular manner. The ideal of any community would be when all of the people can achieve all of their personal and subgroup goals while at the same time achieving the general goals of the community. Naturally, this never occurs in reality because of the diverse nature of the goals of various people and subgroups, and we may understand the success of a community by determining how close to this ideal the community is. In the Psych City community it is obvious that in the beginning the interests and goals of the members of the community will not only be different but very often will be in conflict. This conflict will occur not only between different people and subgroups, but will also be seen when one person has goals and interests which conflict with one another. For instance, if the white middle-class teacher was afraid of black students, she might experience some conflict between her desire to provide a good education for everyone and her fear of losing personal security if more blacks attended her school.

Assuming most participants in Psych City behave in a manner consistent with their role assignments, you should obtain increasingly accurate expectations of how these people will act. These expectations should lead you to develop different kinds of relationships with various people in the simulation. You will discover that there are people in the group who are attempting to achieve the same goals as you; there will be others whose goals are in opposition to yours. People in some roles will be necessary or useful to you for goal attainment, others will inhibit this process. These expectancies are likely to lead to the formation of subgroups or coalitions of various roles, formed to the achievement of similar ends. If the role you have been assigned is that of a minority group militant parent, you are more likely to interact in a positive manner with someone whose role describes him as a Peace and Freedom Party representative than with someone who is described as a middle-class, white bank manager. This is only a relative prediction, however, since goals may change, and some situations may dictate a closer relationship with the white bank manager.

It is these expectancies, interactions, and conflicts which provide the major basis for constructing a field map which will help us understand the various patterns of behavior within the community. The achievement of the overall community goal may be accomplished in one of two ways. Either the personal and subgroup goals of all members of the community must be satisfied and integrated to some extent, or the dominant factions must subjugate or destroy the persons or groups whose interests and goals are in conflict with their own.

The readings in this section provide fictional and nonfictional examples of how role expectancies influence the behavior of persons enacting roles, and the people who come in contact with them.

A NOT-SO-FREE ASSOCIATION*

Robert Cohen

This short story by Robert Cohen shows how role expectancies shape the perceptions and behavior of two people toward each other. Often people will hide behind their roles to keep themselves from becoming personally involved with others. This story is a fictional example of how a professional uses his particular role as a safeguard against personal relationships.

We talked about what roles are and the behaviors of people when in those roles. However, to fully understand a person's motives in Psych City, you must be aware of how he uses his role. The adoption of specific roles (e.g. physician, carpenter, student) may assist people in their quest for developing self-identity, but these roles, if taken too literally, may also serve to mask the human qualities which people have in common with each other. This mask may be used to avoid certain situations (i.e. others finding out what kind of person I really am); or it may be used to gain certain advantages (i.e. I should be given more respect because of my status).

Dr. Sigfried Aural was a prominent psychoanalyst, born in Brooklyn, and trained in Vienna. After six years of exhausting analytic training, he established himself in a plush office, overlooking Central Park. His thriving practice indicated human suffering was in vogue. He heard about infantile regression, anal fixation, and paranoid projection from 8:00 in the morning to 9:00 at night. If not for his obligation to the P.T.A., and the Wednesday evening Bridge Game, the couch would have rarely been vacant.

*Copyright © 1973 by Robert Cohen.

On this sunny June morning, Dr. Aural arrived at his office on schedule. He entered the consultation room, absorbed in *The New York Times* crossword puzzle, and was startled by a noise at the other end of the room. Looking up, he saw a slightly-built, middle-aged man gazing out the window. The doctor addressed the man in a professional manner, "Won't you please make yourself comfortable by reclining on the couch?"

Eyeing him suspiciously, the man walked to the couch, tested the cushion gingerly with his finger, and lay down. The doctor noted the suspicious glance, and leaning forward, said, "Before we get started I want to get everything straight. I am expensive, but good. Fifty dollars an hour and if hardship can be demonstrated, I have no qualms about dropping to forty-five. Of course, I do not have to tell you these things because you were either recommended and know how good I am, or you just picked me out of the phone book, in which case you would not know how good I am. Okay, forget that I just said that. I admit it was not professional. Let us start over.

"Here is how this business works. I either tell you to say the first thing that comes to mind, or if you have trouble with that, I ask pertinent questions to loosen you up. You just do what I tell you. Do not worry— you are paying big money, but you are getting the best."

There was silence for three seconds before Aural broke in with, "That is called resistance. Some analysts will accept that silent bit, but it really drives me buggy. That is another rule. Talk or else. I am not saying what happens if you do not talk, but it will not be pleasant, and unpleasant things do not help treatment."

The man on the couch sat up and turned toward the analyst. "What time do you get here in the morning?" he asked.

"Very clever," Aural snapped. "Turn everything around on the analyst. Oh, you are some clever guy, you are. Too bad I am not some wet-behind-the-ears doctor, just out of Medical School. Then you could really have me spinning. But I am not falling for any of that stuff, so you had better cut it out now!"

"You know, for a doctor you talk pretty funny," said the man. "I mean, who would ever think a doctor could get all hot and bothered over a simple little question."

Aural was squirming around in his chair, trying to get into a comfortable position, and did not seem to hear what was said. In a soft, well-controlled voice he said, "Now, as you were saying?"

"I wasn't saying anything," replied the man. "I'm just trying to get a few facts straight and you keep throwing this mumbo-jumbo at me." For the first time he appeared nervous. He looked down at the floor, and as if to justify the action, scooped up an imaginary object and dropped it into the ashtray stand. Wanting to get rid of the invisible evidence, he pushed down the little button and the jaws of the ashtray opened and snapped shut. The doctor cringed slightly.

"Mister . . . what is your name by the way?" asked Dr. Aural.

"Simpton. Barney Simpton."

"Yes. Well, Mr. Simpton, tell me — what are you thinking about at this moment?"

"Nothing."

"Come now, Mr. Simpton, you know, of course, that we are always thinking about something. You may have difficulty articulating your feelings, and there may be defense mechanisms trying to keep things unconscious, but I am prepared to help you to battle with your psyche, and in the end everything will come bursting forth in a beautiful flood of therapeutic emotion. In the end, everything will come out. Everything! — Do you understand? — Everything! So stop fighting me and help me unleash your real self."

Mr. Simpton seemed impressed with this authoritative approach, and responded quickly. "Okay, you want to know what I'm thinking. Here goes. I'm thinking that I would like to punch my fist into your fat face. I'd like to lay it in there real hard, without holding up at the shoulder. You're really making me mad and when I get that way I'm a pretty tough guy. I get really mean and all that. . . . There, I told you. You asked me what I'm thinking and I told you, so don't blame me."

He sat back against the wall, and then, as if exhausted, he swung his feet up on the couch and lay with his right arm hanging over the side, and his left arm draped across his eyes.

Leaning forward, Dr. Aural said excitedly, "Excellent, excellent. At last you have grasped the essence of analysis. Don't you feel relieved? Can't you feel the enormous pressure disappearing as the juices of health bathe your starved, barren being? Ah, the forces of harmony are setting in!"

The man on the couch rolled toward the wall, brought his knees up to his chest and buried his head between his arms.

"Now comes regression. A necessary phase of treatment in which you revert to more primitive forms of behavior. In this case, a return to the fetal position. Do not worry. You are in a safe, comfortable environment, just like your mother's womb, and you do not have anything to fear."

"Leave my mother out of this," yelled Simpton, springing to his feet and facing the analyst in a crouch. His fists were clenched, and a protruding vein in the middle of his forehead warned of the violent potential behind it. After standing rigidly for a few seconds, Simpton began to tremble slightly. Noticing this, he quickly returned to the couch and sat stiffly with his hands resting awkwardly in his lap.

Aural, noticing that the danger of physical assault was no longer present, leaned across his desk and said, "Okay. You were not ready for that one. I admit it. I jumped the gun. But that is no reason for acting that way. You really should watch yourself or you might do something you will regret later."

"I thought you said anything goes."

"That is a good point. Let me see. It seems I remember reading something about that issue. Give me a minute and I will come up with a rule of thumb." He leaned back in his chair, making a number of grunting and groaning noises, then plunged his head down between his knees. After several seconds he raised his reddened face, and explained somewhat breathlessly, "There are three things to remember in this case. First, I am an expert in human emotions. Second, whatever I say has been backed up scientifically by other analysts. Third, when I tell you something, it is for your own good. There. . . . I hope that clears things up for you. Now, getting back to where we were. . . ."

"But you didn't tell me why I couldn't do what I did," broke in Simpton. "That's not fair. You said you would tell me and then you didn't. What kind of guy are you anyway, a bad sport? I don't think I like you."

"You don't really mean that, do you?"

"I'm serious. I don't think I like you. Nothing personal, but you can be a real pain in the ass, and that's not my idea of the kind of guy I like."

A warm spurt of professional duty shot through the doctor, numbing his bruised feelings. Without any noticeable change, he shifted into another approach. "Tell me Mr. Simpton, have you ever had any traumatic experiences? I mean do you remember anything ever happening to you that was so frightening that you cannot remember it?"

"Huh?"

"Let me put it this way. Some people have been exposed to terrifying situations in their childhood, which have resulted in damage to their personalities. Usually these people think they have forgotten, but they are wrong, because lots of things are going on inside their heads, making their lives very miserable. We psychoanalysts are able to assist in these cases by helping the patient remember the event, thus taking away all the burden from the unconscious."

Simpton looked puzzled, as he asked in a confused tone, "But, what good does that do? If the guy remembers won't he just become upset again?"

"No, no," said Aural, shaking his head. "You do not understand. If the patient is a mature adult, he will realize this was only a memory distorted by his undeveloped mind during childhood, and will see that there is no longer any danger."

"But, what if he is not a mature adult?"

"Then. . . ." The doctor coughed and cleared his throat. "Then . . . that person had no business being in analysis in the first place." Feeling that he had handled this problem adequately, Aural pulled out a long, dark cigar. He stripped off the cellophane in two strokes, and thrust the oblong object into his mouth. Reaching down into his pocket, he pulled out a shining silver lighter, and in what seemed to be one smooth motion, opened and ignited it. Aural lit the cigar, and puffed vigorously on it. When the tip was a glowing orange ember, he pulled it from his mouth and pointed it at Simpton.

"What comes to your mind when I say the word *red*?" asked Aural.

"*Fire*?" replied Simpton in questioning tone.

Dr. Aural did not seem to be satisfied. "There are no right or wrong answers. Just say what comes to mind. Do not worry about what you say. One reply is as good as another."

"Then why go through this thing if it doesn't matter what I say?" asked Simpton.

"Do not be absurd, Mr. Simpton. The purpose of this technique is to loosen the bowels of your unconscious so that you may function in a natural and healthy manner."

"Oh, I get it now! Sort of like Exlax, huh?" Simpton offered, with a big grin.

The doctor squirmed in his seat, saying with some annoyance, "Not exactly. Now will you be kind enough to follow my instructions . . . I am going to show you Unconditional Positive Regard to which you will respond by feeling good all over, and dropping your inhibitions. By doing this, you will be able to relate your innermost thoughts and feelings to me. If there are no questions we will proceed. First, what is . . . "

"Wait a second . . . let's not go so fast . . . how do you mean it's not exactly like Exlax? I'd like you to explain that to me, please. If I'm going to get involved in this thing I want to know what it's all about. Ya know what I mean?"

As Mr. Simpton finished his assertive statement, the sonic boom of a silver jet plane brushed against the window in its desperate attempt to catch up to the swift, streamlined plane. The pane of glass shook briefly and the two men simultaneously glanced in that direction. The doctor tried to cover his awkward move by wincing and scratching an imaginary irritation on his neck. Mr. Simpton also placed his hand on his neck, but instead of scratching, he leaned on his elbow and said, "I'll be damned! A silly old jet, and it nearly scared the wits out of me. Boy am I jumpy! I better get some help before people start calling me some sort of nut . . . ."

"Do not say that," pleaded Aural. "You must not use that kind of language. There is too much misunderstanding . . . too much ignorance . . . too much intolerance . . . too much . . . ."

"What are you talking about?" asked Simpton.

"That . . . that word you used . . . *nut*! It is not right. We must understand that a disturbed person acts the way he does because he is *sick*. He does not have control over himself and cannot function properly until he understands what is at the root of his problem. If we call him names, and make no effort to help him he will shrivel and fade, as a babe without breast . . . Say, I like that, — a babe without breast. I must remember it . . . I can use it in my next lecture at the Analytic Society."

Simpton stared incredulously at the doctor. When he realized the oratory was finished, he started to rise from the couch. Seeing this, Aural quickly left his preparation of the forthcoming speech, and stepped in front of Simpton, blocking his path to the door.

"Wait . . . you cannot leave yet. There are twenty minutes remaining."

Simpton began to walk around the doctor, but seeing the anguished face of this man, he changed his mind, and returned to the couch. "You know," he said gently, "you really look lousy. I mean, you don't look good. Why don't you take a vacation, or something. It might cool you off a little."

It seemed for a second as if Aural might respond to this offer of concern, but he abruptly pushed up his glasses, straightened his tie, and clearing his throat, continued his monologue. ". . . As I was saying, your problems are indeed severe, but there is no reason they cannot be worked through, if you will obediently follow the rules of free association, and trust in me completely. Of course, this will require great sacrifice for both of us, and you cannot be impatient, since a great deal of time is necessary. I tell you this because I want you to be aware of what lies ahead for you. After all, honesty is the cardinal principle of analysis."

"Do you really believe that bullshit you're handing me?" asked Simpton. "I mean, you're a grown man, and a doctor and all that — and you can still sit there and tell me that with a straight face. Aren't you ashamed of yourself?"

Aural did not seem to be phased by this accusation. "Particularly in the early stages of analysis we are likely to see resistance. Then the patient understands that it is not the therapist, but some significant figure in his childhood toward whom he feels anger, the resistance will disappear, and treatment will proceed smoothly again."

Rising from the couch, Simpton started around the desk.

"Ah, resistance Mr. Simpton."

Simpton continued past the desk.

"We must not give in to our infantile urges to avoid reality," taunted the doctor.

Without slowing his pace, the slightly-built man proceeded toward the door.

In a slightly strained voice, Aural warned, "This will not help you Mr. Simpton."

As he reached the door, Simpton stopped, as if to reconsider. He scanned the room slowly, before walking to the window. There, he turned to the doctor and said thoughtfully, "Look, maybe it would be better if I come back some other day to wash the windows." Then, picking up his bucket, he walked briskly out of the office.

CASE STUDY OF A NONCONSCIOUS IDEOLOGY: TRAINING THE WOMAN TO KNOW HER PLACE*

Sandra Bem and Daryl J. Bem

Recently, attention has been focused on the role of women in our society. Women have expressed increased dissatisfaction with the roles which they play. Attempts have been made to define and put into practice a new alternative range of behaviors for women. Liberation groups have demanded equal opportunities for women in all areas of society. They have demanded that men treat them as whole human beings, not as servants and sexual objects.

A look at the new women's magazines forcibly illustrates this trend. There are no articles on the best way to apply eyeshadow, or the latest hairstyles. Rather, the feelings and ideas of women are emphasized. Numerous colleges and universities throughout the country have

*From Daryl J. Bem. *Beliefs, Attitudes, and Human Affairs.* Copyright © 1970 by Wadsworth Publishing Company, Inc. Reprinted by permission of the publisher, Brooks/Cole Publishing Company, Monterey, California.

initiated courses about the changing role of women in our culture. Controversy has arisen over how children should be raised to eliminate this discrimination against women.

Mr. and Ms. Bem's article is a cogent and articulate argument for their theory of how roles for women are inculcated in society.

In Psych City, many of the roles can be interpreted for either sex. We encourage some participants to be the other sex in their roles. Some men could play women, and vice versa.

One wonders how future communities will look due to this consciousness of women about their changing roles. The percentages of women delegates to the Democratic convention provide some indication. In 1968, 13% of the delegates were women; in 1972, women constituted more than 36% of the total number of delegates (*Newsweek*, June 26, 1972, page 21).

We have seen what happens when an individual's reference groups conflict. Alternative ideologies are suddenly brought into his awareness, and he is forced to select explicitly his beliefs and attitudes from among the competing alternatives. But what happens when all his reference groups agree, when his religion, his family, his peers, his teachers, and the mass media all disseminate the same message? The consequence is a nonconscious ideology, a set of beliefs and attitudes which he accepts implicitly but which remains outside his awareness because alternative conceptions of the world remain unimagined. As we noted earlier, only a very intellectual fish is aware that his environment is wet. After all, what else could it be? Such is the nature of a nonconscious ideology.

A society's ability to inculcate this kind of ideology into its citizens is the most subtle and most profound form of social influence. It is also the most difficult kind of social influence to challenge because it remains invisible. Even those who consider themselves sufficiently radical or intellectual to have rejected the basic premises of a particular societal ideology often find their belief systems unexpectedly cluttered with its remnants.

In our view, there is no ideology which better exemplifies these points than the beliefs and attitudes which most Americans hold about women. Not only do most men and women in our society hold hidden prejudices about the woman's "natural" role, but these nonconscious beliefs motivate a host of subtle practices that are dramatically effective at keeping her "in her place." Even many liberal Americans, who insist that a black skin should not uniquely qualify its owner for janitorial and domestic service, continue to assume that the possession of a uterus uniquely qualifies its owner for precisely that.

Consider, for example, the first student rebellion at Columbia University, which took place in the spring of 1968. You will recall that students from the radical left took over some administration buildings in the name of equalitarian ideals which they accused the university of flouting. Here were the most militant spokesmen one could hope to find in the cause of equalitarian ideals. But no sooner had they occupied the buildings than the male militants blandly turned to their sisters-in-arms and assigned them the task of preparing the food, while they—the menfolk—would presumably plan further strategy. The reply they received was the reply they deserved, and the fact that domestic tasks behind the barricades were desegregated across the sex line that day is an everlasting tribute to the class consciousness of the ladies of the left.

But these coeds are not typical, for the nonconscious assumptions about woman's "natural" role are at least as prevalent among women as they are among men. Philip Goldberg (1968) demonstrated this by asking female students to rate a number of professional articles from each of six fields. The articles were collated into two equal sets of booklets, and the names of the authors were changed so that the identical article was attributed to a male author (e.g., John T. McKay) in one set of booklets and to a female author (e.g., Joan T. McKay) in the other set. Each student was asked to read the articles in her booklet and to rate them for value, competence, persuasiveness, writing style, and so forth.

As he had anticipated, Goldberg found that the same article received significantly lower ratings when it was attributed to a female author than when it was attributed to a male author. He had predicted this result for articles from professional fields generally considered the province of men, such as law and city planning, but to his surprise the female students downgraded articles by female authors drawn from the fields of dietetics and elementary school education. In other words, these women rated the male authors as better at everything, agreeing with Aristotle that "we should regard the female nature as afflicted with a natural defectiveness." We repeated this experiment informally in our own classrooms and discovered that male students show the same implicit prejudice against female authors that Goldberg's female students showed. Such is the nature of a nonconscious ideology!

It is significant that examples like these can be drawn from the college world, for today's college generation has the least investment in perpetuating the established ways of looking at most issues, including the role of women. As we noted in our discussion of sexual conduct, today's college students have been quick to reject those attitudes of their parents which conflict explicitly with the students' major values. But as the above examples suggest, they will find it far more difficult to shed some of the more subtle aspects of a sex-role ideology which — as we shall now attempt to demonstrate — conflicts just as surely with their existential values as any of the explicit parental commands to which they have so effectively raised objection. It is thus by examining America's sex-role ideology within the framework of values held by the most aware and sensitive of today's youth that we can best illustrate the power and pervasiveness of the social influences that produce nonconscious ideologies in a society.

The Ideology Versus the Value of Self-Fulfillment

The dominant values of today's student culture concern personal growth, on the one hand, and interpersonal relationships, on the other. Accordingly, one subset of these values emphasizes the importance of individuality and self-fulfillment; the other stresses openness, honesty, and equality in all human relationships.

The major corollary of the self-fulfillment value is that each human being, male or female, is to be encouraged to "do his own thing." Men and women are no longer to be stereotyped by society's definitions. If sensitivity, emotionality, and warmth are desirable human characteristics, then they are desirable for men as well as for women. (John Wayne is no longer an idol of the young, but their pop satire.) If independence, assertiveness, and serious intellectual commitment are desirable human characteristics, then they are desirable for women as well as for men. The major prescription of this college generation is that each individual should be encouraged to discover and fulfill his own unique potential and identity, unfettered by society's presumptions.

But society's presumptions enter the scene much earlier than most people suspect, for parents begin to raise their children in accord with popular stereotypes from the very beginning. Boys are encouraged to be aggressive, competitive, and independent, whereas girls are rewarded for being passive and dependent (Barry, Bacon, & Child, 1957; Sears, Maccoby, & Levin, 1957). In one study, six-month-old infant girls were already being touched and spoken to more by their mothers than were infant boys. When they were thirteen months old, these girls were more reluctant than the boys to leave their mothers; they returned more quickly and more frequently to them; and they remained closer to them throughout the entire session. When a physical barrier was placed between mother and child, the girls tended to cry and motion for help; the boys made more active attempts to get around the barrier (Goldberg & Lewis, 1969). There is no way of knowing for sure to what extent these sex differences at the age of thirteen months can be attributed to the differences in the mothers' behavior at the age of six months, but it is hard to believe that the two are unconnected.

As children grow older, more explicit sex-role training is introduced. Boys are encouraged to take more of an interest in mathematics and science. Boys, not girls, are given chemistry sets and microscopes for Christmas. Moreover, all children quickly learn that mommy is proud to be a moron when it comes to mathematics and science, whereas daddy knows all about those things. When a young boy returns from school all excited over a biology class, he is almost certain to be encouraged to think of becoming a physician. A girl with similar enthusiasm is told that she might want to consider nurse's training later so she can have "an interesting job to fall back upon in case — God forbid — she ever needs to support herself." A very different kind of encouragement. And a girl who doggedly persists in her enthusiasm for science is likely to find her parents as horrified by the prospect of a permanent love affair with physics as they would be by the prospect of an interracial marriage.

These socialization practices have their effect. By the ninth grade, 25% of the boys, but only 3% of the girls, are considering careers in science and engineering. (In the Soviet Union, approximately 35% of the engineers are women.) When they apply for college, boys and girls are about equal on verbal aptitude tests, but boys score significantly higher on mathematical aptitude tests — about 60 points higher on the College Board examinations, for example (Brown, 1965, p. 162). Those who would attribute such differences to feminine hormones should know that girls improve their mathematical performance if problems are reworded so that they deal with cooking and gardening, even though the abstract reasoning required for their solutions remains the same (Milton, 1958). It would appear that both motivation and ability have been affected.

The effects in mathematics and science are only part of the story. A girl's long training in passivity and dependence appears to exact a similar toll from her overall motivation to achieve, to search for new and independent ways of doing things, and to welcome the challenge of new and unsolved problems. Psychologists have found that elementary school girls are more likely to search for a novel solution not provided by the adult (McDavid, 1959). Furthermore, when given the opportunity to return to puzzles a second time, girls are more likely to rework those they had already solved, whereas the boys are more likely to try puzzles they had been unable to solve previously (Crandall & Rabson, 1960). One almost expects to hear an audible sigh of relief when a woman marries and retires from the outside world of novel and unsolved problems. This, of course, is the most conspicuous outcome of all: the majority of American women become full-time homemakers.

Such are the consequences of a nonconscious ideology.

But how does all of this militate against the goal of self-fulfillment? First of all it should be clear that the value of self-fulfillment is not necessarily being violated just because some people may regard the role of homemaker as inferior to other roles. That is not the point. Rather, the point is that our society is managing to consign a large segment of its population to the role of homemaker solely on the basis of sex just as inexorably as it has in the past consigned individuals with black skin to the roles of janitor and domestic. It is not the role itself which is at issue here, but the fact that, in spite of their unique identities, the majority of America's women end up in the *same* role.

Even if this is so, however, there are several arguments which can be advanced to counter the claim that America's socialization of its women violates the value of self-fulfillment. The three most common arguments invoke respectively (1) freewill, (2) biology, and (3) complementarity.

1. The freewill argument proposes that a 21-year-old woman is perfectly free to choose some other role if she cares to do so; no one is standing in her way. But this argument overlooks the fact that society, which has spent twenty years carefully marking the woman's ballot for her, has nothing to lose in the twenty-first year by pretending that she may cast it for the alternative of her choice. Society has controlled not her alternatives, but her motivation to choose any but one of those alternatives. The so-called freedom to choose is illusory and cannot be invoked when the society controls the motivation to choose.

2. The biological argument suggests that there may really be physiological differences between men and women in, say, aggressiveness or mathematical ability. Or that there may be biological factors (beyond the fact that women can become pregnant and nurse children) which uniquely dictate that women, but not men, should stay home all day and shun serious outside commitment. Maybe female hormones really are somehow responsible. One difficulty with this argument is that female hormones would have to be different in the Soviet Union, where women comprise 75% of the physicians and, as noted above, about 35% of the engineers, and where only one married woman in twenty is a full-time homemaker. Female physiology is different, and it may account for some

of the psychological differences between the sexes, but most psychologists, including us, continue to believe that it is America's sex-role ideology which causes so few women to emerge from childhood with the motivation to seek out any role other than the one that society has dictated.

But even if there really were biological differences between the sexes along these lines, the biological argument would still be irrelevant. The reason can best be illustrated with an analogy.

Those who subscribe to the value of self-fulfillment would be outraged, we submit, if every black American boy were to be socialized to become a jazz musician on the assumption that he has a "natural" talent in that direction, and if black parents should subtly discourage their sons from other pursuits because it is "inappropriate" for black men to become physicians or physicists. But suppose that it *could* be demonstrated that black Americans, *on the average*, did possess an innate better sense of rhythm than white Americans. Would that change outrage to acquiescence? Would that argue that a *particular* black youngster should have his unique characteristics ignored from the very beginning and that he should be specifically socialized to become a musician? We don't think so. Similarly, as long as a woman's socialization does not nurture her uniqueness, but treats her only as a member of a group on the basis of some assumed *average* characteristic, she will not be prepared to realize her own potential in the way that the values of today's college students imply she should.

The irony of the biological argument is that it does not take biological differences seriously enough. That is, it fails to recognize the range of biological differences between individuals within the same group category. Thus, recent research has revealed that biological factors help determine many personality traits of dominance and submissiveness have been found to have large inheritable components; that is, biological factors have the potential for partially determining how dominant or submissive an individual, male or female, will turn out to be. But this potential is realized more frequently in males (Gottesman, 1963). Apparently, only the males in our culture are raised with sufficient flexibility, with sufficient latitude given to their biological differences, for their "natural" or biologically determined potential to shine through. The females, it would appear, are subjected to a socialization which so ignores their unique attributes that even the effects of biology are swamped. In sum, the biological argument for continuing America's homogenization of its women gets hoist with its own petard.

3. Many people recognize that most women do end up as full-time homemakers because of their socialization and that these women exemplify the failure of our society to raise girls as unique individuals. But, they point out, the role of the homemaker is not inferior to the role of the professional man: it is complementary but equal.

This argument is usually bolstered by pointing to the joys of taking care of small children. Indeed, mothers *and* fathers find child-rearing rewarding. But the argument appears weak when one considers that the average American woman now lives to age 74 and has her last child in her late twenties; thus, by the time the woman is 33 or so, her children all have more important things to do with their daytime hours than spend them entertaining an adult woman who has nothing to do during the second half of her life-span. As for the other "joys" of homemaking, many writers (e.g., Friedan, 1963) have persuasively argued that the role of the homemaker has been glamorized far beyond its intrinsic worth. This charge becomes plausible when one considers that the average American homemaker spends the equivalent of a man's working day, 7.1 hours, in preparing meals, cleaning house, laundering, mending, shopping, and doing other household tasks. In other words, 43% of her waking time is spent in work that commands an hourly wage on the open market well below the federally set minimum wage for menial industrial work.

The point is not how little she would earn if she did these things in someone else's home, but that this use of time is virtually the same for homemakers with college degrees and for those with less than a grade school education, for women married to professional men and for women married to blue-collar workers. Talent, education, ability, interests, motivations — all are irrelevant. In our society, being female uniquely qualifies an individual for domestic work.

It is true, however, that the American homemaker has, on the average, 5.1 hours of leisure time per day, and it is here, we are told, that each woman can express her unique identity. Thus, politically interested women can join the League of Women Voters; women with humane interests can become part-time Gray Ladies; women who love music can raise money for the symphony; and so forth.

But politically interested men run for Congress. Men with humane interests become physicians or clinical psychologists; men who love music play in the symphony; and so forth. In other words, in our society a woman's unique identity most often determines only the periphery of her life rather than its central core.

Again, the important point is not that the role of homemaker is necessarily inferior, but that the woman's unique identity has been rendered irrelevant. Consider the following "predictability test." When a boy is born, it is difficult to predict what he will be doing 25 years later. We cannot say whether he will be an artist or a doctor or a college professor because he will be permitted to develop and to fulfill his own unique identity, particularly if he is white and middle-class. But if the newborn child is a girl, we can usually predict with confidence how she will be spending her time 25 years later. Her individuality doesn't have to be considered because it will be developed.

The socialization of the American male has closed off certain options for him too. Men are discouraged from developing certain traits such as tenderness and sensitivity just as surely as women are discouraged from being assertive and "too bright." Young boys are encouraged to be incompetent at cooking and child care just as surely as young girls are urged to be incompetent at mathematics and science.

One of the errors of the early feminist movement in this country was that it assumed that men had all the goodies and that women could attain self-fulfillment merely by being like men. But that is hardly the utopia that today's college students envision. Rather, the logical extension of their value of self-fulfillment would require that society raise its children so that some men might emerge with the motivation, the ability, and the opportunity to stay home and raise children without bearing the stigma of being peculiar. If homemaking is as glamorous as the women's magazines portray it, then men too should have the option of becoming homemakers. Even if homemaking isn't all that glamorous, it would probably still be more fulfilling for some men than the jobs in which they now find themselves.

And if biological differences really do exist between men and women in "nurturance," in their innate motivations to care for children, then this will show automatically in the final distribution of men and women across the various roles: relatively fewer men will choose to stay at home. The value of self-fulfillment therefore, does not imply that there must be equality of outcome, an equal number of men and women in each role. It does not imply that there should be the widest possible variation in outcome consistent with the range of individual differences among people, regardless of sex. At the very least, the value of self-fulfillment would seem to imply that the society should raise its males so that they could fulfill their own identities in activities that might be less remunerative than those being pursued by their wives without feeling that they were "living off their wives." One rarely hears it said of a woman that she is "living off her husband."

Thus, it is true that men's options are also limited by our society's sex-role ideology, but as the "predictability test" reveals, it is still the women in our society whose identities are rendered irrelevant by America's socialization practices. In 1954 the United States Supreme Court declared that a fraud and hoax lay behind the slogan "separate but equal." It is unlikely that any court will ever do the same for the more subtle motto that successfully keeps the woman in her place: "complementary but equal."

References

Barry, H., III, Bacon, M. K., & Child, I. L. A cross-cultural survey of some sex differences in socialization. *Journal of Abnormal and Social Psychology*, 1957, **55**, 327–332.

Brown, R. *Social psychology*. New York: Free Press, 1965.

Crandall, V. J., & Rabson, A. Children's repetition choices in an intellectual achievement situation following success and failure. *Journal of Genetic Psychology*, 1960, **97**, 161–168.

Friedan, B. *The feminine mystique*. New York: Norton, 1963.

Goldberg, P. Are women prejudiced against women? *Transaction*, April 1968, **5**, 28–30.

Goldberg, S., & Lewis, M. Play behavior in the year-old infant: Early sex differences. *Child Development*, 1969, **40**, 21–31.

Gottesman, I. I. Heritability of personality: A demonstration. *Psychological Monographs*, 1963, **31**, 58–64.

McDavid, J. W. Imitative behavior in preschool children. *Psychological Monographs*, 1959, 73 (Whole No. 486).

Milton, G. A. Five studies of the relation between sex role identification and achievement in problem-solving. Technical Report No. 3, Yale University, December 1958.

Sears, R. R., Maccoby, E. E., & Levin, H. *Patterns of child rearing*. Evanston, Ill.: Row-Peterson, 1957.

THE WARM-COLD VARIABLE IN FIRST IMPRESSIONS OF PERSONS*

Harold H. Kelley

Harold Kelly's article is one of the early attempts to relate specific psychological variables to people's perceptions of others. His study demonstrated that what someone tells you about a person will significantly affect your behavior toward that person.

Though Kelly uses a laboratory approach, you can look at how pre-information about roles affects attitudes toward people in the simulation. Consider your own reactions to people, merely on the basis of knowing certain things about them, such as their religion, or occupation.

*From the *Journal of Personality*, 1950, **18**, 431–439. Reprinted with permission of the author and publisher.

This experiment is one of several studies of first impressions (Kelley, 1948), the purpose of the series being to investigate the stability of early judgments, their determinants, and the relation of such judgments to the behavior of the person making them. In interpreting the data from several nonexperimental studies on the stability of first impressions, it proved to be necessary to postulate inner-observer variables which contribute to the impression and which remain relatively constant through time. Also some evidence was obtained which directly demonstrated the existence of these variables and their nature. The present experiment was designed to determine the effects of one kind of inner-observer variable, specifically, *expectations* about the stimulus person which the observer brings to the exposure situation.

That prior information or labels attached to a stimulus person make a difference in observers' first impressions is almost too obvious to require demonstration. The expectations resulting from such preinformation may restrict, modify, or accentuate the impressions he will have. The crucial question is: What changes in perception will accompany a given expectation? Studies of stereotyping, for example, that of Katz and Braly (1947), indicate that from an ethnic label such as "German" or "Negro," a number of perceptions follow which are culturally determined. The present study by Asch (1946) which demonstrates that certain crucial labels can transform the entire impression of the person, leading to attributions which are related to the label on a broad cultural basis or even, perhaps, on an autochthonous basis.

Asch read to his subjects a list of adjectives which purportedly described a particular person. He then asked them to characterize that person. He found that the inclusion in the list of what he called *central* qualities, such as "warm" as opposed to "cold," produced a widespread change in the entire impression. This effect was not adequately explained by the halo effect since it did not extend indiscriminately in a positive or negative direction to all characteristics. Rather, it differentially transformed the other qualities, for example, by changing their relative importance in the total impression. Peripheral qualities (such as "polite" versus "blunt") did not produce effects as strong as those produced by the central qualities.[1]

---

[1]Since the present experiment was carried out, Mensh and Wishner (1947) have repeated a number of Asch's experiments because of dissatisfaction with his sex and geographic distribution. Their data substantiate Asch's very closely. Also, Luchins (1948) has criticized Asch's experiments for their artificial methodology, repeated some of them and challenged some of the kinds of interpretations Asch made from his data. Luchins also briefly reports some tantalizing conclusions from a number of studies of first impressions of actual persons.

The present study tested the effects of such central qualities upon the early impressions of *real* persons, the same qualities, "warm" vs. "cold," being used. They were introduced as preinformation about the stimulus person before his actual appearance; so presumably they operated as expectations rather than as part of the stimulus pattern during the exposure period. In addition, information was obtained about the effects of the expectations upon the observers' behavior toward the stimulus person. An earlier study in this series has indicated that the more incompatible the observer initially perceived the stimulus person to be, the less the observer initiated interaction with him thereafter. The second purpose of the present experiment, then, was to provide a better controlled study of this relationship.

No previous studies reported in the literature have dealt with the importance of first impressions for behavior. The most relevant data are found in the sociometric literature, where there are scattered studies of the relation between choices among children having some prior acquaintance and their interaction behavior. For an example, see the study by Newstetter, Feldstein, and Newcomb (1938).

Procedure

The experiment was performed in three sections of a psychology course (Economics 70) at the Massachusetts Institute of Technology.[2] The three sections provided 23, 16, and 16 subjects respectively. All 55 subjects were men, most of them in their third college year. In each class the stimulus person (also a male) was completely unknown to the subjects before the experimental period. One person served as stimulus person in two sections, and a second person took this role in the third section. In each case the stimulus person was introduced by the experimenter, who posed as a representative of the course instructors and who gave the following statement:

> Your regular instructor is out of town today, and since we of Economics 70 are interested in the general problem of how various classes react to different instructors, we're going to have an instructor today you've never had before, Mr. —————. Then, at the end of the period, I want you to fill out some forms about him. In order to give you some idea of what he's like, we've had a person who knows him write up a little biographical note about him. I'll pass this out to you now and you can read it before he arrives. *Please read these to yourselves and don't talk about this among yourselves until the class is over so that he won't get wind of what's going on.*

[2]Professor Mason Haire of the University of California provided valuable advice and help in executing the experiment.

Two kinds of these notes were distributed, the two being identical except that in one the stimulus person was described among other things as being "rather cold" whereas in the other form the phrase "very warm" was substituted. The content of the "rather cold" version is as follows:

> Mr. —————— is a graduate student in the Department of Economics and Social Science here at M.I.T. He has had three semesters of teaching experience in psychology at another college. This is his first semester teaching Ec. 70. He is 26 years old, a veteran, and married. People who know him consider him to be a rather cold person, industrious, critical, practical and determined.

The two types of preinformation were distributed randomly within each of the three classes and in such a manner that the students were not aware that two kinds of information were being given out. The stimulus person then appeared and led the class in a twenty-minute discussion. During this time the experimenter kept a record of how often each student participated in the discussion. Since the discussion was almost totally leader-centered, this participation record indicates the number of times each student initiated verbal interaction with the instructor. After the discussion period, the stimulus person left the room, and the experimenter gave the following instructions:

> Now, I'd like to get your impression of Mr. ——————. This is not a test of you and can in no way affect your grade in this course. This material will not be identified as belonging to particular persons and will be kept strictly confidential. It will be of most value to us if you are completely honest in your evaluation of Mr. ——————. Also please understand that what you put down will not be used against him or cause him to lose his job or anything like that. This is not a test of him but merely a study of how different classes react to different instructors.

The subjects then wrote free descriptions of the stimulus person and finally rated him on a set of 15 rating scales.

Results and Discussion

1. *Influence of Warm-Cold Variable on First Impressions*

The differences in the ratings produced by the warm-cold variable were consistent from one section to another even where different stimulus persons were used. Consequently, the data from the three sections were combined by equating means (the S.D.'s were approximately equal) and the results for the total group are presented in Table 1. Also in this table is presented that part of Asch's data which refers to the qualities included in our rating scales. From this table it is quite clear that those given the

Table 1 Comparison of "Warm" and "Cold" Observers in Terms of Average Ratings Given Stimulus Persons.

Item	Low End of Rating Scale	High End of Rating Scale	Average Rating		Level of Significance of Warm-Cold Difference	Asch's Data: Per Cent of Group Assigning Quality at Low End of Our Rating Scale*	
			Warm N = 27	Cold N = 28		Warm	Cold
1	Knows his stuff	Doesn't know his stuff	3.5	4.6			
2	Considerate of others	Self-centered	6.3	9.6	1%		
3†	Informal	Formal	6.3	9.6	1%		
4†	Modest	Proud	9.4	10.6			
5	Sociable	Unsociable	5.6	10.4	1%	91%	38%
6	Self-assured	Uncertain of himself	8.4	9.1			
7	High intelligence	Low Intelligence	4.8	5.1			
8	Popular	Unpopular	4.0	7.4	1%	84%	28%
9†	Good natured	Irritable	9.4	12.0	5%	94%	17%
10	Generous	Ungenerous	8.2	9.6		91%	08%
11	Humorous	Humorless	8.3	11.7	1%	77%	13%
12	Important	Insignificant	6.5	8.6		88%	99%
13†	Humane	Ruthless	8.6	11.0		86%	31%
14†	Submissive	Dominant	13.2	14.5	5%		
15	Will go far	Will not get ahead	4.2	5.8			

*Given for all qualities common to Asch's list and this set of rating scales.
†These scales were reversed when presented to the subjects.

"warm" preinformation consistently rated the stimulus person more favorably than do those given the "cold" preinformation. Summarizing the statistically significant differences, the "warm" subjects rated the stimulus person as more considerate of others, more informal, more sociable, more popular, better natured, more humorous, and more humane. These findings are very similar to Asch's for the characteristics common to both studies. He found more frequent attribution to his hypothetical "warm" personalities of sociability, popularity, good naturedness, generosity, humorousness, and humaneness. So these data strongly support his finding that such a central quality as "warmth" can greatly influence the total impression of a personality. This effect is found to be operative in the perception of real persons.

This general favorableness in the perceptions of the "warm" observers as compared with the "cold" ones indicates that something like a halo effect may have been operating in these ratings. Although his data are not completely persuasive on this point, Asch was convinced that such a general effect was *not* operating in his study. Closer inspection of the present data makes it clear that the "warm-cold" effect cannot be explained altogether on the basis of simple halo effect. In Table 1 it is evident that the "warm-cold" variable produced differential effects from one rating scale to another. The size of this effect seems to depend upon the closeness of relation between the specific dimension of any given rating scale and the central quality of "warmth" or "coldness." Even though the rating of intelligence may be influenced by a halo effect, it is not influenced to the same degree to which considerateness is. It seems to make sense to view such strongly influenced items as considerateness, informality, good naturedness, and humaneness as dynamically more closely related to warmth and hence more perceived in terms of this relation than in terms of a general positive or negative feeling toward the stimulus person. If first impressions are normally made in terms of such general dimensions as "warmth" and "coldness," the power they give the observer in making predictions and specific evaluations about such disparate behavior characteristics as formality and considerateness is considerable (even though these predictions may be incorrect or misleading).

The free report impression data were analyzed for only one of the sections. In general, there were few sizable differences between the "warm" and "cold" observers. The "warm" observers attributed more nervousness, more sincerity, and more industriousness to the stimulus person. Although the frequencies of comparable qualities are very low because of the great variety of descriptions produced by the observers, there is considerable agreement with the rating scale data.

Two important phenomena are illustrated in these free description protocols, the first of them having been noted by Asch. *Firstly*, the characteristics of the stimulus person are interpreted in terms of the precognition of warmth or coldness. For example, a "warm" observer writes about a rather shy and retiring stimulus person as follows: "He makes friends slowly but they are lasting friendships when formed." In another instance, several "cold" observers describe him as being ". . . intolerant: would be angry if you disagree with his views. . ."; while several "warm" observers put the same thing this way: "Unyielding in principle, not easily influenced or swayed from his original attitude." *Secondly*, the preinformation about the stimulus person's warmth or coldness is evaluated and interpreted in the light of the direct behavioral data about him. For example, "He has a slight inferiority complex which leads to his coldness," and "His conscientiousness and industriousness might be mistaken for coldness." Examples of these two phenomena occurred rather infrequently, and there was no way to evaluate the relative strengths of these countertendencies. Certainly some such evaluation is necessary to determine the conditions under which behavior which is contrary to a stereotyped label resists distortion and leads to rejection of the label.

A comparison of the data from the two different stimulus persons is pertinent to the last point in so far as it indicates the interaction between the properties of the stimulus person and the label. The fact that the warm-cold variable generally produced differences in the same direction for the two stimulus persons, even though they are very different in personality, behavior, and mannerisms, indicates the strength of this variable. However, there were some exceptions to this tendency as well as marked differences. For example, stimulus person A typically appears to be anything but lacking in self-esteem and on rating scale 4 he was generally at the "proud" end of the scale. Although the "warm" observers tended to rate him as they did the other stimulus person (i.e., more "modest"), the difference between the "warm" and "cold" means for stimulus person A is very small and not significant as it is for stimulus person B. Similarly, stimulus person B was seen as "unpopular" and "humorless," which agrees with his typical classroom behavior. Again the "warm" observers rated him more favorably on these items, but their ratings were not significantly different from those of the "cold" observers, as was true for the other stimulus person. Thus we see that the strength or compellingness of various qualities of the stimulus person must be reckoned with. The stimulus is not passive to the forces arising from the label but actively resists distortion and may severely limit the degree of influence exerted by the preinformation.[3]

2. *Influence of Warm-Cold Variable on Interaction with the Stimulus Person*

In the analysis of the frequency with which the various students took part in the discussion led by the stimulus person, a larger proportion of those given the "warm" preinformation participated than of those given the "cold" preinformation. Fifty-six per cent of the "warm" subjects entered the discussion, whereas only 32 per cent of the "cold" subjects did so. Thus the expectation of warmth not only produced more favorable early perceptions of the stimulus person but led to greater initiation of interaction with him. This relation is a low one, significant at between the 5 per cent and 10 per cent level of confidence, but it is in line with the general principle that social perception serves to guide and steer the person's behavior in his social environment.

As would be expected from the foregoing findings, there was also a relation between the favorableness of the impression and whether or not the person participated in the discussion. Although any single item yielded only a small and insignificant relation to participation, when a number are combined the trend becomes clear cut. For example, when we combine the seven items which were influenced to a statistically significant degree by the warm-cold variable, the total score bears considerable relation to participation, the relationship being significant as well beyond the 1 per cent level. A larger proportion of those having favorable total impressions participated than of those having unfavorable impressions, the biserial correlation between these variables being .34. Although this relation may be interpreted in several ways, it seems most likely that the unfavorable perception led to a curtailment of interaction. Support for this comes from one of the other studies in this series (Kelley, 1948). There it was found

---

[3]We must raise an important question here: Would there be a tendency for "warm" observers to distort the perception in the favorable direction regardless of how much the stimulus deviated from the expectation? Future research should test the following hypothesis, which is suggested by Gestalt perception theory (Krech, D., and Crutchfield, R. S., 1948, pp. 95–98): If the stimulus differs but slightly from the expectation, the perception will tend to be *assimilated* to the expectation; however, if the difference between the stimulus and expectation is too great, the perception will occur by contrast to the expectation and will be distorted in the opposite direction.

that those persons having unfavorable impressions of the instructor at the end of the first class meeting tended less often to initiate interactions with him in the succeeding four meetings than did those having favorable first impressions. There was also some tendency in the same study for those persons who interacted least with the instructor to change least in their judgments of him from the first to later impressions.

It will be noted that these relations lend some support to the autistic hostility hypothesis proposed by Newcomb (1947). This hypothesis suggests that the possession of an initially hostile attitude toward a person leads to a restriction of communication and contact with him which in turn serves to preserve the hostile attitude by preventing the acquisition of data which could correct it. The present data indicate that a restriction of interaction is associated with unfavorable preinformation and an unfavorable perception. The data from the other study support this result and also indicate the correctness of the second part of the hypothesis, that restricted interaction reduces the likelihood of change in the attitude.

What makes these findings more significant is that they appear in the context of a discussion class where there are numerous *induced* and *own* forces to enter the discussion and to interact with the instructor. It seems likely that the effects predicted by Newcomb's hypothesis would be much more marked in a setting where such forces were not present.

Summary

The warm-cold variable had been found by Asch to produce large differences in the impressions of personality formed from a list of adjectives. In this study the same variable was introduced in the form of expectation about a real person and was found to produce similar differences in first impressions of him in a classroom setting. In addition, the differences in first impressions produced by the different expectations were shown to influence the observers' behavior toward the stimulus person. Those observers given the favorable expectation (who, consequently, had a favorable impression of the stimulus person) tended to interact more with him than did those given the unfavorable expectation.

References

Asch, S. E. Forming impressions of personality. *J. abnorm. soc. Psychol.*, 1946, **41**, 258–290.

Katz, D., and Braly, K. W. Verbal stereotypes and racial prejudice. In T. M. Newcomb and E. L. Hartley (Eds.), *Readings in social psychology*. New York: Holt, Rinehart and Winston, 1947. Pp. 204–210.

Kelley, H. H. First impressions in interpersonal relations. Ph.D. thesis, Massachusetts Institute of Technology, Cambridge, Mass. Sept., 1948.

Krech, D., and Crutchfield, R. S. *Theory and problems of social psychology.* New York: McGraw-Hill, 1948.

Luchins, A. S. Forming impressions of personality: a critique. *J. abnorm. soc. Psychol.*, 1948, **48**, 318–325.

Mensh, I. N., and Wishner, J. Asch on "Forming impressions of personality": further evidence. *J. Pers.*, 1947, **16**, 188–191.

Newcomb, T. M. Autistic hostility and social reality. *Hum. Relat.*, 1947, **1**, 69–86.

Newstetter, W. I., Feldstein, M. J., and Newcomb, T. M. *Group adjustment: a study in experimental sociology.* Cleveland: Western Reserve University, 1938.

EXERCISES AND DISCUSSION TOPICS FOR CHAPTER 6

For Role Expectancies, as in the other chapters, we have listed some exercises and discussion topics related to the areas covered. They are meant to be used as guidelines for you to integrate your experiences in the simulation. They are only suggestions; you might want to develop your own exercises and discuss other relevant issues not mentioned here.

Exercises

1. Find a person who fits the description of the role you are playing. Spend at least an hour talking with this person in order to find out what he or she is like. Write a one-page description of this person. Include his (her) major interests, attitudes, and habits. Write what you believe makes sense for this person, knowing what you do about the character. If possible, find out the person's attitudes toward the issues you are dealing with in the simulation (integration, welfare, etc.) and include these at the end of your written description.

   Read your description to other participants with the exception of the person's attitudes toward those issues you are dealing with in the simulation. Have the other participants state what they think the person's attitudes on specific issues are, based on your written description.

2. List the major goals of the person whose role you are playing for each of the following areas: personal, subgroup and community. Get together with other participants in the group who have similar goals and discuss a topic or issue related to the simulation.

Discussion Topics

Discuss variables other than Kelley's "warm-cold" variable that influence our perceptions of others. Share your personal experiences regarding how preinformation affects attitudes toward people. What are some of your expectancies of Psych City characters based on preinformation? Discuss the major factors that determine whether or not preinformation will influence you. Kelley's article investigates the short-term effect of preinformation. How long do you think preinformation has an effect? How would you study the long-term effect of preinformation on our perceptions of others? Discuss some ways of reducing the effect of preinformation if that is desirable.

Talk about the role of women in our society. How is the traditional role of women changing? What is a "liberated" woman? Discuss ways of child-rearing that could eliminate discrimination against women.

Compare the differences in expectancies in and out of your role in the simulation. How do you expect the police chief to act? How would you expect the person who plays the role of police chief to act outside of the simulation? How successfully can you discriminate between expectancies of people in role and in real life? What role do other people perceive *you* as having in role and in real life? How would your character perceive you outside of the simulation?

CHAPTER 7

Interpersonal Perception

The process of role playing involves a number of behaviors and has a number of effects. To adequately play your role you should first understand it intellectually and see what behaviors it implies. Relationships between your role and others in the simulation will provide you with some of this information since you are dependent on the other role players in reaching your goals. Over time you should begin to see how roles are interrelated, which behaviors are or are not consistent with these roles and the viewpoints logically associated with each role. If your role is that of the police chief, it would be inconsistent for you to support a violent demonstration proposed by minority group students but consistent to support a parents group seeking order in the schools.

Playing a role effectively also involves an emotional component. You should try to feel toward issues and other roles as someone who occupies your role in real life would feel. This may be somewhat different from your own feelings and may be more difficult to accomplish than intellectual understanding. Most people have had the experience of thinking that they understood another person's problem or situation until they have found themselves in a similar position and discovered it to be quite different from what they anticipated. If this kind of involvement is achieved in playing your role, your perceptions and feelings about issues or other participants may be different from those you might have if you were not highly involved.

Many factors can influence our perception of people and things. Some of these factors are: (1) physical, (2) biological, (3) cultural, and (4) psychological. People will see things differently if the weather is bad. This is an example of physical factor influencing perception. Other factors are bio-

logical; you are more likely to perceive things that will satisfy your immediate needs (e.g. man who sees an oasis while lost in the desert). A big
problem may not seem so hopeless after a good night's sleep. Culture
might influence the way in which we perceive things. It might seem very
strange to dispose of waste by using garbage cans to a group of people
from a primitive rural area who have always disposed of their garbage by
feeding it to animals. Psychological biases often color the way we see
people and things. Someone who has had bad experiences with people of
the opposite sex often mistrust everyone of that sex. These factors can
have transitory (e.g. weather) or more permanent (e.g. psychological)
effects on our perceptions. In the Psych City simulation, you can identify
these factors operating on different characters' perceptions of other people
and situations. A wealthy person from the east side of the city will look at
a problem differently than a lower-class black laborer would.

Involvement in a position different from your own forces you to become
familiar with arguments or information that you normally might ignore.
Many people can tell the differences between many shades of opinion that
are similar to their own opinions but see the same amount of variation in
opposing opinions as essentially the same. By looking for these shades of
difference in opinions, you are more likely to be in a better position to
enact your own role. How you use this new information in your own role
behavior will affect how other participants react to you and in turn help
determine the nature of how you relate to these other participants.

IS THERE A RED CHINA?*

Art Buchwald

The field of international relations is a rich source for studying the problems of people's perceptions of others. In his satirical essay on diplomatic recognition, Mr. Buchwald illustrates, through exaggeration, the
distortion and confusion which ensue when individuals choose to view
another group of persons as objects and political abstractions rather than
as human beings.

Looking at this essay in relation to our own communities (simulated
and real), we might consider the effect of such factors as geographic distance, physical dissimilarity, cultural difference, and political persuasion
on the perceptions of any community member toward other people or
groups.

One of the most astounding discoveries in history was made the other day when a group of American State Department people found a new country named Red China. For years there had been rumors that there was a country in the Far East with a population of 800 million people. Yet no one in the United States would believe it.

But an expedition of Senators led by Marco Fulbright came across it accidentally while looking for a new route to North Vietnam.

When the existence of Red China was reported, a meeting of all the top policy people in the State Department was called.

"If this is true," said one of the Assistant Secretaries, "that means the world is round."

"Hogwash," said another Secretary. "We all know there is a country called China already, so how could there be another China? Look at our maps. China is right here in the Formosa Strait."

"That's right," a Secretary said. "And our maps are all up to date."

"What's that large land mass across the water from it?" someone asked.

"It's marked 'unexplored.'"

"Perhaps that's where Red China is."

"I'm an old China hand, and I say there is no place called Red China. The only China is located on the island of Formosa."

"What proof do we have that there really is a country with 800 million people in it, except for the word of a few disgruntled Senators?" an Under-secretary demanded. "They're only trying to discredit our foreign policy anyway."

"There is no proof," a Far East expert said, "except the West Germans have announced they plan to build a $150 million steel mill there. I don't think they'd put in that kind of money if the country didn't exist."

The Secretary of State spoke up. "That is a point. The only thing I can't understand is how we could have missed it all these years."

"Perhaps there is a cloud cover over it all the time," someone suggested.

"Does the CIA have anything on it?"

"No, sir. They're as much in the dark as we are. The French, the British, and the Canadians have all reported that they believe there is a Red China, but the Russians now claim it isn't there."

The old China hand spoke up. "Mr. Secretary, I believe we're only looking for trouble by following up the rumor. We already have a China. It's *our* kind of China. Another China would only mean trouble."

"But," said one of the other men, "if the reports are true that this land mass contains 800 million people, won't we have to deal with it sooner or later? I think we should announce that we don't believe there is a Red China, but if there is, we intend to contain it, but not isolate it."

The Secretary of State said, "That's a good phrase, 'containment but not isolation.' I think I'll use it in my next press conference. Our only problem is that if we admit there is such a place, we might be forced to admit her to the United Nations."

"Precisely, sir," a Secretary spoke out. "Besides, we've told the American people for seventeen years that there is no Red China. If we admit there is a Red China now, we would only confuse them."

One of the advisers said, "Seventeen years ago, the American people didn't believe in flying saucers, either. Perhaps we could announce the existence of Red China and flying saucers at the same time."

THEY SAW A GAME: A CASE STUDY*

Albert H. Hastorf and Hadley Cantril

Flouting the often expressed axiom that scientific study and reporting are by necessity sterile and uninteresting, Messrs. Hastorf and Cantril have produced a description of an empirical research project which combines popular "real life" phenomena, sound research procedures and readily understandable explanation.

Their description of the differential perceptions of Princeton and Dartmouth students viewing a football game between these two schools underscores the importance of considering characteristics of the perceiver when attempting to understand how events and people are perceived. In this case, the emotional and social identification and affiliation of the perceiver are critical.

On a brisk Saturday afternoon, November 23, 1951, the Dartmouth football team played Princeton in Princeton's Palmer Stadium. It was the last game of the season for both teams and rather special significance because the Princeton team had won all its games so far and one of its players, Kazmaier, was receiving All-American mention and had just appeared as the cover man on *Time* magazine, and was playing his last game.

A few minutes after the opening kick-off, it became apparent that the game was going to be a rough one. The referees were kept busy blowing their whistles and penalizing both sides. In the second quarter, Princeton's star left the game with a broken nose. In the third quarter, a Dartmouth

*Albert H. Hastorf and Hadley Cantril, "They saw a game: a case study," *Journal of Abnormal and Social Psychology*, XLIX, 1954, 129–34. Copyright© 1954 by the American Psychological Association, and reproduced by permission.

player was taken off the field with a broken leg. Tempers flared both during and after the game. The official statistics of the game, which Princeton won, showed that Dartmouth was penalized 70 yards, Princeton 25, not counting more than a few plays in which both sides were penalized.

Needless to say, accusations soon began to fly. The game immediately became a matter of concern to players, students, coaches, and the administrative officials of the two institutions, as well as to alumni and the general public who had not seen the game but had become sensitive to the problem of big-time football through the recent exposures of subsidized players, commercialism, etc. Discussion of the game continued for several weeks.

One of the contributing factors to the extended discussion of the game was the extensive space given to it by both campus and metropolitan newspapers. An indication of the fervor with which the discussions were carried on is shown by a few excerpts from the campus dailies.

For example, on November 27 (four days after the game), the *Daily Princetonian* (Princeton's student newspaper) said:

> This observer has never seen quite such a disgusting exhibition of so-called "sport." Both teams were guilty but the blame must be laid primarily on Dartmouth's doorstep. Princeton, obviously the better team, had no reason to rough up Dartmouth. Looking at the situation rationally, we don't see why the Indians should make a deliberate attempt to cripple Dick Kazmaier or any other Princeton player. The Dartmouth psychology, however, is not rational itself.

The November 30th edition of the *Princeton Alumni Weekly* said:

> But certain memories of what occurred will not be easily erased. Into the record books will go in indelible fashion the fact that the last game of Dick Kazmaier's career was cut short by more than half when he was forced out with a broken nose and a mild concussion, sustained from a tackle that came well after he had thrown a pass.
>
> This second-period development was followed by a third quarter outbreak of roughness that was climaxed when a Dartmouth player deliberately kicked Brad Glass in the ribs while the latter was on his back. Throughout the often unpleasant afternoon, there was undeniable evidence that the losers' tactics were the result of an actual style of play, and reports on other games they have played this season substantiate this.

Dartmouth students were "seeing" an entirely different version of the game through the editorial eyes of the *Dartmouth* (Dartmouth's undergraduate newspaper). For example, on November 27 the *Dartmouth* said:

> However, the Dartmouth–Princeton game set the stage for the other type of dirty football. A type which may be termed as an unjustifiable accusation.

Dick Kazmaier was injured early in the game. Kazmaier was the star, an All-American. Other stars have been injured before, but Kazmaier had been built to represent a Princeton idol. When an idol is hurt there is only one recourse—the tag of dirty football. So what did the Tiger Coach Charley Caldwell do? He announced to the world that the Big Green had been out to extinguish the Princeton star. His purpose was achieved.

After this incident, Caldwell instilled the old see-what-they-did-go-get-them attitude into his players. His talk got results. Gene Howard and Jim Miller were both injured. Both had dropped back to pass, had passed, and were standing unprotected in the backfield. Result: one bad leg and one leg broken.

The game was rough and did get a bit out of hand in the third quarter. Yet most of the roughing penalties were called against Princeton while Dartmouth received more of the illegal-use-of-the-hands variety.

On November 28 the *Dartmouth* said:

Dick Kazmaier of Princeton admittedly is an unusually able football player. Many Dartmouth men traveled to Princeton, not expecting to win—only hoping to see an All-American in action. Dick Kazmaier was hurt in the second period, and played only a token part in the remainder of the game. For this, spectators were sorry.

But there were no such feelings for Dick Kazmaier's health. Medical authorities have confirmed that as a relatively unprotected passing and running star in a contact sport, he is quite liable to injury. Also, his particular injuries—a broken nose and slight concussion—were no more serious than is experienced almost any day in any football practice, where there is no more serious stake than playing the following Saturday. Up to the Princeton game, Dartmouth players suffered about 10 known nose fractures and face injuries, not to mention several slight concussions.

Did Princeton players feel so badly about losing their star? They shouldn't have. During the past undefeated campaign they stopped several individual stars by a concentrated effort, including such mainstays as Frank Hauff of Navy, Glenn Adams of Pennsylvania and Rocco Calvo of Cornell.

In other words, the same brand of football condemned by the *Prince*—that of stopping the big man—is practiced quite successfully by the Tigers.

Basically, then, there was disagreement as to what had happened during the "game." Hence we took the opportunity presented by the occasion to make a "real life" study of a perceptual problem.[1]

Procedure

Two steps were involved in gathering data. The first consisted of answers to a questionnaire designed to get reactions to the game and to learn something of the climate of opinion in each institution. This questionnaire was administered a week after the game to both Dartmouth and Prince-

[1]We are not concerned here with the problem of guilt or responsibility for infractions, and nothing here implies any judgment as to who was to blame.

ton undergraduates who were taking introductory and intermediate psychology courses.

The second step consisted of showing the same motion picture of the game to a sample of undergraduates in each school and having them check on another questionnaire, as they watched the film any infraction of the rules they saw and whether these infractions were "mild" or "flagrant."[2] At Dartmouth, members of two fraternities were asked to view the film on December 7; at Princeton, members of two undergraduate clubs saw the film early in January.

The answers to both questionnaires were carefully coded and transferred to punch cards.[3]

Results

Table 1 shows the questions which received different replies from the two student populations on the first questionnaire.

Questions asking if the students had friends on the team, if they had ever played football themselves, if they felt they knew the rules of the game well, etc., showed no differences in either school and no relation to answers given to other questions. This is not surprising since the students in both schools come from essentially the same type of educational, economic, and ethnic background.

Summarizing the data of Tables 1 and 2, we find a marked contrast between the two student groups.

Nearly all Princeton students judged the game as "rough and dirty" — not one of them thought it "clean and fair." And almost nine-tenths of them thought the other side started the rough play. By and large they felt that the charges they understood were being made were true; most of them felt the charges were made in order to avoid similar situations in the future.

When Princeton students looked at the movie of the game, they saw the Dartmouth team make over twice as many infractions as their own team made. And they saw the Dartmouth team make over twice as many

[2]The film shown was kindly loaned for the purpose of the experiment by the Dartmouth College Athletic Council. It should be pointed out that a movie of a football game follows the ball, is thus selective, and omits a good deal of the total action on the field. Also, of course, in viewing only a film of a game, the possibilities of participation as spectator are greatly limited.

[3]We gratefully acknowledge the assistance of Virginia Zerega, Office of Public Opinion Research, and J. L. McCandless, Princeton University and E. S. Horton, Dartmouth College, in the gathering of the data.

Table 1 Data from First Questionnaire.

Question	Dartmouth Students (N = 163)	Princeton Students (N = 161)
	(per cent)	
1. Did you happen to see the actual game between Dartmouth and Princeton in Palmer Stadium this year?		
Yes	33	71
No	67	29
2. Have you seen a movie of the game or seen it on television?		
Yes, movie	33	2
Yes, television	0	1
No, neither	67	97
3. (Asked of those who answered "yes" to either or both of above questions.) From your observations of what went on at the game, do you believe the game was clean and fairly played, or that it was unnecessarily rough and dirty?		
Clean and fair	6	0
Rough and dirty	24	69
Rough and fair*	25	2
No answer	45	29
4. (Asked of those who answered "no" on both of the first questions.) From what you have heard and read about the game, do you feel it was clean and fairly played, or that it was unnecessarily rough and dirty?		
Clean and fair	7	0
Rough and dirty	18	24
Rough and fair*	14	1
Don't know	6	4
No answer	55	71
(Combined answers to questions 3 and 4 above)		
Clean and fair	13	0
Rough and dirty	42	93
Rough and fair*	39	3
Don't know	6	4
5. From what you saw in the game or the movies, or from what you have read, which team do you feel started the rough play?		
Dartmouth started it	36	86
Princeton started it	2	0
Both started it	53	11
Neither	6	1
No answer	3	2

Table 1   (*continued*)

	Dartmouth Students (N = 163)	Princeton Students (N = 161)
Question	(per cent)	
6. What is your understanding of the charges being made?†		
Dartmouth tried to get Kazmaier	71	47
Dartmouth intentionally dirty	52	44
Dartmouth unnecessarily rough	8	35
7. Do you feel there is any truth to these charges?		
Yes	10	55
No	57	4
Partly	29	35
Don't know	4	6
8. Why do you think the charges were made?		
Injury to Princeton star	70	23
To prevent repetition	2	46
No answer	28	31

*This answer was not included on the checklist but was written in by the percentage of students indicated.

†Replies do not add to 100% since more than one charge could be given.

infractions as were seen by Dartmouth students. When Princeton students judged these infractions as "flagrant" or "mild," the ratio was about two "flagrant" to one "mild" on the Dartmouth team, and about one "flagrant" to three "mild" on the Princeton team.

As for the Dartmouth students, while the plurality of answers fell in the "rough and dirty" category, over one-tenth thought the game was "clean and fair" and over a third introduced their own category of "rough and fair" to describe the action. Although a third of the Dartmouth stu-

Table 2   Data from Second Questionnaire Checked While Seeing Film.

		Total Number of Infractions Checked Against—			
		Dartmouth Team		Princeton Team	
Group	N	Mean	SD	Mean	SD
Dartmouth students	48	4.3*	2.7	4.4	2.8
Princeton students	49	9.8*	5.7	4.2	3.5

*Significant at the .01 level.

Interpersonal Perception   123
Interpersonal Perception   **123**

dents felt that Dartmouth was to blame for starting the rough play, the majority of Dartmouth students thought both sides were to blame. By and large, Dartmouth men felt that the charges they understood were being made were not true, and most of them thought the reason for the charges was Princeton's concern for its football star.

When Dartmouth students looked at the movie of the game they saw both teams make about the same number of infractions. And they saw their own team make only half the number of infractions the Princeton students saw them make. The ratio of "flagrant" to "mild" infractions was about one to one when Dartmouth students judged the Dartmouth team, and about one "flagrant" to two "mild" when Dartmouth students judged infractions made by the Princeton team.

It should be noted that Dartmouth and Princeton students were thinking of different charges in judging their validity and in assigning reasons as to why the charges were made. It should also be noted that whether or not students were spectators of the game in the stadium made little difference in their responses.

Interpretation: The Nature of a Social Event[4]

It seems clear that the "game" actually was many different games and that each version of the events that transpired was just as "real" to a particular person as other versions were to other people. A consideration of the experiential phenomena that constitute a "football game" for the spectator may help us both to account for the results obtained and illustrate something of the nature of any social event.

Like any other complex social occurrence, a "football game" consists of a whole host of happenings. Many different events are occurring simultaneously. Furthermore, each happening is a link in a chain of happenings, so that one follows another in sequence. The "football game," as well as other complex social situations, consists of a whole matrix of events. In the game situation, this matrix of events consists of the actions of all the players, together with the behavior of the referees and linesmen, the action on the sidelines, in the grandstands, over the loudspeaker, etc.

Of crucial importance is the fact that an "occurrence" on the football field or in any other social situation does not become an experiential "event" unless and until some significance is given to it: an "occurrence" becomes an "event" only when the happening has significance. And a

[4]The interpretation of the nature of a social event sketched here is in part based on discussions with Adelbert Ames, Jr., and is being elaborated in more detail elsewhere.

happening generally has significance only if it reactivates learned significances already registered in what we have called a person's assumptive
form-world.

Hence the particular occurrences that different people experienced in
the football game were a limited series of events from the total matrix
of events potentially available to them. People experienced those occurrences that reactivated significances they brought to the occasion; they
failed to experience those occurrences which did not reactivate past
significances. We do not need to introduce "attention" as an "intervening
third" (to paraphrase James on memory) to account for the selectivity of
the experiential process.

In this particular study, one of the most interesting examples of this
phenomenon was a telegram sent to an officer of Dartmouth College by a
member of a Dartmouth alumni group in the Midwest. He had viewed the
film which had been shipped to his alumni group from Princeton after its
use with Princeton students, who saw, as we noted, an average of over
nine infractions by Dartmouth players during the game. The alumnus,
who couldn't see the infractions he had heard publicized, wired:

> Preview of Princeton movies indicates considerable cutting of important part please
> wire explanation and possibly air mail missing part before showing scheduled for
> January 25 we have splicing equipment.

The "same" sensory impingements emanating from the football field,
transmitted through the visual mechanism to the brain, also obviously
gave rise to different experiences in different people. The significances
assumed by different happenings for different people depend in large part
on the purposes people bring to the occasion and the assumptions they
have of the purposes and probable behavior of other people involved. This
was amusingly pointed out by the *New York Herald Tribune*'s sports
columnist, Red Smith, in describing a prize fight between Chico Vejar and
Carmine Fiore in his column of December 21, 1951. Among other things,
he wrote:

> You see, Steve Ellis is the proprietor of Chico Vejar, who is a highly desirable tract of
> Stamford, Conn., welterweight. Steve is also a radio announcer. Ordinarily there is no
> conflict between Ellis the Brain and Ellis the Voice because Steve is an uncommonly
> substantial lump of meat who can support both halves of a split personality and give
> away weight on each end without missing it.
>   This time, though, the two Ellises met head-on, with a sickening, rending crash. Steve
> the Manager sat at ringside in the guise of Steve the Announcer broadcasting a dis-
> passionate, unbiased, objective report of Chico's adventures in the ring. . . .
>   Clear as mountain water, his words came through, winning big for Chico. Winning?
> Hell, Steve was slaughtering poor Fiore.

Watching and listening, you could see what a valiant effort the reporter was making to remain cool and detached. At the same time you had an illustration of the old, established truth that when anybody with a preference watches a fight, he sees only what he prefers to see.

That is always so. That is why, after any fight that doesn't end in a clean knockout, there always are at least a few hoots when the decision is announced. A guy from, say, Billy Graham's neighborhood goes to see Billy fight and he watches Graham all the time. He sees all the punches Billy throws, and hardly any of the punches Billy catches. So it was with Steve.

"Fiore feints with a left," he would say, honestly believing that Fiore hadn't caught Chico full on the chops. "Fiore's knees buckle", he said, "and Chico backs away." Steve didn't see the hook that had driven Chico back. . .

In brief, the data here indicate that there is no such "thing" as a "game" existing "out there" in its own right which people merely "observe." The "game" "exists" for a person and is experienced by him only in so far as certain happenings have significances in terms of his purpose. Out of all the occurrences going on in the environment, a person selects those that have some significance for him from his own egocentric position in the total matrix.

Obviously in the case of a football game, the value of the experience of watching the game is enhanced if the purpose of "your" team is accomplished, that is, if the happening of the desired consequence is experienced — i.e., if your team wins. But the value attribute of the experience can, of course, be spoiled if the desire to win crowds out behavior we value and have come to call sportsmanlike.

The sharing of significances provides the links except for which a "social" event would not be experienced and would not exist for anyone.

A "football game" would be impossible except for the rules of the game which we bring to the situation and which enable us to share with others the significances of various happenings. These rules make possible a certain repeatability of events such as first downs, touchdowns, etc. If a person is unfamiliar with the rules of the game, the behavior he sees lacks repeatability and consistent significance and hence "doesn't make sense."

And only because there is the possibility of repetition is there the possibility that a happening has a significance. For example, the balls used in games are designed to give a high degree of repeatability. While a football is about the only ball used in games which is not a sphere, the shape of the modern football has apparently evolved in order to achieve a higher degree of accuracy and speed in forward passing than would be obtained with a spherical ball, thus increasing the repeatability of an important phase of the game.

The rules of a football game, like laws, rituals, customs, and mores, are registered and preserved forms of sequential significances enabling people to share the significances of occurrences. The sharing of sequential significances which have value for us provides the links that operationally make social events possible. They are analogous to the forces of attraction that hold parts of an atom together, keeping each part from following its individual, independent course.

From this point of view it is inaccurate and misleading to say that different people have different "attitudes" concerning the same "thing." For the "thing" simply is not the same for different people whether the "thing" is a football game, a presidential candidate, Communism, or spinach. We do not simply "react to" a happening or to some impingement from the environment in a determined way (except in behavior that has become reflexive or habitual). We behave according to what we bring to the occasion, and what each brings to the occasion is more or less unique. And except for these significances which we bring to the occasion, the happenings around us would be meaningless occurrences, would be "inconsequential."

From the transactional view, an attitude is not a predisposition to react in a certain way to an occurrence or stimulus "out there' that exists in its own right with certain fixed characteristics which we "color" according to our predisposition. That is, a subject does not simply "react to" an "object." An attitude would rather seem to be a complex of registered significances reactivated by some stimulus which assumes its own particular significances for us in terms of our purposes. That is, the object as experienced would not exist for us except for the reactivated aspects of the form-world which provide particular significance to the hieroglyphics of sensory impingements.

READINESS TO PERCEIVE VIOLENCE AS A RESULT OF POLICE TRAINING*

Hans H. Toch and Richard Schulte

In their study Hastorf and Cantril demonstrated the influence of affiliation and identification on the perception of events. Using a laboratory research approach, Messrs. Toch and Schulte focus on the role of train-

*From *Social Perception* by Hans H. Toch and Henry Clay Smith © 1968 by Litton Educational Publishing, Inc. Reprinted by permission of Van Nostrand-Reinhold Company.

ing in social perception. The authors compare the abilities of first year and advanced police administration students and introductory psychology students to perceive "violent" pictures when they are presented at the same time as "nonviolent" pictures. They infer from their results that training may serve to sensitize people to certain cues in a situation which others may not be aware of.

This study has many implications for our attempt to understand and improve our communities. It relates to the nature of the education we offer to our citizens, the difficulty of establishing common bases of perception in groups with members who have diverse experiential backgrounds and the dangers inherent in overtraining people in special fields to the extent that their personal perceptions (and actions) are strongly influenced by their professional training (e.g. soldiers who bring their combat training into their civilian lives and psychologists who tend to analyze everyone).

The present study was designed to test the hypothesis that specific past experiences acquired under particular conditions or training could "sensitive" a person to related content in a binocular rivalry situation. The content category selected for the study was that of violence and crime. Relevant training was available in undergraduate programmes offered by the School of Police Administration and Public Safety of Michigan State University. The explicit purpose of these programmes, as described in the *Catalog* (Michigan State University, 1960), is "to develop professional competence in the fields of law enforcement administration, police science, the prevention and control of delinquency and crime, correctional administration, industrial security administration, and highway traffic safety administration" (p. 113).

In our experiment, sixteen advanced police administration students were tested. They were compared with two control groups — one consisting of 27 introductory psychology students, and another comprising 16 first-year students in police administration.

Apparatus

The apparatus used for the study was a modified stereoscope designed by Engel (1956). This stereoscope is completely enclosed, and the fields are subject to variable illumination. In the present experiment, the light intensity was maintained at 0.2 candles/ft.^{2} in both fields.

An interval timer was attached to the stereoscope to permit control of the exposure times of stimulus figures. Exposures of 0.05 sec. were used throughout the study.

Stimulus Figures

Nine stereograms were made up of eighteen figures selected out of a collection of pictograms. One figure in each pair represented a scene of violence or crime. The subject-matter of these figures comprised three murders, two suicides, an act of theft, an imprisoned convict and a policeman. Each of these "violent" figures was carefully matched with a "neutral" one corresponding to it in size and outline, and covering roughly the same area in the visual field. These stimuli include a farmer, a worker operating a drill press, a radio announcer, a mailman and two women.

Procedure

The nine pairs of slides were presented in the same order to each subject. "Violent" figures were alternately presented to the left and right eye, as a control for eye dominance. As additional control, the entire series was presented a second time, with the order of alternation reversed. Thus, each eye of each subject was exposed to all eighteen figures.

The slide holder of the stereoscope was individually adjusted for optimal fusion. No attempt was made to test for visual abnormalities, but subjects were questioned about the condition of their eyes, and were requested to wear glasses if needed.

All subjects were told that the experiment was concerned with "visual recognition of objects under specific conditions," and that the aim was to ascertain "how well each of the objects can be recognized." The subjects were also told that similarities might exist among some of the pictures, but that they were to watch for differentiating details. Whenever one exposure did not permit confident identification, the subject was permitted to view the slide again.

Results

Except for a negligible number of fusions or confusions, subjects had no difficulty in perceiving a single picture for each stereogram presented to them. This figure, as described by the subject, almost always clearly corresponded to one of the monocular fields.

Table 1 contains a summary of the number of times the "violent" figure was described. The group of 27 psychology students (Control Group 1) yielded from 1 to 7 anti-social percepts; the largest number of "violent" pictures perceived by anyone in the group was 7. The average subject in the group saw 4 "violent" pictures. The 16 first-year police administra-

Table 1   Number of "violent" pictures seen in eighteen stereoscopic presentations by the experimental group and two control groups.

	Number of "violent" percepts		
	Lowest no. in group	Highest no. in group	Average for group
Control Group 1 ($N = 27$)	1	7	4.03
Control Group 2 ($N = 16$)	2	9	4.69
Advanced Police Ad. Students ($N = 16$)	6	15	9.37

tion students (Control Group 2) performed very similarly: they saw between 2 and 9 of the 18 violent figures; their group mean is 4.69. (For both control groups, the Mode and the Median were 4.)

The Experimental Group (the advanced police administration students) saw an average of 9.37 "violent" figures. The lowest number of "violent" percepts reported was 6, and the highest was 15 out of 18 presentations. Only 9 of the 43 subjects in both Control Groups saw enough "violent" figures to overlap with the Experimental Group. Inspection of the data therefore suggests that there is a difference in the proportion of violent percepts achieved by the experimental and control subjects.

The significance of the difference was separately tested for each Control Group. In each case, the scores of the Control Group and those of the Experimental Group were combined, and a Median Test was applied to this combined distribution. The difference between control and experimental subjects falling above and below the Median in each case proved significant beyond the 0.01 level.

Discussion

Students who are exposed to several years of police training appear not only to have acquired information, but also to have sustained other effects. Given a task in which others predominantly perceive non-violent content, subjects with police schooling have become relatively aware of violent content.

We can assume that the difference in perceived violence is indeed an expression of increased "awareness," because there was no time or opportunity in our task for interpretation or selection. The subject "sees" only one figure; the stimulus in the other monocular field never "reaches" him.

In other words, our experimental subjects seemed to have different data mediated to them by their perceptual process from that mediated to our controls. The question which faces us is, what accounts for the difference?

One explanation which suggests itself is that individuals who enter law enforcement as a profession are motivationally predisposed toward violence, and could therefore be relatively sensitive to it. But we may recall that our two control groups yielded very similar results. If persons with "aggressive" needs were drawn into police work, should not our first-year students show evidence of it?

The difference in the proportion of perceived violence thus seems to be produced during training. What type of change could be involved? One possibility is that law enforcement training removes inhibitions which ordinarily "defend" people against the perception of material "loaded" in favor of hostile, anti-social impulses. By providing the person with the opportunity to externalize aggression, law enforcement training could make violence less objectionable, and reduce the need selectively to exclude percepts having "violent" connotations.

Advocates of this "perceptual defence" view could point to the fact that our Experimental Group reported *precisely* the number of violent percepts expected *by chance* if the monocular fields are structurally comparable. Since the Control Groups saw only *half* the number of violent figures expected by chance, could not "defence" have excluded the rest?

Quite possibly. However, the same data can lead to a different explanation: the person with run-of-the-mill experience is, after all, very infrequently exposed to extreme anti-social conduct. As a consequence, most people may unconsciously have come to assign a low probability to open violence in their expectations of reality. They may have formed the conception that violence is unusual, whereas more routinely experienced themes are likely to recur.

In ambiguous situations such prognoses become relevant. Given a choice of interpretation, the most commonly experienced occurrence becomes the best "bet." Perceptual experiments show that familiar meaning connotations determine perception under non-optimal conditions (Allport & Pettigrew, 1957) or when structure is neutral (Toch & Ittelson, 1956).

A momentary exposure of rival fields in a stereoscope presents a perceptual task in which one set of meanings must be elaborated at the expense of another. If the fields are mutually exclusive (so that they cannot "fuse"), and if neither fields asserts itself through structural advantages (such as those of a strongly articulated figure competing with a vaguely outlined one), familiarity clearly becomes the only remaining basis of choice.

Assuming that extremely violent scenes are comparatively unfamiliar, we would thus expect violence to be relatively infrequently perceived in true binocular rivalry. We would predict the type of result we obtained from our Control Groups.

We could assume that law enforcement training *supplements* this experiential deficit in the area of violence and crime. Unusual experiences, after all, become "familiar" in the course of *any* specialization. The funeral director or the medical intern, for instance, may learn to accept corpses as part and parcel of everyday experience. The dedicated nudist may acquire a special conception of familiar attire. The air pilot may come to find nothing unusual about glancing down out of a window at a bank of clouds.

In the same fashion, law enforcement training can produce a revision of unconscious expectations of violence and crime. This does not mean that the law enforcer necessarily comes to exaggerate the prevalence of violence. It means that the law enforcer may come to accept crime *as a familiar personal experience*, one which he himself is not surprised to encounter. The acceptance of crime as a familiar experience in turn increases the *ability or readiness to perceive violence where clues to it are potentially available*.

An "increased readiness to perceive" is highly functional. It permits the person to cope with otherwise improbable situations. The law enforcer thus learns to differentiate within violent scenes — to "detect" or "investigate" crimes; the mechanic becomes able to react with dispatch to unusual noises; the sonar operator can efficiently respond to infrequent underwater sounds.

Further research with marginal or ambiguous perceptual situations might shed light on this process. Such research could also deal with the relative "effectiveness" of different phases of training, and with the impact of various kinds of practical experience.

If subsequent work confirms our hunch that police officers are "trained" to perceive violence with relative ease, this should not lead to the conclusion that law enforcement training is a danger to the community and requires drastic modifications. To the extent to which vocational training affects perception, it helps to accomplish its purpose. It increases the trainee's readiness to act in the sort of world he is likely to face.

If a person is to deal with non-everyday occurrences, he must first be able to reduce these to workaday reality. In Goethe's words, he must be able to convert "deficiencies" into "events." Our data suggest that this task can be facilitated through intensive familiarization.[1]

References

Allport, G. W. and Pettigrew, T. F. (1957). Cultural influence on the perception of movement: The trapezoidal illusion among Zulus. *J. Abnorm. Soc. Psychol.* **55**, 104–13.
Bagby, J. W. (1957). A cross-cultural study of perceptual predominance in binocular rivalry. *J. Abnorm. Soc. Psychol.* **54**, 331–34.
Engel, E. (1956). The role of content in binocular resolution. *Amer. J. Psychol.* **69**, 87–91.
Hastorf, A. H. and Myro, G. (1959). The effect of meaning on binocular rivalry. *Amer. J. Psychol.* **72**, 393–400.
Michigan State University (1960). *Catalog, 1960–1961.* East Lansing: Michigan State University.
Toch, H. and Ittelson, W. H. (1956). The role of past experience in apparent movement: A revaluation. *Brit. J. Psychol.* **47**, 195–207.

EXERCISES AND DISCUSSION TOPICS FOR CHAPTER 7

Exercises

1. Choose two or three public figures in your community. Find out these persons' stands on a particular issue. Discuss the differences in perception of this issue by these people. What are the sources of these differences?
2. Using the issue you are dealing with in the simulation (drugs, integration, welfare) write a description of how your character would perceive this issue. Find other people in the simulation whose characters have similar attitudes. Get together with these people; discuss why each of you have this particular viewpoint in the simulation.
3. Write a description of how you in real life would perceive certain issues. What is your stand on busing, welfare, use of drugs, equal employment of women, etc.?

Discussion Topics

Identify sources of your own perceptions in real life and the perceptions of your character in the simulation. Discuss differences and similarities.

[1]The experiment reported in this paper was partly supported by a research grant from Michigan State University. The authors are grateful to Professor Harold Sheehan and other staff members and students of the School of Police Administration and Public Safety, whose cooperation made the study possible.

How might the example from Hastorf's article be applied to simulated and real communities on the positions of different groups? Discuss how the findings of social science can be applied to understanding situations in communities.

How do you differentiate between more important and less important factors that influence perception?

Faced with two diverging groups, which see the same issue differently, what are some techniques or methods used to bring people toward agreement on an issue? Discuss how perceptual differences can be resolved.

CHAPTER 8

Communication

The pattern and amount of communication among participants in the simulation may be a function of the particular role assigned to each participant and the manner in which that role is played. People occupying certain roles are naturally more likely to initiate and receive more communications. An example of this is the mayor of Psych City. Since he has a formal relationship with everyone in the simulation as well as a position of authority, it is likely that he will be frequently addressed by other participants and find it necessary to communicate both with individuals and the group as a whole. Someone filling the role of a student in the simulation, on the other hand, has fewer formal relationships with others as defined by his role. His initiated communications may be fewer in number and more selective. People will also be less likely to address him since his role carries less influence than that of the mayor. It will probably require more effort for the student to get his ideas heard or accepted than it would for someone occupying a higher status role. Generally, high status people give and receive more communications than others (Bales, 1952; Cohen, 1958; Kelly, 1951).

In playing your role you will have to compensate for the status deficiency of your role if you are to achieve your goals. One way of doing this is to talk more. Some research has shown (Bales, 1952) that people who talk a great deal receive more communications from others. Too much talking may have a negative effect. It has been discovered (Bales, 1952) that people who are expressive and talkative are often well liked but not if they talk too much. Another way to circulate your ideas is to establish communication with as many subgroups as possible and attempt to channel their efforts in a direction which will maximize your own goals. Increased communication may elevate your status in the simulation beyond that implicit in your role. The degree to which your goals in Psych City are realized depends on how well you develop the social power given to you in your role and how well you exploit the natural relationship your role has with others.

The preceding discussion involved factors which are external to the people who are communicating with each other. You should be aware of additional factors which reside within the individual communicators and those who receive the communications. In order to make the communication process both clear and understandable a very basic model can be used. It consists of three basic elements: the person who says something (the sender), the medium through which he says it (the channel), and the person who hears him (the recipient).

For the communication process to occur, someone has to send out some information which is intended to increase another's knowledge or persuade him to a point of view. This information (the message) is shaped by a filtering process which includes the sender's intentions, motives, or attitudes. In other words, the sender communicates for a reason which is shaped by the goals he is trying to attain, his attitudes, his social position, and his perception of the person he intends to communicate with. Therefore, when evaluating a message it can be useful to try to reconstruct the filter through which the sender is transmitting his message. What is his role in the simulation? What does he want to accomplish through his message? Are his intentions the same or different from your goals in the simulation? It helps to read the message plus the excess baggage supplied by the sender's particular needs. This should be easy since most people do it everyday, but in this case try to be more aware of the process than usual.

The second important element is the channel through which the communication is sent. Usually this will simply be open space since most Psych City communications will be direct. There will be occasions where you will receive messages from a third or fourth party. You should be aware that the greater the number of people through which a message must pass, the greater is the probability that the message will be altered in some form. If a statement originally made by the mayor of Psych City passes through a Black Panther and the S.D.S. representative, it is likely to come out different than if it had passed through the police chief and a city councilwoman. This is the process that shapes and maintains a rumor in the outside world. It is important that you deal with accurate information in the simulation and are able to make the appropriate corrections or alterations in messages which you do not receive directly from the sender. It may be useful to you tactically to start your own rumor within the simulation at a place where it will be shaped to your own advantage.

The third element in the communication process is the person who hears the message. Just as the sender emits his message through attitudinal filters, the receiver also hears the message through his own, similar filters. Many people may hear the same message, but essentially understand it to mean completely different things. The receiver's attitudes influence his interpretation; people often hear what they want or expect to hear. People generally do not expect the police chief to advocate rebellion or a left-wing radical to espouse law and order. When this does occur, recipients of the communication may interpret it in a manner which is consistent with the role of the sender.

There seems to be a general tendency for people to keep their opinions consistent with one another. This is important when attempting to persuade someone within the simulation to your point of view on a subject. If you know he thinks or believes the opposite of what you are advocating, there is little possibility that you will change him. To do this it may be necessary to play him off another person or idea. For example, if you are a radical and are trying to convince the mayor that a mass demonstration on an issue is important to the community, you may not have much luck. If you point out that the police chief and two councilmen also think your way, you may have an easier time of it. If he respects the judgment of these people and sees them as being in a similar position as himself (i.e. city officials) it is somewhat less inconsistent for him to agree with your position. This is an extreme example, but you should have little difficulty applying the principle to your own situation within Psych City.

Finally, there is a technique that you can use over time in the simulation which may allow you to get support from someone who ordinarily would be difficult to persuade. It is based upon the assimilation-contrast effect first researched by Sherif and Hovland (1961). It is this type of technique that Secretary of Defense, Clark Clifford is reported to have used in convincing President Lyndon Johnson to halt the bombing of North Vietnam. The first step involves finding exactly where the person you want to persuade stands on an issue. When you know this, you then try to persuade him to adopt a position just *slightly* closer to your own than it already is. Stop there. When he begins to accept the new position as his own, repeat the same maneuver. Using a variety of techniques, you can often convert someone to your point of view if you do it in small steps, over time, and making it appear that the person is making the change of his own accord.

In sum, influencing other people involves a great many variables. Some of these exist outside the people involved in the form of roles and status. Other variables are concerned with states within the person. Finally, some influencing variables are intrinsic to the communication process itself. The degree to which you are attentive to these variables and able to use knowledge of them will contribute to or inhibit your success in Psych City.

MACHINES TAKE OVER *

Art Buchwald

The nature and style of public communication has been strongly influenced by technological progress. The development of superspeed transportation has expanded the potential range of face-to-face contacts enormously; television has made it possible for us to have direct visual experience with events occurring in all parts of the universe.

In the process of utilizing machinery in almost all of our communication processes, we seem to have created some side effects which many would consider undesirable. Dependence upon "gadgetry" and equipment has increased along with a diminished inclination toward old-fashioned person-to-person communication. Because of the predictability and nonconfrontative qualities of machinery, there is a fear that people will seek security through relating even more frequently to machines at the expense of their interpersonal relationships. The following essay explores the limits of this trend.

People don't realize it, but it won't be very long before teaching machines are perfected to the point where it won't be necessary to have teachers at all. The teaching-machine industry is working night and day to perfect new machines which will not only help make up for the teacher shortage in the United States but will also cut down on the cost of hiring new teachers. It is not too far-fetched to predict that in ten or twenty years our children will be sitting in teacherless classes, their work programmed for them by computers, graded by IBM cards, and scolded for sloppy work by closed-television monitors fifty miles away.

While there are great advantages to learning by machine, we should never lose sight of the human element. It is for this reason that we have perfected the Robot Teaching Machine, which will combine all the advantages of machine learning with those of being taught by a teacher in the room. The Robot Teaching Machine would work as follows: each seat would be magnetized, and there would be a small piece of metal sewn into the seat of each student's clothes. When the class was in session, the student would not be able to get out of his seat.

If a child had to go to the bathroom, he would push a button on his desk. The computer in front of the room would then break the field of magnetism and allow the child to go to the bathroom, providing there was only one pupil out of the room at a time.

If a child misbehaved in class, the computer would send out a slight shock which would be the equivalent of a rapped knuckle. If the child still refused to behave and the shock treatment were not enough punishment, he would be lifted out of his seat by a conveyor belt and carried to the principal's office. There the principal computer would deal with the pupil. When the pupil arrived at the principal computer's office, the machine would automatically sound an alarm in the home of the pupil's parents and one of them would have to come to school and discuss his child with the computer. The principal computer would have stored in it several lectures on tape, and would play the one most suitable for the occasion.

The Robot Teaching Machine would be as humane as possible. If a little boy or little girl started to cry in class, the machine would start dispensing facial tissue. If the child continued to cry, there would be a portable lap on the side of the machine where the child could find comfort.

During lunch periods the computer would turn into a vending machine where the student could buy milk, sandwiches, hot soup, and candy bars. The profits from these would go into buying athletic machines for recreational purposes.

Now, someone is going to raise the question of how you can prevent cheating on tests without a teacher in the room. Quite simple. Before each child hands in his IBM paper, he will attach a blood-pressure valve to his arm and take a lie-detector test. If the graph shows he cheated, he gets three shocks and has to take the test over again.

The object of the machine is to make the child love and respect it. Some machines will be better than others. If a machine breaks down, a substitute machine will teach for the day.

Some children may want to show their affection for a teaching computer. Instead of bringing the machine an apple or flowers, the child could bring it a can of oil or a new transistor.

COMMUNICATION, A SOCIAL TOOL*

Dennis Angelini

It is possible that communication is the most important basic tool which people may use in solving the problems they encounter within their communities. With good communication, many alternative channels of resolution are available; without adequate communication most attempts to deal with social problems are doomed to failure.

Mr. Angelini explores various forms of communication and the purposes they serve. In his essay, he discusses how the components of communication affect the process and outcome of communication.

As man wrestles with his ever-present adversary, the environment, he develops tools which make this struggle less difficult. He translates genetic potential into manpower by developing his capabilities in one direction or another in congruence with environmental conditions. One of the major social tools man has enlarged upon is communication.

When one views communication as observations and responses made by a party of respondents, human communication appears as part of a continuum of animal behavior, not a separate dimension. Communication is not unique to mankind. Nonhumans communicate, although their forms are less voluntary, less complex and less dependent on verbal components than human communication.

Nonhuman communication appears to be more dependent on movement, color changes, and odors than human behavior. Particular gyrations may communicate sexual or aggressive interests. Changes in color of parts of the body may be interpreted by species as indicating the onset of some inter-organism activity. These movements and color changes may be involuntary and species specific, and understanding of these cues may be partially inherited; however, they do serve as communication for nonhuman parties.

At the human level, verbal variations are a major means of communication. Nevertheless, any sensory channel can be used. Variations in the intensity of a hand on a shoulder can communicate different messages. Color changes, such as blushing and paling, reveal things to others. Body movements such as shrugging of shoulders, bowed head or fidgety fingers convey information from one to another. These nonverbal aspects of

*Prepared especially for this book.

human communication form a field or background in which language is imbedded. Understanding of both background and figure is important to the success of total communication processes.

Whether the communication is used to express beliefs or needs, to transfer information or to entertain, communication is an integral part of human activity. It is a fundamental social tool for increasing competence in dealing with the social and physical environment. The expression of beliefs and needs and the transmission of knowledge directly increase man's ability to effectively deal with his surroundings. Entertainment may also function in a more indirect manner. For example, humorous communication is funny when the unexpected or forbidden occurs in a situation. Therefore, in a roundabout way, humor reaffirms appropriate or competent activity in a situation by emphasizing the inappropriate or incompetent.

Verbal and nonverbal behavior are the bases of total communication. The amount of each component can vary with different communication processes. Language is not always necessary for successful communication. Once during testing trials of a submarine I was awakened from a restless sleep by the loud blasts of alarms and the feel of the boat at a steep down angle. Since this was the first night I had ever spent below the surface of the sea in a submarine I was concerned about the situation in which I found myself. With pounding heart I quickly glanced around the torpedo room and then rolled over and went back to sleep. Having seen no signs of panic or stress in the crew's nonverbal behavior, I assumed a test dive and not an emergency condition was in effect. In this crisis situation I sought a message in actions not words to get a basic understanding of the situation.

The use of language improves communication but it must be language which is appropriate to the context in which it occurs or else problems can arise. For example, a diabetic neighbor of mine was shopping with her two-year-old daughter when she felt a coma developing. In order to prevent the coma and avoid a scene she sought aid from a nearby woman who happened to be using the telephone. In the few moments it took to reach her would-be benefactress, my neighbor's speech became somewhat slurred. The diabetic took hold of her "savior's" arm, told her she was a diabetic and needed help. The woman became alarmed when this strange lady with a slurring voice grabbed hold of her arm. She started screaming that a crazy woman was after her. In desperation the sick woman slapped the lady, hoping to bring her to her senses; however, it only aggravated the situation.

My neighbor wanted to let the gathering people know that she was diabetic and needed some orange juice but by this time the symptoms were much stronger. All she could say was that she needed juice. Because she was wobbly, because her speech was slurred and because her "protector"-to-be panicked, her plea for juice was interpreted by the gathering crowd as a plea for booze or wine. At this time, several men, thinking she was in an alcoholic frenzy grabbed her and roughly threw her to the ground. This treatment forced her coat to open revealing her six-month pregnant condition. Women took her child from her and kept them separated. As she defended herself against these assaults and continued her plea for juice she was pinned to the ground, her child was screaming, she was becoming hysterical and the police were called.

A passerby, attracted by this wild commotion, went to the scene and recognized my neighbor as a previous acquaintance. Kneeling she spoke softly to her in Ukranian, their native tongue, and asked what was happening. The sound of her native language had a soothing effect on the diabetic; she was able to tell her friend of her condition and her need for orange juice.

Upon hearing this, the passerby rose and yelled "Get the hell off this woman, she's diabetic and pregnant and you're killing her on the ground." People now rushed to call an ambulance and to get some juice. They returned her daughter to her. And some, who had manhandled her, quickly disappeared into the crowd.

Clearly this woman's communication system did not function properly. She had hoped to get assistance and avoid a scene, and neither event occurred. Her messages did not result in competently handling the situation. Obviously there was a breakdown among the components of communication.

As discussed in the introduction to this section, there are three basic components in the communication process. They are the sender, the receiver, and the message which travels between them. Characteristics of each component contribute to the success or failure of the communication process. This process may be one way with messages coming from one sender or it may be more complex with messages coming from several senders or it may be multidirectional with senders and receivers exchanging messages. In all types of communication the three components will be found.

The sender's credibility, in terms of his qualifications and objectivity, have a major influence on the effect of communication. Credibility gaps develop when there are doubts about these characteristics of the sender.

Additionally, attractiveness, power, and prestige of the sender lend support to or weaken his message. In the example of the diabetic woman her messages were misinterpreted and devalued not only because of their limited clarity but undoubtedly also because of reductions in her credibility, attractiveness, prestige, and power as a result of being labeled a drunkard.

The tone of the message also influences its effectiveness. Different levels of emotionality and different kinds of emotional appeals are tonal characteristics which are found in messages. Communicators use emotional appeals which match the aim or purpose of the message. Political and military messages frequently contain messages of patriotism, bravery, and survival, whereas religious groups load their messages with love appeals. These appeals serve to arouse emotions and hence make the messages more appealing.

Obviously the clarity and precision of the words used in a message will effect the success of the communication. Jargon, fifty-cent words or words with multiple meanings may be a handicap in communication. In the example of the diabetic woman, her language was limited and she aggravated the situation by using words which were less than precise. Her words led to alternative interpretations of the message.

It is the third factor in the communication process, the receiver, which often shapes many of the qualities of the sender and the message. Sender qualities such as credibility, attractiveness, power, and prestige are not always clearly labeled. The receiver has to infer these characteristics. Not only must the receiver guess at senders' characteristics but the values of various receivers differ. Consequently, attractiveness and prestige differ, causing variations in the success of the communication process as receivers change. Additionally, the tone a sender selects for his message will vary with different receivers.

Receiver dependency does not mean there are no constancies in communication processes across different senders and receivers. The point is that the process is interactive and the degree of success depends upon the degree of understanding between the two communicators. Incongruities in verbal or behavioral styles of the participants may lead to incorrect inferences about each other with negative effects on the success of the communication process.

As individuals collect in groups and form communities, communication becomes more complex. Community life involves a variety of communication processes. Some messages are meant for total community such as government and commercial messages. Other messages are aimed at specific subgroups of people, such as union members or stamp collectors.

Some messages are sent to just one other person. Daily we participate in a maze of communication involving the use of these various kinds of messages.

Communicators seek different media for their messages. Generally, community-wide messages appear in newspapers or on radio and television. They are presented in standard English, usually in a logical objective manner. Emotionality tends to be de-emphasized in mass media messages unless direct quotes or such occur. Gossip columns, editorials, and subgroup messages are other places where departures from standard English may occur in mass media. The most conspicuous departure is the use of a foreign language by ethnic subgroups. The use of dialects and jargon by subgroups reduces the range of the communication as does the use of jargon by ethnic languages. Unless one is familiar with the jargon of sport, work, science, or art, one has difficulty with their communications which appear on mass communication channels.

Subgroup communication often uses less extensive channels than newspapers and television. Pamphlets carry messages for neighborhoods, churches, clubs and schools. Bulletin boards hold scores of messages. Barbershops, taverns, laundromat, and coffee machines function as face-to-face communication centers. Telephones, porch steps, and fences assist the transmission of messages. The style of these messages becomes less dependent on standard English and more characteristic of the subgroup. This transformation is most likely to occur at the personal level of communication which adds nonverbal components to the interaction.

A member of a subgroup and a community is clearly exposed to a multitude of messages. He must become familiar with the communication processes in his community, how they function and how they differ. He must know which channels are open and credible and why others are closed and unreliable. He must understand communication styles from other reference groups in his community. Awareness and control of the communication process is necessary or man may find this tool has turned against him.

References and Suggested Readings

Katz, D. Functional approaches to the study of attitudes. In E. Hollander and P. Hunt (Eds.) *Current perspectives in social psychology.* New York: University Press, 1967. Pp. 336–346.

Rasnov, R. and Robinson, E. *Experiments in persuasion.* New York: Academic Press, 1967.

Watson, G. and Johnson, D. *Social psychology: Insight and association.* Philadelphia: J. B. Lippincott Co., 1972. Pp. 222–253.

EXERCISES AND DISCUSSION TOPICS FOR CHAPTER 8

Exercises

1. Plan to attend some event in your community. This could be a public meeting (e.g. PTA), a football game, or a cultural event. Follow the different media's coverage of this event — radio, television, newspapers, magazines. Discover how information is communicated to the public. Compare and contrast the different media coverage of the event with your own perceptions.
2. On five (or more) 3 × 5 in. index cards print a series of words, numbers or symbols. Each card should have a different set of symbols, with one symbol in common with the rest of the cards.

Example:

Card 1	□	★	Z	W	+
Card 2	★	Z	W	+	○
Card 3	Z	W	+	○	□
Card 4	W	+	○	□	★
Card 5	+	○	□	★	Z

Common symbol —   +

Divide the group into three or more groups of five people in each group. Have one group sit in a circle, another group sit in a straight line, a third group sit in a Y-shaped configuration, and a fourth group sit in a wheel.

```
     A              A           A   B          A     B
                    B                                C
 B       C          C               C
                    D               D           D     E
   D   E            E               E
  Circle          Line          Y-shape         Wheel
```

Each person in a group receives one of the index cards. The group's task is to find the one common symbol that each of them has on their cards. To discover the common symbol, people can send only *written* messages to people sitting adjacent to them. In the circle, each person can pass messages to the people on their left and right; in the line network, *A* and *B* can pass messages only to the one person adjacent to them; *A* and *B* in the Y-shaped network can communicate only with *C*; in the wheel only *C* can receive and send messages to all the other members in the network.

No talking is allowed. Record the time it takes the group to solve the problem. (Adapted from Leavitt, 1951.)

Discuss the relevance of using only written communication to the simulation. Talk about what happened in the networks and apply this to the simulation and the real world.

Discussion Topics

Who in Psych City would have the most influence over you in the simulation? In real life? List the reasons why this person would influence you (personality, role attributes).

Discuss the purpose of communication in various situations: Cocktail parties, political rallies, classrooms. What are the purposes of communication in the simulation? In the simulated and real community, what are some ways of facilitating communication?

Many people believe a large percentage of information is communicated by nonverbal means. What is nonverbal communication? When and how is it used?

Some people believe that mass media not only report the news but, in a sense, create it. How does the medium shape the message? Does mass media facilitate public communication?

Discuss how nonhuman objects which humans relate to (i.e. Buchwald's article) affect person-to-person communication?

CHAPTER 9

Norms and Reference Groups

Everyone participating in Psych City will find that he or she belongs to one or more groups within the simulation, just as in everyday life. Although the term "groups" is familiar to everyone, it will be helpful to define the term a little more precisely, so that it will be easier to identify groups within the simulation. Once identification of various groups in Psych City is possible, the groups can be observed by each participant and used for the prediction and manipulation of the other participants' behavior. Your success in the simulation will be influenced by your ability to use your knowledge of groups in planning your own behavior.

Two social scientists (Cartwright and Zander, 1968, p. 48) currently writing in the field of group behavior, list ten possible characteristics that can be used in identifying groups and group behavior. They propose that the term group be used to refer to "any collection of interdependent people" characterized by one or more of the following statements:

1. They engage in frequent interaction.
2. They define themselves as members of a group.
3. They are defined by others as belonging to a group.
4. They share norms concerning matters of common interest.
5. They participate in a system of interlocking roles.
6. They identify with one another as a result of having set up the same ideals.
7. They find the group to be rewarding.
8. They pursue promotively interdependent goals.
9. They have a collective perception of their unity.
10. They tend to act in a unitary way toward their environment.

Various collections of people who are participating in Psych City fit one or more of the above descriptions. Psych City as a whole can be defined as a group. Participants engage in frequent interaction, are seen as a group by the instructor, if not by themselves, participate in a system of interlocking (albeit artificial) roles, and have possibly other characteristics that define themselves as a group. Since you are one of these participants, you are part of the group called Psych City. You also belong to other, smaller groups, simultaneously. If your role prescription is that of councilman, you belong to a group of city administrators, and other people in Psych City react to you as such. Perhaps you are a minority group councilman and therefore belong to a minority group as well as administrators. The overlapping groups to which you belong may be few or many; and, as with the roles which help define groups, different people will expect different things from you depending upon which group or groups *they* think you belong to. Finally, since you belong to more than one group, the goals of your groups are likely to come into conflict. The goals of minority group members in the simulation may not always be the same as those of the city administrators. Which goals you work toward achieving are likely to depend upon which group is more important to you.

After you are able to identify and observe various groups in Psych City, one thing should become apparent. This is the regularity in the way people within each group deal with each other. People tend to work out patterns of dealing with each other over a period of time which are implicitly agreed- upon by the people involved. Sometimes these regularities are formalized, as will be most obvious in the Town Meeting. Here all or most of the people agree on standards of behavior which allow at least some of the group's goals to be accomplished such as Roberts Rules of Order. Agreed upon regularities of behavior are usually called social *norms*. The notion of social norms can become more inclusive, but generally they allow other members and outsiders to be able to predict some of the behavior of the group members. It also helps to guide member behavior by giving some standards regarding what behaviors are "right" or expected by other members, and what behaviors are considered "wrong." The existence of group norms facilitates the functioning of the group as a whole as long as the norms are realistic and are adapted to the situation in which the group is operating.

Since Psych City is a society which begins only when the participants assemble for the first time, you may have the opportunity to see how group norms form. They should form in a manner which is very similar to the way in which the norms which control a large part of your life outside the simulation were originally constructed. Norms will come into being out of the interests and goals of the groups' members. Social pressures will be exerted by various members to get other participants to behave in a fashion which maximizes the success of the group (or some of its individual members) in the simulation. These needs in turn will be dependent upon the roles assigned to each individual. Conformity to the emerging norms should be enforced by the withholding of cooperation or approval from the offending members.

Conformity to the social norms of a particular group can be viewed in terms of what each member is likely to gain or lose by conforming or failing to conform (Thibaut and Kelley, 1959; Homans, 1961). Each person may differ from other group members in the degree to which the group is able to satisfy his needs. Simply being able to interact with other members may be sufficiently rewarding to some people that withholding his opportunity constitutes a loss to be avoided. Other members need the group to validate their ideas or opinions. Still others may require more tangible rewards such as the group's assistance in obtaining status or material possessions. The rewards and losses provided by the group may vary from person-to-person, but each individual will be attracted to the group to the extent that it meets his needs. The more alternatives the individual has for the satisfaction of his needs, the less control any single group has over his behavior.

While participating in Psych City, it may be useful to you to speculate about what other participants want from the groups to which they belong. By satisfying the right needs and withholding desired rewards, you should increase the probability of achieving your own goals within the simulation.

Areas to be on the lookout for in attempting to control other's behavior in Psych City are: (1) How much of the other participants' behavior is visible and therefore open to control? (2) To what extent can you give or withhold favors relative to their behavior? (3) How much can you use individual needs to be wanted, liked, admired, needed, or useful? (4) How much power does your Psych City role place at your disposal, for aiding or obstructing attainment of other people's goals?

Everyone lives in a context of group pressure and control. Some people are more controlled by the groups to which they belong than are other people. It is hoped that your experience in Psych City helps you to understand how group pressures operate. Ideally this should assist you in developing some ability to use the natural processes of group behavior to your own advantage rather than be used by them. You should be able to generalize your experience beyond the simulation itself, into your own everyday affairs.

FOOD FOR ALL HIS DEAD*

Frank Chin

The often cited "generation gap" may be attributed to many experiential factors. One of the more common sources of difference between parent and offspring is the cultural groups with which the older and younger person identifies. These groups may be ethnic in nature (old country versus American), or they may relate to more subtle sources of lifestyle identification (Negro versus Black or Ms. versus Miss). In the transition from the old to the new reference groups many internal as well as external conflicts arise. Change does not usually take place in a smooth, linear fashion. Instead, the person entering the new group experiences a great deal of conflict and pain as he attempts to integrate his feelings and attitudes toward his parents and their culture, with his new reference group, which will help him gain a unique identity.

Mr. Chin describes the process of identity formation in his powerful story of a young Chinese–American and his relationship to his family and friends.

"Jus' forty-fie year 'go, Doctah Sun Yat-sen Free China from da Manchus. Dats' why all us Chinee, all ovah da woil are celebrate Octob' tan or da Doubloo Tan. . . !"

The shouted voice came through the open bathroom window. The shouting and music was still loud after rising through the night's dry air; white moths jumped on the air, danced through the window over the voice, and lighted quickly on the wet sink, newly reddened from his father's attack. Johnny's arms were around his father's belly, holding the man upright against the edge of the sink to keep the man's mouth high enough to spit lung blood into the drain. . . .

The man's belly shrank and filled against Johnny's arms as the man breathed and spat, breathed and spat, the belly shrinking and filling. The breaths and bodies against each other shook with horrible rhythms that could not be numbed out of Johnny's mind. "Pride," Johnny thought, "Pa's pride for his reputation for doing things . . . except dying. He's not proud of dying, so it's a secret between father and son. . . ." At the beginning of the man's death, when he had been Johnny's father, still commanding and large, saying, "Help me. I'm dying; don't tell," and removing his jacket and walking to the bathroom. Then came the grin — pressed lips

---

twisted up into the cheeks — hiding the gathering blood and drool. Johnny had cried then, knowing his father would die. But now the man seemed to have been always dying and Johnny always waiting, waiting with what he felt was a coward's loyalty to the dying, for he helped the man hide his bleeding and was sick himself, knowing he was not waiting for the man to die but waiting for the time after death when he could relax.

"*. . .free from da yoke of Manchu slab'ry, in'epen'ence, no moah queue on da head! Da's wha'fo' dis big a parade! An' here, in San Francisco, alla us Chinee–'mellican're, pwowd! . . .*"

"It's all gone . . . I can't spit any more. Get my shirt, boy. I'm going to make a speech tonight. . . ." The man slipped from the arms of the boy and sat on the toilet lid and closed his mouth. His bare chest shone as if washed with dirty cooking oil and looked as if he should have been chilled, not sweating, among the cold porcelain and tile of the bathroom.

To the sound of herded drums and cymbals, Johnny wiped the sweat from his father's soft body and dressed him without speaking. He was full of the heat of wanting to cry for his father but would not.

His father was heavier outside the house.

They staggered each other across the alleyway to the edge of Portsmouth Square. They stood together at the top of the slight hill, their feet just off the concrete onto the melted fishbone grass, and could see the brightly lit reviewing stand, and they saw over the heads of the crowd, the dark crowd of people standing in puddles of each other, moving like oily things and bugs floating on a tide; to their left, under trees, children played and shouted on swings and slides; some ran toward Johnny and his father and crouched behind their legs to hide from giggling girls. And they could see the street and the parade beyond the crowd. The man stood away from the boy but held tightly to Johnny's arm. The man swallowed a greasy sound and grinned. "I almost feel I'm not dying now. Parades are like that. I used to dance the Lion Dance in China, boy. I was always in the parades."

Johnny glanced at his father and saw the man's eyes staring wide with the skin around the eyes stretching for the eyes to open wider, and Johnny patted his father's shoulder and watched the shadows of children running across the white sand of the play area. He was afraid of watching his father die here; the man was no longer like his father or a man; perhaps it was the parade. But the waiting, the lies and waiting, waiting so long with a flesh going to death that the person was no longer real as a life but a parody of live things, grinning. The man was a fish drying and shrinking inside its skin on the sand, crazy, mimicking swimming, Johnny thought, thrown to cats; for his father, Johnny could only wait and help the man stay alive without helping him die. "That's probably where you got the disease," Johnny said.

"Where, boy?"

"Back in China."

"No, I got it here. I was never sick for one day in China." The man began walking down the hill toward the crowd. "Back in China. . . ."

They walked down the hill, the man's legs falling into steps with his body jerking after his falling legs; Johnny held his father, held the man back to keep him from falling over his own feet. The man's breath chanted dry and powdered out of his mouth and nostrils to the rhythm of the drums, and his eyes showed brickcolored teeth in his grin. "Not so fast, *ah-bah!*" Johnny shouted and pulled at his father's arm. He was always frightened at the man's surges of nervous life.

"Don't run," Johnny said, feeling his father's muscles stretch as he pulled Johnny down the hill toward the crowd. "Stop running, pa!" And his father was running and breathing out fog into the hot night and sweating dirty oil, and trembling his fleshy rump inside his baggy trousers, dancing in stumbles with dead senses. "Pa, not so fast, dammit! You're going to have another attack! Slow down!"

"I can't stop, boy."

They were in the shadow of the crowd now, and children chased around them.

"Look! There they are!" the man said.

"*Dere you're, ladies and genullmans! Eben da lion are bow in respack to us tonigh'!*"

The crowd clapped and whistled, and boys shoved forward to see. Old women, roundbacked in their black overcoats, lifted their heads to smile; they stood together and nodded, looking like clumps of huge beetles with white faces.

"Closer to the platform, boy; that's where I belong," the man said. He leaned against Johnny's shoulder and coughed out of his nostrils. Johnny heard the man swallow and cringed. The man was grinning again, his eyes anxious, the small orbs jumping scared spiders all over the sockets. "Aren't you happy you came, boy? Look at all the people."

"Take time to catch your breath, *ah-bah*. Don't talk. It's wrong for you to be here anyhow."

"Nothing's wrong, boy, don't you see all your people happy tonight? As long as . . ." he swallowed and put his head against Johnny's cheek, then made a sound something like laughter, "As I've been here ... do you understand my Chinese?" Then slowly in English, catching quick breaths between his words, "I be here, allabody say dere chillren're gonna leab Chinatong and go way, but 'snot so, huh?" His voice was low, a guttural monotone. "Look a'em all; dey still be Chinee. I taught da feller dat teach dem to dance how to do dat dancer boy. Johnny? dis're you home, here, an' I know you gat tire, but alla you fran's here, an' dey likee you." His face was speaking close to Johnny and chilled the boy's face with hot breath.

The boy did not look at his father talking to him but stared stiffly out to the street, watching the glistening arms of boys jerking the bamboo skeletons of silk-hided lions over their heads. His father was trying to save him again, Johnny thought, trying to be close like he had been to him now long ago when his father was a hero from the war. The man spoke as if he had saved his life to talk to his son now, tonight, here among the eyes and sounds of Chinese.

"I'm sorry, *ah-bah*, I can't help it ..." was all Johnny could answer sincerely. He knew it would be cruel to say, "Pa, I don't want to be a curiosity like the rest of the Chinese here. I want to be something by myself," so he did not, not only because of the old man, but because he was not certain he believed himself; it had been easy to believe his own shouted words when he was younger and safe with his parents; it had been easy not to like what he had then — when he knew he could stay; then, when the man was fat and not dying, they were separate and could argue, but not now; now he was favored with the man's secret; they were horribly bound together now. The old man was dying and still believing in the old ways, still sure — even brave, perhaps — and that meant something to Johnny.

"An' you see dam bow in respack now, an' da's good lucks to ev'eybody!"

The lion dancers passed, followed by a red convertible with boys beating a huge drum on the back seat.

Johnny knew the parades; the lion dancers led the wait for the coming of the long dragon, and the end. The ends of the parades with the dragon were the most exciting, were the loudest moment before the chase down the streets to keep the dragon in sight. He was half aware of the air becoming brittle with the noise of the dances and the crowd, and, with his father now, was almost happy, almost anxious, dull, the way he felt when he was tired and staring in a mirror, slowly realizing that he was looking at his own personal reflection; he felt pleased and depressed, as if he had just prayed for something.

"You know," the man said, "I wan' you to be somebody here. Be doctor, mak' moneys and halp da Chinee, or lawyer, or edgenerer, make moneys and halp, and people're respack you." He patted the boy's chest. "You tall me now you won' leab here when I die, hokay?"

"I don't know, pa." The boy looked down to the trampled grass between his feet and shrugged off what he did not want to say. They were hopeless to each other now. He looked over his shoulder to his father and could not answer the chilled face and they stared a close moment onto each other and were private, holding each other and waiting.

Policemen on motorcycles moved close to the feet of the crowd to move them back. The boys wearing black-and-red silk trousers and white sweatshirts, coaxing the clumsy dragon forward with bells and shafts could be seen now; they were dancing and shouting past the reviewing stand. The dragon's glowing head lurched side to side, rose and fell, its jaw dangling after the goading boys. As the dragon writhed and twisted about itself, boys jumped in and out from under its head and belly to keep the dragon fresh.

"Maybe I'm not Chinese, pa! Maybe I'm just a Chinese accident. You're the only one that seems to care that I'm Chinese." The man glared at the boy and did not listen. "Pa, most of the people I don't like are Chinese. They even *laugh* with accents, Christ!" He turned his head from the man, sorry for what he said. It was too late to apologize.

"You dare talk to your father like that?" the man shouted in Chinese. He stood back from the boy, raised himself and slapped him, whining through his teeth as his arm swung heavily toward the boy's cheek. "You're no son of mine! No son! I'm ashamed of you!"

The shape of the bamboo skeleton was a shadow within the thinly painted silk of the dragon, and boys were shouting inside.

"Pa, *ah-bah*, I'm sorry."

"Get me up to the platform, I gotta make a speech."

"Pa, you've got to go home."

"I'm not dead yet; you'll do as I say."

"All right, I'll help you up because you won't let me help you home. But I'll leave you up there, pa. I'll leave you for ma and sister to bring home."

"From da Pres'den, of da United State' 'mellica! 'To alla ob da Chinee–'mellican on da celebrate ob dere liberate from da Manchu . . . .'"

"I'm trying to make you go home for your own good."

"You're trying to kill me with disgrace. All right, leave me. Get out of my house, too."

"Pa, I'm trying to help you. You're dying!" The boy reached for his father, but the man stepped away. "You'll kill ma by not letting her take care of you."

"Your mother's up on the platform waiting for me."

"Because she doesn't know how bad you are. I do. I have a right to make you go home."

"It's my home, not yours. Leave me alone." The man walked the few steps to the edge of the platform and called his wife. She came down and helped him up. She glanced out but did not see Johnny in the crowd. Her cheeks were made up very pink and her lipstick was still fresh; she looked very young next to Johnny's father, but her hands were old, and seemed older because of the bright nail polish and jade bracelet.

Johnny knew what his father would tell his mother and knew he would have to trust them to be happy without him. Perhaps he meant he would have to trust himself to be happy without them . . . the feeling would pass; he would wait and apologize to them both, and he would not have to leave, perhaps. Everything seemed wrong, all wrong, yet, everyone, in his own way, was right. He turned quickly and walked out of the crowd to the children's play area. He sat on a bench and stretched his legs straight out in front of him. The dark old women in black coats stood by on the edges of the play area watching the nightbleached faces of children flash in and out of the light as they ran through each other's shadows. Above him, Johnny could hear the sound of pigeons in the trees. Chinatown was the same and he hated it now. Before, when he was younger, and went shopping with his mother, he had enjoyed the smells of the shops and seeing colored toys between the legs of walking people; he had been proud to look up and see his mother staring at the numbers on the scales that weighed meat to see the shopkeepers smile and nod at her. And at night, he had played here, like the children chasing each other in front of him now.

"What'sa wrong, Johnny? Tire?" He had not seen the girl standing in front of him. He sat up straight and smiled. "You draw more pitchers on napkin for me tonigh'?"

"No, I was with pa." He shrugged. "You still got the napkins, huh?"

"I tole you I want dem. I'm keeping 'em." She wore a short white coat over her red *cheongsam* and her hair shook down over her face from the wind.

"I wanta walk," he said. "You wanta walk?"

"I gotta gat home before twalve."

"Me too."

"I'll walk for you dan, okay?" She smiled and reached a hand down for him.

"You'll walk *with* me, not *for* me. You're not a dog." He stood and took her hand. He enjoyed the girl; she listened to him; he did not care if she understood what he said or knew what he wanted to say. She listened to him, would listen with her eyes staring with a wide frog's stare until he stopped speaking, then her body would raise and she would sigh a curl of girl's voice and say, "You talk so nice . . . ."

The tail of an embroidered dragon showed under her white coat and seemed to sway as her thigh moved. "You didn' come take me to the parade, Johnny?"

"I was with pa." Johnny smiled. The girl's hand was dry-feeling, cold and dry like a skin of tissue-paper covered with flesh. They walked slowly, rocking forward and back as they stepped up the hill. "I'm always with pa, huh?" he said bitterly, "I'm sorry."

"'sall right. Is he still dying?"

"Everyone's dying here; it's called the American's common cold."

"Don' talk you colleger stuff to me! I don' unnerstan' it, Johnny."

"He's still dying . . . always. I mean, sometimes I think he won't die or is lying and isn't dying."

"Wou'n't that be good, if he weren't dying? And if it was all a joke? You could all laugh after."

"I don't know, Sharon!" He whined on the girl's name and loosened her hand, but she held.

"Johnny?"

"Yeah?"

"What'll you do if he dies?"

Johnny did not look at the girl as he answered, but lifted his head to glance at the street full of lights and people walking between moving cars. Grant Avenue. He could smell incense and caged squabs, the dank smell of damp fish heaped on tile from the shops now. "I think I'd leave. I know what that sounds like, like I'm waiting for him to die so I can leave; maybe it's so. Sometimes I think I'd kill him to stop all this waiting and lifting him to the sink and keeping it a secret. But I won't do that."

"You won' do that . . ." Sharon said.

"An' now, I like to presan' da Pres'den ob da Chinee Benabolen' . . . ."

"My father," Johnny said.

The girl clapped her hands over her ears to keep her hair from jumping on the wind. "You father?" she said.

"I don't think so," Johnny said. They walked close to the walls, stepped almost into doorways to allow crowding people to pass them going down the hill toward the voice. They smelled grease and urine of open hallways, and heard music like birds being strangled as they walked over iron gratings.

"You don't think so what?" Sharon asked, pulling him toward the crowd.

"I don't think so what you said you didn't think so . . . ." He giggled, "I'm sort of funny tonight. I was up all last night listening to my father practice his speech in the toilet and helping him bleed when he got mad. And this morning I started to go to classes and fell asleep on the bus; so I didn't go to classes, and I'm still awake. I'm not tired but kind of stupid with no sleep, dig, Sharon?"

The girl smiled and said, "I dig, Johnny. You the same way every time I see you almos'."

"And I hear myself talking all this stupid stuff, but it's sort of great, you know? Because I have to listen to what I'm saying or I'll miss it."

"My mother say you cute."

They were near the top of the street now, standing in front of a wall stand with a fold-down shelf covered with Chinese magazines, nickel comic books, postcards and Japanese souvenirs of Chinatown. Johnny, feeling ridiculous with air between his joints and his cheeks tingling with the anxious motion of the crowd, realized he was tired, then realized he was staring at the boy sitting at the wall stand and staring at the boy's leather cap.

"What are you loo' at, huh?" the boy said in a girl's voice. Sharon pulled at Johnny and giggled. Johnny giggled and relaxed to feeling drunk and said:

"Are you really Chinese?"

"What're you ting, I'm a Negro soy sauce chicken?"

"Don't you know there's no such thing as a real Chinaman in all of America? That all we are are American Indians cashing in on a fad?"

"Fad? Don' call me fad. You fad yourselv."

"No, you're not Chinese, don't you understand? You see it all started when a bunch of Indians wanted to quit being Indians and fighting the cavalry and all, so they left the reservation, see?"

"In'ian?"

"And they saw that there was this big kick about Chinamen, so they braided their hair into queues and opened up laundries and restaurants and started reading Margaret Mead and Confucius and Pearl Buck and became respectable Chinamen and gained some self-respect."

"Chinamong! You battah not say Chinamong."

"But the reservation instinct stuck, years of tradition, you see? Something about needing more than one Indian to pull off a good rain dance or something, so they made Chinatown! And here we are!"

He glanced around him and grinned. Sharon was laughing, her shoulders hopping up and down. The boy blinked then pulled his cap lower over his eyes. "It's all right to come out now, you see?" Johnny said. "Indians are back in vogue and the Chinese kick is wearing out . . . ." He laughed until he saw the boy's confused face. "Aww nuts," he said, "this is no fun."

He walked after Sharon through the crowd, not feeling the shoulders and women's hips knocking against him. "I'd like to get outta here so quick, Sharon; I wish I had something to do! What do I do here? What does anybody do here? I'm bored! My mother's a respected woman because she can tell how much monosodium glutamate is in a dish by smelling it, and because she knows how to use a spittoon in a restaurant. Everybody's Chinese here, Sharon."

"Sure!" the girl laughed and hopped to kiss his cheek. "Didn' you like that?"

"Sure, I liked it, but I'm explaining something. You know, nobody shoulda let me grow up and go to any school outside of Chinatown." They walked slowly, twisting to allow swaggering men to pass. "Then, maybe everything would be all right now, you see? I'm stupid, I don't know what I'm talking about. I shouldn't go to parades and see all those kids. I remember when I was a kid. Man, then I knew everything. I knew all my aunts were beautiful, and all my cousins were small, and all my uncles were heroes from the war and the strongest guys in the world that smoked cigars and swore, and my grandmother was a queen of women." He nodded to himself. "I really had it made then, really, and I knew more then than I do now."

"What' d'ya mean? You smart now! You didn't know how to soun' or spall, or nothin'; now you in colleger."

"I had something then, you know? I didn't have to ask about anything; it was all there; I didn't have questions, I knew who I was responsible to, who I should love, who I was afraid of, and all my dogs were smart."

"You lucky, you had a dog!" The girl smiled.

"And all the girls wanted to be nurses; it was fine! Now, I'm just what a kid should be — stupid, embarrassed. I don't know who can tell me anything.

"Here, in Chinatown, I'm undoubtedly the most enlightened, the smartest fortune cookie ever baked to a golden brown, but out there . . . God!" He pointed down to the end of Grant Avenue, past ornamented lamps of Chinatown to the tall buildings of San Francisco. "Here, I'm fine — and bored stiff. Out there — Oh, Hell, what'm I talking about. You don't know either; I try to tell my father, and he doesn't know, and he's smarter'a you."

"If you don't like stupids, why'd you talk to me so much?"

"Because I like you. You're the only thing I know that doesn't fight me. . . . You know I think I've scared myself into liking this place for awhile. See what you've done by walking with me? You've made me a good Chinese for my parents again. I think I'll sell firecrackers." He was dizzy now, overwhelmed by the sound of too many feet and clicking lights. "I even like you, Sharon!" He swung her arm and threw her ahead of him and heard her laugh. "Christ! my grandmother didn't read English until she watched television and read 'The End'; that's pretty funny, what a kick!" They laughed at each other and ran among the shoulders of the crowd, shouting "Congratulations!" in Chinese into the shops, "Congratulations!" to a bald man with long hair growing down the edges of his head.

"Johnny, stop! You hurt my wrist!"

It was an innocent kiss in her hallway, her eyes closed so tight the lashes shrank and stitched like insect legs, and her lips puckered long, a dry kiss with closed lips. "Goodnight, Johnny . . . John," she said. And he waved and watched her standing in the hallway, disappearing as he walked down the stairs; then, out of sight, he ran home.

He opened the door to the apartment and hoped that his father had forgotten. "Fine speech, pa!" he shouted.

His little sister came out of her room, walking on the toes of her long pajamas. "Brother? Brother, *ah-bah*, he's sick!" she said. She looked straight up to Johnny as she spoke and nodded. Johnny stepped past his sister and ran to the bathroom and opened the door. His mother was holding the man up to the sink with one hand and holding his head with the other. The man's mess spattered over her *cheongsam*. The room, the man, everything was uglier because of his mother's misery in her bright *cheongsam*. "*Ah-bah?*" Johnny said gently as if calling the man from sleep for dinner. They did not turn. He stepped up behind the woman. "I can do that, *ah-mah*, I'm a little stronger than you."

"Don't you touch him! You!" She spoke with her cheek against the man's back and her eyes closed. "He told me what you did, what you said, you're killing him! If you want to leave, just go! Stop killing this man!"

"Not me, ma. He's been like this a long time. I've been helping him almost every night. He told me not to tell you."

"You think I don't know? I've seen you in here with him when I wanted to use the bathroom at night, and I've crept back to bed without saying anything because I know your father's pride. And you want to go and break it in a single night! First it's your telling everybody how good you are! Now go and murder your father. . . ."

"Ma, I'm sorry. He asked me, and I tried to make him understand. What do you want me to do, lie? I'll call a doctor."

"Get out, you said you're going to leave, so get out," the man said, lifting his head.

"I'll stay, ma, *ah-bah*, I'll stay."

"It's too late," his mother said, "I don't want you here." The time was wrong . . . nobody's fault that his father was dying; perhaps, if his father was not dying out of his mouth Johnny could have argued and left or stayed, but now, he could not stay without hate. "Ma, I said I'm calling a doctor. . . ."

After the doctor came, Johnny went to his room and cried loudly, pulling the sheets from his bed and kicking at the wall until his foot became numb. He shouted his hate for his father and ignorant mother into his pillow until his face was wet with tears. His sister stood next to his bed and watched him, patting his ankle and saying over and over, "Brother, don't cry, brother . . . ."

Johnny sat up and held the small girl against him. "Be a good girl," he said. "You're going to have my big room now. I'm moving across the bay to school." He spoke very quietly to his sister against the sound of their father's spitting.

Sharon held his sister's elbow and marched behind Johnny and his mother. A band played in front of the coffin, and over the coffin was a large photograph of the dead man. Johnny had a miniature of the photograph in his wallet and would always carry it there. Without being told, he had dressed and was marching now beside his mother behind the coffin and the smell of sweet flowers. It was a parade of black coats and hats, and they all wore sunglasses against the sun; the sky was green, seen through the glasses, and the boys playing in Portsmouth Square had green shadows about them. A few people stopped on the street and watched.

CLASS AND CONFORMITY: *
AN INTERPRETATION
Melvin Kohn

Social class is one of the reference group categories which has received considerable attention in social science literature. In this selection which is taken from Mr. Kohn's book on the issue of values and social class, the author attempts to demonstrate how the experiences associated with different social class lifestyles influence the manner in which people view the world. It is the author's contention that membership in a social class reference group affects conformity attitudes and behaviors as a function of the experiential opportunities which are made available or denied to members of each subgroup.

In trying to understand the beliefs and actions of members of your community, it is important to take into account social class variables. While these factors are not always as visible as other reference group classifications (e.g. race, age, sex) they often contribute substantially to the formation of attitude and behavior patterns.

Our thesis — the central conclusion of our studies — is that social class is significant for human behavior because it embodies systematically-differentiated conditions of life that profoundly affect men's views of social reality.

The essence of higher-class position is the expectation that one's decisions and actions can be consequential; the essence of lower-class position is the belief that one is at the mercy of forces and people beyond one's control, often, beyond one's understanding. Self-direction — acting on the basis of one's own judgment, attending to internal dynamics as well as to external consequences, being open-minded, being trustful of others, holding personally responsible moral standards — this is possible only if the actual conditions of life allow some freedom of action, some reason to feel in control of fate. Conformity — following the dictates of authority, focusing on external consequences to the exclusion of internal processes, being intolerant of nonconformity and dissent, being distrustful of others, having moral standards that strongly emphasize obedience to the letter of the law — this is the inevitable result of conditions of life that allow little freedom of action, little reason to feel in control of fate.

*Reprinted with permission from Melvin Kohn, *Class and Conformity: An Interpretation* (Homewood, Ill.: The Dorsey Press, 1969) pp. 17–37.

Self-direction, in short, requires opportunities and experiences that are much more available to people who are more favorably situated in the hierarchical order of society; conformity is the natural consequence of inadequate opportunity to be self-directed.

In interpreting the consistent relationships of class to values and orientation, it is useful to recall the many conditions that our analyses have shown to have little or no explanatory relevance. The relationship of class to parental values is not a function of parental aspirations, family structure, or—insofar as we have been able to measure them—family dynamics. The relationships of class to values and orientation in general are clearly not a function of such class-correlated dimensions of social structure as race, religion, or national background. Nor are they to be explained in terms of such facets of stratification as income and subjective class identification, or of conditions that impinge on only part of the class hierarchy, or of class origins or social mobility. Finally, the class relationships do not stem from such important (but from our point of view, tangential) aspects of occupation as the bureaucratic or entrepreneurial setting of jobs, time-pressure, job dissatisfaction, or a host of other variables. Any of these might be important for explaining the relationship of class to other social phenomena; none of them is important for explaining why class is consistently related to values and orientation.[1]

By contrast, we have substantial evidence that any interpretation of the relationships of class to values and orientation must take into account the cumulative impact of education and occupational position and must recognize that occupational self-direction is importantly implicated in these relationships.

Our interpretation of these facts is that the conformist values and orientation held by people in the lower segments of the class hierarchy are a product of the limited education and constricting job conditions to which they are subject. Education is important because self-direction requires more intellectual flexibility and breadth of perspective than does conformity; tolerance of nonconformity, in particular, requires a degree of analytic ability that is difficult to achieve without formal education. But

---

[1]It could be argued that the class relationships stem not from currently applicable structural conditions, but from historically derived cultural traditions. "Working-class culture," in this view, is derived from the historical tradition of the working class, rather than stemming from the realistic conditions of today's working class. But explanations of class culture based either on accidental origins or on past structural conditions that no longer hold sway seem to us to be insufficient. We want to know: Why does a historically derived class culture persist under present conditions?

education is not all that is involved. The conformity of people at lower social class levels is in large measure a carry-over from the limitations of their occupational experiences. Men of higher-class position, who have the opportunity to be self-directed in their work, want to be self-directed off the job, too, and come to think self-direction possible. Men of lower-class position, who do not have the opportunity for self-direction in work, come to regard it a matter of necessity to conform to authority, both on and off the job. The job does mold the man—it can either enlarge his horizons or narrow them. The conformity of the lower social classes is only partly a result of their lack of education; it results also from the restrictive conditions of their jobs.

The Efficacy of Education

Self-directed values and orientation require that one look beyond externals, think for oneself. Education does not insure the development of these capacities, but lack of education must seriously impede their development. For most people, self-directed values and orientation require formal educational experience.

The effects of education on values and orientation are not immutable—men who are subject to occupational conditions different from those normally experienced at their educational level are likely to have somewhat different values and orientation from those of their educational peers. Nevertheless, the relationship of education to values and orientation is not greatly affected by occupational experience or by any other experiences that we have examined. The importance of education for men's values and orientation—at least under the conditions of life in the United States in the mid-1960's—is great, no matter what conditions men subsequently encounter.

Implicit in this interpretation is the assumption that the predominant direction of effect is *from* education *to* values and orientation, rather than the reverse. We do not argue that men's values have no effect on their educational attainment. Quite the contrary: It is probably that self-directed values and orientation are a powerful impetus for educational attainment. In the actual circumstances of most people's lives, though, values and orientation probably have less effect upon educational attainment than educational attainment has upon values and orientation. This is in part because critical, often irreversible, decisions about education are made in behalf of children and adolescents by parents and other adults (and thus reflect the adults' values). In larger part, it is because of the inequitable distribution of social resources. Educational opportunities – good schools, stimulating teachers – and the economic resources to take advantage of such opportunities are not equally distributed, nor are children of varying class backgrounds always treated equally even within the same school. This issue is so much at the forefront of informed public attention that it need hardly be pursued further here.

Values and orientation undoubtedly influence educational attainment, but for most people education is primarily a determinant, rather than a consequence, of self-directed values and orientation.[2]

Occupational Position and Occupational Self-Direction

In industrial society, where occupation is central to men's lives, occupational experiences that facilitate or deter the exercise of self-direction come to permeate men's views, not only of work and of their role in work, but of the world and of self. The conditions of occupational life at higher social class levels facilitate interest in the intrinsic qualities of the job, foster a view of self and society that is conducive to believing in the possibilities of rational action toward purposive goals, and promote the valuation of self-direction. The conditions of occupational life at lower social class levels limit men's view of the job primarily to the extrinsic benefits it provides, foster a narrowly circumscribed conception of self and society, and promote the positive valuation of conformity to authority. Conditions of work that foster thought and initiative tend to enlarge men's conceptions of reality, conditions of constraint tend to narrow them.

The processes by which men come to generalize from occupational to nonoccupational realities need not be altogether or even mainly rational; all that we mean to assert is that occupation markedly affects men, not that men rationally decide on values and orientations to fit the facts of their occupational experiences.[3] The essential point was made more than a third of a century ago by Waller (1932: 375–376) in his classic study of teachers and teaching:

> What does any occupation do to the human being who follows it? ... We know that some occupations markedly distort the personalities of those who practice them, that there are occupational patterns to which one conforms his personality as to a Procrustean bed by lopping off superfluous members. Teaching is by no means the only occupation

[2]The point is well illustrated by Rosenberg's (1957) study of changes in students' values during their college years.
[3]Cf. Breer and Locke, 1965, for experimental evidence on how "task experience" affects values and beliefs.

which whittles its followers to convenient size and seasons them to suit its taste. The lawyer and the chorus girl soon come to be recognizable social types. One can tell a politician when one meets him on the street. Henry Adams has expanded upon the unfitness of senators for being anything but senators; occupational molding, then, affects the statesman as much as lesser men. The doctor is always the doctor, and never quite can quit his role. The salesman lives in a world of selling configurations. And what preaching most accomplishes is upon the preacher himself. Perhaps no occupation that is followed long fails to leave its stamp upon the person.

As with education, there is a question of direction of effect.[4] We have assumed — as did Waller — that the job does affect the man, that the relationship between occupational self-direction and values does not simply reflect the propensity of self-directed men to gravitate into self-directed jobs. We recognize the tendency for self-directed men to search out opportunities for occupational self-direction. Nevertheless, there are stringent limitations to men's deciding for themselves how much self-direction they will exercise in their work.

The most important limitation is that occupational choice is dependent on educational qualifications — which are greatly affected by the accidents of family background, economic circumstances, and available social resources. At any educational level, most occupational choice is among jobs of about the same degree of self-direction — men of limited educational background may perhaps choose between factory work and construction work, but neither offers much opportunity for self-direction, and jobs that do are not open to them.

Moreover, the possibilities for enlarging the sphere of self-direction by shifting to other occupations are seriously limited. Most job changes are not radical. Having completed their educations and embarked on their first jobs, few men have the chance to make any substantial change in these occupational conditions.

Furthermore, there are limits to how much men actually can mold their jobs. It is true that men placed in similar occupational positions will play their roles differently, some utilizing every opportunity for self-direction, some being altogether dependent on external direction. But there are structural limitations upon the leeway that jobs provide, and the limits are most severe at the lowest levels.

The reinforcing processes by which jobs affect values and orientation, and values and orientation reflect back on jobs, are undoubtedly more

[4]We intend, in our further research, to try to differentiate the effects of "occupational self-selection" from those of occupational experience. This analysis will have to take account of men's entering and leaving occupations.

complex that we have represented. The thrust of our discussion is not that all influence is in one direction, but rather that the occupational conditions attendant on men's class positions are important in shaping their values and orientation.

Historical Trends

If our interpretation that education and occupational self-direction underlie class differences in values and orientation is valid, it suggests that a major historical trend probably has been — and will continue to be — toward an increasingly self-directed populace.[5] It is well known that educational levels have long been rising and are continuing to do so. What is not so well recognized is that levels of occupational self-direction have also been rising, and almost certainly will continue to rise.

Despite the widely held belief that the industrial revolution substituted a multitude of unskilled operations for an earlier pattern of skilled artisanship, industrialization probably has increased the general level of occupational self-direction (cf. Blauner, 1966: 484). Men have thought otherwise because their images of past and present treated as typical of the times the craftsmanship of preindustrial days and the assembly-line worker of today. The facts, though, are that most men in preindustrial times were agricultural laborers, not craftsmen, and that the degradation of work on the assembly line is far from typical of industrial occupations today. Even in automobile plants, most men do not work on the line (cf. Walker and Guest, 1952; Chinoy, 1955). What is more important, the assembly line has never become the dominant type of industrial organization (cf. Blauner, 1964) and is clearly not the model for present and future industrial development.

The industrial model for the future, automation, far from extending the assembly-line practice of dividing skilled jobs into a series of unskilled jobs, gives mindless tasks to the machines and substitutes for mere drudgery, newly created thinking tasks (cf. Blauner, 1964; Walker, 1957). Automation builds on the rising levels of education of the population and markedly increases the opportunities and requirements for occupational

[5]Moreover, the industrialization of non-Western countries is probably having much the same effect today. There is growing evidence from Inkeles's (1966) research on underdeveloped countries that everywhere the movement of peasants into industrial occupations results in changes in attitudes, values, and beliefs (changes which Inkeles calls "modernization") that are altogether consonant with the effects we attribute to occupational self-direction. Inkeles sees education and occupational experience as independently contributing to these effects.

self-direction. The introduction of automation comes at high social cost — ever-shrinking employment opportunities for the less educated and the untrained. The long range prospect, though, is for a better educated society of men whose jobs require substantially more judgment, thought, and initiative than did those of any past era.

The United States and Other Industrial Nations

Is our interpretation as applicable to other industrialized societies as to the United States? It has been said, for example, that the family is a weak institution in the United States, easily penetrated by the occupational system. Perhaps occupational experiences are less relevant, and family more, in other countries. Perhaps occupational self-direction is a less critical aspect of life in societies that have a less activist ethos. Or perhaps class identification matters more and objective occupational conditions less in societies where class ideologies are more pronounced. Unfortunately, there are only limited data with which to examine these possibilities.

The most important data are those compiled by Inkeles in "Industrial Man: the Relation of Status to Experience, Perception, and Value" (1960). His thesis is that industrialization has everywhere produced comparable effects on man, manifested especially in similar relationships of class to perceptions, attitudes, and values in all industrialized countries. In support of this thesis, he has gathered evidence from a great diversity of sources and countries. For example, in the United States, Italy, West Germany, Norway, the Soviet Union, and Sweden, occupational position is consistently related to job satisfaction, with highly placed men always more satisfied. In the United States, Italy, West Germany, Norway, England, France, Australia, Mexico, and the Netherlands, there are fairly consistent relationships between class position and feelings of happiness or psychic well-being: The "better off" are in all instances happier. In 8 of 11 countries for which data on parental values exist, the lowest class (of those studied) is the most likely to value obedience. And in some seven countries, class position is positively related to men's belief in the possibility of change in human nature — which Inkeles takes as an indication of confidence that man can master his environment.

There are additional data in Inkeles's storehouse, but these are sufficient to demonstrate the validity of his assertion that class has similar effects in all industrial societies. What is lacking, as he explicitly states, is evidence that class has similar effects for the same reasons in all these countries.

To our knowledge, the only directly pertinent data are those we have reported from Turin. These data show, not only that class is related to parental values in northern Italy as in the United States, but also that occupational self-direction is as important for explaining the relationship of class to values in northern Italy as in the United States. Occupation penetrates the family in Italy, too.

Valuable as the Turin findings are, they speak only of parental values, not of values and orientation in general. Moreover, although it is invaluable to know that occupational self-direction plays as important a role in the relationship of class to parental values in Italy as in the United States, the same may not be true for non-Western societies, for non-capitalist societies, or even for these same societies under changed economic or social circumstances. Still, we have one critical bit of information (Turin), many pertinent supplementary data (primarily those provided by Inkeles), and considerable tangential evidence (the corpus of studies of social stratification in other societies)—all of which are consistent with the inference that what we have said of the United States is true for industrial societies generally.

Our best guess is that, as more is learned, we shall come to conclude that the American situation represents a perhaps extreme instance of a very general pattern. There may be minor variations on this pattern; class identification, for example, may be of greater importance in societies where class divisions are more recognized and more ideologically relevant. But we doubt that there are any sizeable industrial societies — Western or non-Western, capitalist, socialist, or communist—in which the relationship of class to conformity is much different, or in which occupational self-direction does not play a major part in this relationship.

Values and Behavior

Class differences in values and orientation have far-ranging effects on behavior. That men of higher-class position are more self-directed in their view of social reality and men of lower-class position more conformist, means that they see — and respond to — decidedly different realities.

Granted, men do not simply act out their preconceptions: Behavior is almost always responsive to situational and institutional constraints and, even in areas of high emotional involvement, may be greatly affected by these constraints.[6] Still, there is always some (and often great) latitude for

[6]The evidence comes principally from one arena—race relations—but the lessons are equally applicable to other behavior. (Cf. LaPiere, 1934; Mannheim, 1941; Lohman and Reitzes, 1952; Kohn and Williams, 1956.)

differential perception of the elements of a given situation, differential evaluation of these elements, differential choice, and differential action. The crux of the matter is elegantly summarized in W. I. Thomas's dictum, "If men define situations as real, they are real in their consequences" (Thomas and Thomas, 1928: 572). Class profoundly affects men's definitions of reality and their evaluations of reality so conceived.

Our findings about parental responses to children's misbehavior are especially pertinent in illustrating how class differences in definitions of reality affect behavior. If only the external consequences of children's actions are thought to be real, parents will attend only to external consequences. If parents are oriented to children's internal dynamics, they will try to be attentive to and will respond to what they understand to be the children's motives and feelings. Neither middle- nor working-class parents necessarily follow the rationally appropriate course of action for accomplishing their goals. Nevertheless, class differences in responses to children's misbehavior can best be understood when one realizes how class differences in parental values and orientation affect parents' perceptions and evaluations of children's actions.

Since social scientists understand (and largely share) middle-class values, we find middle-class parental behavior self-evidently reasonable. But, because many of us have not had an adequate grasp of working-class values, it has been less apparent that working-class parental behavior is also reasonable. Some have asserted, for example, that working-class parents are oriented only to the present and give little thought to the effects of their actions on their children's futures. We contend, instead, that working-class parents are as concerned as are middle-class parents about their children's futures, but that social scientists have not sufficiently understood working-class goals. Parental actions that seem, from the middle-class perspective, to be oblivious to the children's needs are, from the working-class perspective, altogether appropriate to parental goals in child rearing.

Similarly, from the point of view of middle-class values, fathers who are not supportive of sons shirk an important responsibility. From the point of view of working-class values, there is no such paternal responsibility.

Even though the evidence in this book deals with only a limited segment of human behavior, this evidence demonstrates that values and orientation provide an important mechanism by which social structure is translated into individual actions. Admittedly, values and orientation are not the only intervening mechanism from class to behavior, in all probability, a variety of other processes reinforce the ones on which we focus. If we over-emphasize the set of processes that leads from class-determined conditions of life, to values and orientation, to behavior, it is because we deem these processes central, our data support this supposition, and previous interpretations have for the most part failed to recognize their importance.

The power of this interpretation lies in its ability to help us understand why class is important for many diverse facets of human behavior. The implications of this one fundamental class difference in values and orientation—the higher valuation of self-direction at higher-class levels and of conformity at lower-class levels—extend to such varied social problems as schizophrenia, the perpetuation of inequality, and political illiberalism.

In discussing these problems, we focus on the negative consequences of conformity. We do this not because we fail to see the virtue of some measure of social order or the dangers of unconstrained individualism, but because we are convinced that conformity poses far more serious problems in the United States (and throughout the industrial world). A creative, democratic society needs more self-direction—and could do with less conformity—than is evident.

Schizophrenia

Class differences in values and orientation may help clarify the problem that originally motivated this research—the relationship of class to schizophrenia. As earlier formulated, the problem revolved around the complex interrelationship of class, family, and schizophrenia; we now suggest that a more fruitful approach would be in terms of the inadequacies of a conformist orientational system for dealing with stress.

There is fairly substantial evidence that the incidence of schizophrenia is especially great at the lowest-class levels.[7] It is not evident from published research reports, however, precisely which lower-class conditions of life actually are relevant to schizophrenia. There is some indication (Rogler and Hollingshead, 1965) that the great stress to which lower-class people are subjected is directly implicated. But more than stress is involved, for as Langner and Michael (1963) discovered, no matter how high the level of stress that people experience, social class continues to be correlated with the probability of mental disturbance. One implication is that people of lower-class position are less prepared to deal with the stresses they encounter.

[7]For comprehensive reviews of the research literature on class and schizophrenia, see Kohn, 1968; Mishler and Scotch, 1963; and Romar and Trice, 1967.

We think that the *family* is relevant to schizophrenia because of its role in preparing children to cope with the stresses of adult life. Because lower-class families teach an orientational system that may be too gross and inflexible for critical circumstances that require subtlety and flexibility, they often fail to prepare children adequately to meet stress.

This formulation reduces the emphasis on the family as uniquely important for schizophrenia, and says instead that the family provides one institutional mechanism — perhaps, but not necessarily, the most important one — for teaching an orientational system that is conducive to schizophrenia. The crucial family processes are less a matter of role-allocation (domineering mothers, for example) than many past discussions have emphasized, and more a matter of how children are taught to perceive, to assess, and to deal with reality.[8] The orientational system that lower-class parents transmit to their children is not likely to provide a sufficient sense of the complexity of life or the analytic tools needed to cope with the dilemmas and problems men encounter. These deficiencies could be overcome by later educational and occupational experience; but often they are not, in part because people who have learned this orientational system are unlikely to want to overcome them, in larger part because circumstances probably would not be propitious even if they were.

Certainly there is a vast gap between the inadequacies of a conformist orientational system and the severe disabilities of schizophrenia. What makes the possibility of a connection seem worth taking seriously, nevertheless, is the pointed correspondence of the two phenomena. Schizophrenia is quintessentially a disorder of orientation — a severe defect in men's ability to accurately comprehend the world about them. If one looks at it clinically, it is a caricature of precisely the outstanding features of the conformist orientation — an over-simple and rigid conception of reality, fearfulness and distrust, and a lack of empathic understanding of other people's motives and feelings. One reason for the disproportionately high incidence of schizophrenia at lower social class levels may be that the disorder builds on an orientational system firmly grounded in the experiences of these social classes.

The more general implication of these speculations is that conformist values and orientation may be personally disastrous to men who are confronted with difficult circumstances that require an innovative response.

[8]This is clearly consistent with the ideas of Wynne and his colleagues on cognitive processes in the families of schizophrenics, and with those of Bateson and Jackson on communication processes in such families. (Cf. Wynne, *et al.*, 1958; Ryckoff, *et al.*, 1959; Bateson, *et al.*, 1956; Mishler and Waxler, 1965.)

The Perpetuation of Inequality

A second implication of class differences in values and orientation is that they contribute to the perpetuation of inequality. Whether consciously or not, parents tend to impart to their children lessons derived from the conditions of life of their own social class — and thus help prepare their children for a similar class position. An obvious factor is the higher educational and occupational aspirations that parents of higher-class position hold for their children. Less obvious but perhaps more important: Class differences in parental values and child-rearing practices influence the development of the capacities that children someday will need for coping with problems and with conditions of change.

The conformist values and orientation of lower- and working-class parents, with their emphases on externals and consequences, often are inappropriate for training children to deal with the problems of middle-class and professional life. Conformist values and orientation are inflexible — not in the sense that people cannot learn to obey new directives, but in the sense that conformity is inadequate for meeting new situations, solving new problems — in short, for dealing with change. Whatever the defects of the self-directed orientation of the middle and upper classes, it is well adapted to meeting the new and be problematic. At its best, it teaches children to develop their analytic and their empathic abilities. These are the essentials for handling responsibility, for initiating change rather than merely reacting to it. Without such skills, horizons are severely restricted.

The family, then, functions as a mechanism for perpetuating inequality. At lower levels of the stratification order, parents are likely to be ill-equipped and often will be ill-disposed to train their children in the skills needed at higher-class levels. Other social institutions — notably, formal educational institution — can counteract this influence, but they do so to only a small extent; as the Coleman study (1966) shows, the capacity of the schools to overcome the limitations of the home is not great.

The result is that family and occupation usually reinforce each other in molding values and orientation. The influence of the family have temporal priority and have commonly been viewed as predominant in importance. Our data argue otherwise, suggesting that where there is conflict between early family experience and later occupational conditions, the latter are likely to prevail. The more important point, though, is that early family and later occupational experiences seldom conflict. No matter how dramatic the exceptions, it is usual that families prepare their offspring for the world as they know it and that the conditions of life eventually faced by the offspring are not very different from those for which they have been prepared.

Political Implications

Our data touch only lightly on political issues, but political implications are clearly evident. Conformity, as we conceive and index it, includes a strong component of intolerance of nonconformity. This conception is based on Stouffer's demonstration, in *Communism, Conformity, and Civil Liberties* (1955), that generalized conformity necessarily entails an unwillingness to permit other people to deviate from paths of established belief; conformist beliefs are necessarily anti-civil-libertarian.

Stouffer's analysis focuses on intolerance of political dissent; our analysis, particularly as embodied in the index of authoritarian conservatism, is addressed to intolerance of any behavior at odds with the dictates of authority. A self-directed orientation includes (but is not confined to) a willingness to allow others to deviate, within some broad limits, from the prescribed; a conformist orientation includes an unwillingness to permit others to step out of narrowly defined limits of what is proper and acceptable. Thus, a conformist orientation implies not only intolerance of deviant political belief, but also intolerance of any beliefs thought to be threatening to the social order — religious beliefs, ethnic and racial identifications, even beliefs about proper dress and deportment.

The political implications of conformist values and orientation extend beyond issues of civil liberties. As Lipset (1959: 485) points out, people less favorably situated in the class hierarchy tend to be illiberal about many noneconomic issues:

> The poorer everywhere are more liberal or leftist on [economic] issues; they favor more welfare state measures, higher wages, graduated income taxes, support of trade-unions and other measures opposed by those of higher class position. On the other hand, when liberalism is defined in non-economic terms — so as to support, for example, civil liberties for political dissidents, civil rights for ethnic and racial minorities, internationalist foreign policies, and liberal immigration legislation — the correlation is reversed.

Lipset cites an impressive array of evidence from several countries to support his empirical assertion that, on noneconomic issues, people of lower social class position tend to be illiberal. But he is unable to specify the determinants of this illiberalism, thus in effect concluding that *every-thing* about their conditions of life is relevant. Moreover, in choosing the intriguing term, "working-class authoritarianism," to describe these illiberal beliefs, he implies that the beliefs are an expression of authoritarian personality structure. That there are authoritarian components to the beliefs is indisputable, but to label the entire orientational system authoritarian*ism* is to explain its content in terms of the personality structures of those who endorse it.

Our data help explain working-class authoritarianism without requiring the psychodynamic assumptions of past interpretations.[9] We would contend that this illiberalism is an expression of conformist values and orientation—notably, intolerance (and perhaps fear) of nonconformity. Its explanation, we have come to think, lies not in an especially high incidence of authoritarian personality structure at lower levels of the class hierarchy, nor in "everything" about the conditions of life characteristic of these social classes. Rather, the explanation lies specifically in those social structural conditions that we have found to be most determinative of class differences in values and orientation: education and occupational self-direction.

The negative consequences of conformist values and orientation are of great importance, whatever their origins. Our understanding of these beliefs—and of our ability as a society to change them—are increased by recognizing precisely where in the structure of society their sources lie.

References

Bateson, Gregory, Jackson, Don D., Haley, Jay, and Weakland, John. Toward a theory of schizophrenia. *Behavioral Science* 1 October, 1956. 251–264.

Blauner, Robert. *Alienation and Freedom: The Factory Worker and His Industry.* Chicago: University of Chicago Press, 1964.

Blaunder, Robert. Work satisfaction and industrial trends in modern society. in Reinhard Bendix and Seymour Martin Lipset (Eds.), *Class, Status, and Power.* Glencoe, Ill. Free Press, Second edition, 1966, 473–487.

Breer, Paul E. and Locke, Edwin A. *Task Experience as a Source of Attitudes.* Homewood, Ill.: The Dorsey Press, 1965.

Chinoy, Ely. *Automobile Workers and the American Dream.* Garden City, N.Y.: Doubleday, 1955.

[9] As Miller and Riessman (1961) point out, psychological theories developed to explain the personality structure of middle-class authoritarians are probably not valid for explaining the authoritarian beliefs of the working class.

Inkeles, Alex. Industrial man: The relation of status to experience, perception and value. *American Journal of Sociology*, 1960, 66 (July), 1–31.

Inkeles, Alex. The modernization of man. In Myron Weiner (Ed.), *Modernization*. New York: Basic Books, 1966, 138–150.

Kohn, Melvin L. Social class and schizophrenia: A critical review. in David Rosenthal and Seymour S. Kety (Eds.), *The Transmission of Schizophrenia*. Oxford: Pergamon Press, Ltd., 1968, 155–173.

Kohn, Melvin L. and Williams, Robin M. Jr. Situational patterning in intergroup relations. *American Sociological Review*, April 1956, 21, 164–174.

Langner, Thomas S. and Michael, Stanley T. *Life Stress and Mental Health*. New York: The Free Press of Glencoe, 1963.

LaPiere, Richard T. Attitudes vs. actions. *Social Forces*, December 1934, 13, 230–237.

Lipset, Seymour Martin. Democracy and working-class authoritarianism. *American Sociological Review*, August 1959, 24, 482–501.

Lohman, Joseph D. and Reitzes, Dietrich C. Note on race relations in mass society. *American Journal of Sociology*, November 1952, 58, 240–246.

Mannheim, Karl. *Man and Society in an Age of Reconstruction*. New York: Harcourt, Brace, 1941.

Miller, S. M. and Riessman, Frank. The working class subculture: A new view. *Social Problems*, Summer 1961a, 9, 86–97.

Miller, S. M. and Riessman, Frank. Working class authoritarianism: A critique of Lipset. *British Journal of Sociology*, September 1961b, 12, 263–276.

Mishler, Elliot G. and Scotch, Norman A. Sociocultural factors in the epidemiology of schizophrenia: A review. *Psychiatry*, November 1963, 26, 315–351.

Mishler, Elliot G. and Waxler, Nancy E. Family interaction processes and schizophrenia: A review of current theories. *Merrill-Palmer Quarterly of Behavior and Development*, October 1965, 11, 269–315.

Rogler, Lloyd H. and Hollingshead, August B. *Trapped: Families and Schizophrenia*. New York: John Wiley, 1965.

Roman, Paul M. and Trice, Harrison M. *Schizophrenia and the Poor*. Ithaca: New York State School of Industrial and Labor Relations, 1967.

Rosenberg, Morris. Occupations and Values. Glencoe, Ill.: Free Press, 1957.

Ryckoff, Irving, Day, Juliana, and Wynne, Lyman C. Maintenance of stereotyped roles in the families of schizophrenics. *A.M.A. Archives of Psychiatry*, July 1959, 1, 93–98.

Stouffer, Samuel A. *Communism, Conformity, and Civil Liberties: A Cross-Section of the Nation Speaks its Mind*. New York: Doubleday, 1955.

Thomas, W. I. and Thomas, Dorothy S. *The Child in America*. New York: Knopf, 1928.

Walker, Charles R. *Toward the Automatic Factory: A Case Study of Men and Machines*. New Haven: Yale University Press, 1957.

Walker, Charles R. and Guest, Robert H. *The Man on the Assembly Line*. Cambridge, Massachusetts: Harvard University Press, 1952.

Waller, Willard. *The Sociology of Teaching*. New York: Russell and Russell, 1932.

Wynne, Lyman C., Ryckoff, Irving M., Day, Juliana, and Hirsch, Stanley I. Pseudo-mutuality in the family relations of schizophrenics. *Psychiatry*, May 1958, 22, 205–220.

EFFECTS OF GROUP PRESSURE UPON THE MODIFICATION AND DISTORTION OF JUDGMENTS*

S. E. Asch

The utilization of analogue research often helps us isolate the variables and forces which influence social behavior. In an analogue study a "real life" situation is approximated in a laboratory setting where special controls and measurement procedures may be introduced. S. E. Asch was one of the first psychologists to use this approach in studying the dynamics of small group interaction.

In this article, Asch reports his research about sources of group influence on individuals' perceptions and judgments. While it is necessary to be cautious when extrapolating from laboratory situations to complex everyday occurrences, it may be beneficial to look at the findings and derived principles of this and other analogue studies as they relate to the dynamics of your community.

We shall here describe in summary form the conception and first findings of a program of investigation into the conditions of independence and submission to group pressure.[1]

Our immediate object was to study the social and personal conditions that induce individuals to resist or to yield to group pressures when the latter are perceived to be *contrary to fact*. The issues which this problem raises are of obvious consequence for society; it can be of decisive importance whether or not a group will, under certain conditions, submit to existing pressures. Equally direct are the consequences for individuals and our understanding of them, since it is a decisive fact about a person whether he possesses the freedom to act independently, or whether he characteristically submits to group pressures.

*S. E. Asch, (A. Interpersonal Influence), adapted by the author especially for G. E. Swanson, T. M. Newcomb, and E. L. Hartley (Eds.), *Readings in Social Psychology*, Rev. ed., New York: Holt, Rinehart and Winston, 1952, from H. Guetzkow (Ed.), *Groups, Leadership and Men* (Pittsburgh: Carnegie Press, 1951). Reprinted by permission of the author and publishers.
[1]The earlier experiments out of which the present work developed and the theoretical issues which prompted it are discussed in S. E. Asch, *Social Psychology* (Englewood Cliffs, N.J.: Prentice-Hall, Inc., 1952), Ch. 16. A full account of the procedures and data on which the present report is based can be found in S. E. Asch, "Studies of independence and submission to group pressure: I. A minority of one against a unanimous majority." *Psychol. Monogr.*, 1956, **70**.

The problem under investigation requires the direct observation of certain basic processes in the interaction between individuals, and between individuals and groups. To clarify these seems necessary if we are to make fundamental advances in the understanding of the formation and reorganization of attitudes, of the functioning of public opinion, and of the operation of propaganda. Today we do not possess an adequate theory of these central psycho-social processes. Empirical investigation has been predominantly controlled by general propositions concerning group influence which have as a rule been assumed but not tested. With few exceptions investigation has relied upon descriptive formulations concerning the operation of suggestion and prestige, the inadequacy of which is becoming increasingly obvious, and upon schematic applications of stimulus-response theory.

Basic to the current approach has been the axiom that group pressures characteristically induce psychological changes *arbitrarily*, in far-reaching disregard of the material properties of the given conditions. This mode of thinking has almost exclusively stressed the slavish submission of individuals to group forces, has neglected to inquire into their possibilities for independence and for productive relations with the human environment, and has virtually denied the capacity of men under certain conditions to rise above group passion and prejudice. It was our aim to contribute to a clarification of these questions, important both for theory and for their human implications, by means of direct observation of the effects of groups upon the decisions and evaluations of individuals.

The Experiment and First Results

To this end we developed an experimental technique which has served as the basis for the present series of studies. We employed the procedure of placing an individual in a relation of radical conflict with all the other members of a group, of measuring its effect upon him in quantitative terms, and of describing its psychological consequences. A group of eight individuals was instructed to judge a series of simple, clearly structured perceptual relations—to match the length of a given line with one of three unequal lines. Each member of the group announced his judgments publicly. In the midst of this monotonous "test" one individual found himself suddenly contradicted by the entire group, and this contradiction was repeated again and again in the course of the experiment. The group in question had, with the exception of one member, previously met with the experimenter and received instructions to respond at certain points with wrong — and unanimous — judgments. The errors of the majority were large (ranging between $\frac{1}{2}''$ and $1\frac{3}{4}''$) and of an order not encountered under control conditions. The outstanding person — the critical subject — whom we had placed in the position of a *minority of one* in the midst of a *unanimous majority* — was the object of investigation. He faced, possibly for the first time in his life, a situation in which a group unanimously contradicted the evidence of his senses.

This procedure was the starting point of the investigation and the point of departure for the study of further problems. Its main features were the following: (1) The critical subject was submitted to two contradictory and irreconcilable forces — the evidence of his own experience of a clearly perceived relation, and the unanimous evidence of a group of equals. (2) Both forces were part of the immediate situation; the majority was concretely present, surrounding the subject physically. (3) The critical subject, who was requested together with all others to state his judgments publicly, was obliged to declare himself and to take a definite stand vis-à-vis the group. (4) The situation possessed a self-contained character. The critical subject could not avoid or evade the dilemma by reference to conditions external to the experimental situation. (It may be mentioned at this point that the forces generated by the given conditions acted so quickly upon the critical subjects that instances of suspicion were infrequent.)

The technique employed permitted a simple quantitative measure of the "majority effect" in terms of the frequency of errors in the direction of the distorted estimates of the majority. At the same time we were concerned to obtain evidence of the ways in which the subjects perceived the group, to establish whether they became doubtful, whether they were tempted to join the majority. Most important, it was our object to establish the grounds of the subject's independence or yielding — whether, for example, the yielding subject was aware of the effect of the majority upon him, whether he abandoned his judgment deliberately or compulsively. To this end we constructed a comprehensive set of questions which served as the basis of an individual interview immediately following the experimental period. Toward the conclusion of the interview each subject was informed fully of the purpose of the experiment, of his role and of that of the majority. The reactions to the disclosure of the purpose of the experiment became in fact an integral part of the procedure. The information derived from the interview became an indispensable source of evidence and insight into the psychological structure of the experimental situation, and in particular, of the nature of the individual differences. It should be added that it is not justified or advisable to allow the subject to leave without giving him a full explanation of the experimental conditions. The experimenter has a responsibility to the subject to clarify his doubts and to state the reasons for placing him in the experimental situation. When this is done most subjects react with interest, and some express gratification at having lived through a striking situation which has some bearing on them personally and on wider human issues.

Both the members of the majority and the critical subjects were male college students. We shall report the results for a total of fifty critical subjects in this experiment. In Table 1 we summarize the successive comparison trials and the majority estimates. The reader will note that on certain trials the majority responded correctly; these were the "neutral" trials. There were twelve critical trials on which the responses of the majority responded incorrectly.

The quantitative results are clear and unambiguous.

1. There was a marked movement toward the majority. One third of all the estimates in the critical group were errors identical with or in the

Table 1   Lengths of Standard and Comparison Lines.

Trial	Length of Standard Line (in Inches)	Comparison Lines (in Inches)			Correct Response	Group Response	Majority Error (in Inches)
		1	2	3			
1	10	$8\frac{3}{4}$	10	8	2	2	—
2	2	2	1	$1\frac{1}{2}$	1	1	—
3	3	$3\frac{3}{4}$	$4\frac{1}{4}$	3	3	1*	$+\frac{3}{4}$
4	5	5	4	$6\frac{1}{2}$	1	2*	-1.0
5	4	3	5	4	3	3	—
6	3	$3\frac{3}{4}$	$4\frac{1}{4}$	3	3	2*	$+1\frac{1}{4}$
7	8	$6\frac{1}{4}$	8	$6\frac{3}{4}$	2	3*	$1\frac{1}{4}$
8	5	5	4	$6\frac{1}{2}$	1	3*	$+1\frac{1}{2}$
9	8	$6\frac{1}{4}$	8	$6\frac{3}{4}$	2	1*	$-1\frac{3}{4}$
10	10	$8\frac{3}{4}$	10	8	2	2	—
11	2	2	1	$1\frac{1}{2}$	1	1	—
12	3	$3\frac{3}{4}$	$4\frac{1}{4}$	3	3	1*	$\frac{3}{4}$
13	5	5	4	$6\frac{1}{2}$	1	2*	-1.0
14	4	3	5	4	3	3	—
15	3	$3\frac{3}{4}$	$4\frac{1}{4}$	3	3	2*	$+1\frac{1}{4}$
16	8	$6\frac{1}{4}$	8	$6\frac{3}{4}$	2	3*	$-1\frac{1}{4}$
17	5	5	4	$6\frac{1}{2}$	1	3*	$+1\frac{1}{2}$
18	8	$6\frac{1}{4}$	8	$6\frac{3}{4}$	2	1*	$-1\frac{3}{4}$

*Starred figures designate the erroneous estimates by the majority.

direction of the distorted estimates of the majority. The significance of this finding becomes clear in the light of the virtual absence of errors in the control group, the members of which recorded their estimates in writing. The relevant data of the critical and control groups are summarized in Table 2.

2. At the same time the effect of the majority was far from complete. The preponderance of estimates in the critical group (68 percent) was correct despite the pressure of the majority.

3. We found evidence of extreme individual differences. There were in the critical group subjects who remained independent without exception, and there were those who went nearly all the time with the majority. (The maximum possible number of errors was 12, while the actual range of errors was 0–11.) One fourth of the critical subjects was completely independent; at the other extreme, one third of the group displaced the estimates toward the majority in one half or more of the trials.

Table 2 Distribution of Errors in Experimental and Control Groups.

Number of Critical Errors	Critical Group* $(N = 50)$ F	Control Group $(N = 37)$ F
0	13	35
1	4	1
2	5	1
3	6	
4	3	
5	4	
6	1	
7	2	
8	5	
9	3	
10	3	
11	1	
12	0	
Total	50	37
Mean	3.84	0.08

*All errors in the critical group were in the direction of the majority of estimates.

The differences between the critical subjects in their reactions to the given conditions were equally striking. There were subjects who remained completely confident throughout. At the other extreme were those who became disoriented, doubt-ridden, and experienced a powerful impulse not to appear different from the majority.

For purposes of illustration we include a brief description of one independent and one yielding subject.

Independent

After a few trials he appeared puzzled, hesitant. He announced all disagreeing answers in the form of "Three, sir; two, sir"; not so with the unanimous answers on the neutral trials. At Trial 4 he answered immediately after the first member of the group, shook his head, blinked, and whispered to his neighbor: "Can't help it, that's one." His later answers came in a whispered voice, accompanied by a deprecating smile. At one point he grinned embarrassedly, and whispered explosively to his neighbor: "I always disagree—darn it!" During the questioning, this subject's constant refrain was: "I called them as I saw them, sir." He insisted that his estimates were right without, however, committing himself as to whether the others were wrong, remarking that "that's the way I see them and that's the way they see them." If he had to make a practical decision under similar circumstances, he declared, "I would follow my own view, though part of my reason would tell me that I might be wrong." Immediately following the experiment the majority engaged this subject in a brief discussion. When they pressed him to say whether the entire group was wrong and he alone right, he turned upon them defiantly, exclaiming: "You're *probably* right, but you *may* be wrong!" To the disclosure of the experiment this subject reacted with the statement that he felt "exultant and relieved," adding, "I do not deny that at times I had the feeling: 'to heck with it, I'll go along with the rest.'"

Yielding

This subject went with the majority in 11 out of 12 trials. He appeared nervous and somewhat confused, but he did not attempt to evade discussion; on the contrary, he was helpful and tried to answer to the best of his ability. He opened the discussion with the statement: "If I'd been first I probably would have responded differently"; this was his way of stating that he had adopted the majority estimates. The primary factor in his case was loss of confidence. He perceived the majority as a decided group, acting without hesitation: "If they had been doubtful I probably would have changed, but they answered with such confidence." Certain of his errors, he explained, were due to the doubtful nature of the comparisons; in such instances he went with the majority. When the object of the experiment was explained, the subject volunteered: "I suspected about the middle — but tried to push it out of my mind." It is of interest that his suspicion did not restore his confidence or diminish the power of the majority. Equally striking is his report that he assumed the experiment to involve an "illusion" to which the others, but not he, were subject. This assumption too did not help to free him; on the contrary, he acted as if his divergence from the majority was a sign of defect. The principal impression this subject produced was of one so caught up by immediate difficulties that he lost clear reasons for his actions, and could make no reasonable decisions.

A First Analysis of Individual Differences

On the basis of the interview data described earlier, we undertook to differentiate and describe the major forms of reaction to the experimental situation, which we shall now briefly summarize.

Among the *independent* subjects we distinguished the following main categories:

1. Independence based on *confidence* in one's perception and experience. The most striking characteristic of these subjects is the vigor with which they withstand the group opposition. Though they are sensitive to the group, and experience the conflict, they show a resilience in coping with it, which is expressed in their continuing reliance on their perception and the effectiveness with which they shake off the oppressive group opposition.
2. Quite different are those subjects who are independent and *withdrawn*. These do not react in a spontaneously emotional way, but rather on the basis of explicit principles concerning the necessity of being an individual.
3. A third group of independent subjects manifests considerable tension and doubt, but adhere to their judgment on the basis of a felt necessity to deal adequately with the task.

The following were the main categories of reaction among the *yielding* subjects, or those who went with the majority during one half or more of the trials.

1. *Distortion of perception* under the stress of group pressure. In this category belong a very few subjects who yield completely, but are not aware that their estimates have been displaced or distorted by the majority. These subjects report that they came to perceive the majority estimates as correct.
2. *Distortion of judgment.* Most submitting subjects belong to this category. The factor of greatest importance in this group is a decision the subjects reach that their perceptions are inaccurate, and that those of the majority are correct. These subjects suffer from primary doubt and lack of confidence; on this basis they feel a strong tendency to join the majority.
3. *Distortion of action.* The subjects in this group do not suffer a modification of perception nor do they conclude that they are wrong. They yield because of an overmastering need not to appear different from or inferior to others, because of an inability to tolerate the appearance of defectiveness in the eyes of the group. These subjects suppress their observations and voice the majority position with awareness of what they are doing.

The results are sufficient to establish that independence and yielding are not psychologically homogeneous, that submission to group pressure and freedom from pressure can be the result of different psychological conditions. It should also be noted that the categories described above, being based exclusively on the subjects' reactions to the experimental conditions, are descriptive, not presuming to explain why a given individual responded in one way rather than another. The further exploration of the basis for the individual differences is a separate task.

Experimental Variations

The results described are clearly a joint function of two broadly different sets of conditions. They are determined first by the specific external conditions, by the particular character of the relation between social evidence and one's own experience. Second, the presence of pronounced individual differences points to the important role of personal factors, or factors connected with the individual's character structure. We reasoned that there are group conditions which would produce independence in all subjects, and that there probably are group conditions which would induce intensified yielding in many, though not all. Secondly, we deemed it reasonable to assume that behavior under the experimental social pressure is significantly related to certain characteristics of the individual.

The present account will be limited to the effect of the surrounding conditions upon independence and submission. To this end we followed the procedure of experimental variation, systematically altering the quality of social evidence by means of systematic variation of the group conditions and of the task.

The Effect of Nonunanimous Majorities

Evidence obtained from the basic experiment suggested that the condition of being exposed *alone* to the opposition of a "compact majority" may have played a decisive role in determining the course and strength of the effects observed. Accordingly we undertook to investigate in a series of successive variations the effects of *nonunanimous* majorities. The technical problem of altering the uniformity of a majority is, in terms of our procedure, relatively simple. In most instances we merely directed one or more members of the instructed group to deviate from the majority in prescribed ways. It is obvious that we cannot hope to compare the performance of the same individual in two situations on the assumption that they remain independent of one another; at best we can investigate the effect of an earlier upon a later experimental condition. The comparison of different experimental situations therefore requires the use of different but comparable groups of critical subjects. This is the procedure we have followed. In the variations to be described we have maintained the conditions of the basic experiment (e.g., the sex of the subjects, the size of the majority, the content of the task, and so on) save for the specific factor that was varied. The following were some of the variations studied.

1. *The presence of a "true partner."* (a) In the midst of the majority were *two* naive, critical subjects. The subjects were separated spatially, being seated in the fourth and eighth positions, respectively. Each therefore heard his judgments confirmed by one other person (provided the other person remained independent), one prior to, the other after announcing his own judgment. In addition, each experienced a break in the unanimity of the majority. There were six pairs of critical subjects. (b) In a further variation the "partner" to the critical subject was a member of the group who had been instructed to respond correctly throughout. This procedure permits the exact control of the partner's responses. The partner was always seated in the fourth position; he therefore announced his estimates in each case before the critical subject.

The results clearly demonstrate that a disturbance of the unanimity of the majority markedly increased the independence of the critical subjects. The frequency of promajority errors dropped to 10.4 percent of the total number of estimates in variation (a), and to 5.5 percent in variation (b). These results are to be compared with the frequency of yielding to the unanimous majorities in the basic experiment, which was 32 percent of the total number of estimates. It is clear that the presence in the field of *one other* individual who responded correctly was sufficient to deplete the power of the majority, and in some cases to destroy it. This finding is all the more striking in the light of other variations which demonstrate the effect of even small minorities provided they are unanimous. Indeed, we have been able to show that a unanimous majority of 3 is, under the given conditions, far more effective than a majority of 8 containing 1 dissenter. That critical subjects will under these conditions free themselves of a majority of 7 and join forces with one other person in the minority is, we believe, a result significant for theory. It points to a fundamental psychological difference between the condition of being alone and having a minimum of human support. It further demonstrates that the effects obtained are not the result of a summation of influences proceeding from each member of the group; it is necessary to conceive the results as being relationally determined.

2. *Withdrawal of a "true partner."* What will be the effect of providing the critical subject with a partner who responds correctly and then withdrawing him? The critical subject started with a partner who responded correctly. The partner was a member of the majority who had been instructed to respond correctly and to "desert" to the majority in the middle of the experiment. This procedure permits the observation of the same subject in the course of the transition from one condition to another. The withdrawal of the partner produced a powerful and unexpected result. We had assumed that the critical subject, having gone through the experience of opposing the majority with a minimum of support, would maintain his independence when alone. Contrary to this expectation, we found that the experience of having had and then lost a partner restored the majority effect to its full force, the proportion of errors rising to 28.5 percent of all judgments, in contrast to the preceding level of 5.5 percent. Further experimentation is needed to establish whether the critical subjects were responding to the sheer fact of being alone, or to the fact that the partner abandoned them.

3. *Late arrival of a "true partner."* The critical subject started as a minority of 1 in the midst of a unanimous majority. Toward the con-

clusion of the experiment one member of the majority "broke" away and began announcing correct estimates. This procedure, which reverses the order of conditions of the preceding experiment, permits the observation of the transition from being alone to being a member of a pair against a majority. It is obvious that those critical subjects who were independent when alone would continue to be so when joined by a partner. The variation is therefore of significance primarily for those subjects who yielded during the first phase of the experiment. The appearance of the late partner exerts a freeing effect, reducing the level of yielding to 8.7 percent. Those who had previously yielded also became markedly more independent, but not completely so, continuing to yield more than previously independent subjects. The reports of the subjects do not cast much light on the factors responsible for the result. It is our impression that some subjects, having once committed themselves to yielding, find it difficult to change their direction completely. To do so is tantamount to a public admission that they had not acted rightly. They therefore follow to an extent the precarious course they had chosen in order to maintain an outward semblance of consistency and conviction.

4. *The presence of a "compromise partner."* The majority was consistently extremist, always matching the standard with the most unequal line. One instructed subject (who, as in the other variations, preceded the critical subject) also responded incorrectly, but his estimates were always intermediate between the truth and the majority position. The critical subject therefore faced an extremist majority whose unanimity was broken by one more moderately erring person. Under these conditions the frequency of errors was reduced but not significantly. However, the lack of unanimity determined in a strikingly consistent way the *direction* of the errors. The preponderance of the errors, 75.7 percent of the total, was moderate, whereas in a parallel experiment in which the majority was unanimously extremist (i.e., with the "compromise" partner excluded), the incidence of moderate errors was 42 percent of the total. As might be expected, in a unanimously moderate majority, the errors of the critical subjects were without exception moderate.

The Role of Majority Size

To gain further understanding of the majority effect, we varied the size of the majority in several different variations. The majorities, which were in each case unanimous, consisted of 2, 3, 4, 8, and 10–15 persons, respectively. In addition, we studied the limiting case in which the critical subject was opposed by one instructed subject. Table 3 contains the mean and the range of errors under each condition.

With the opposition reduced to 1, the majority effect all but disappeared. When the opposition proceeded from a group of 2, it produced a measurable though small distortion, the errors being 12.8 percent of the total number of estimates. The effect appeared in full force with a majority of 3. Larger majorities did not produce effects greater than a majority of 3.

The effect of a majority is often silent, revealing little of its operation to the subject, and often hiding it from the experimenter. To examine the range of effects it is capable of inducing, decisive variations of conditions are necessary. An indication of one effect is furnished by the following variation in which the conditions of the basic experiment were simply reversed. Here the majority, consisting of a group of 16, was naïve; in the midst of it we placed a single individual who responded wrongly according to instructions. Under these conditions the members of the naïve majority reacted to the lone dissenter with amusement. Contagious laughter spread through the group at the droll minority of 1. Of significance is the fact that the members lacked awareness that they drew their strength from the majority, and that their reactions would change radically if they faced the dissenter individually. These observations demonstrate the role of social support as a source of power and stability, in contrast to the preceding investigations which stressed the effects of social opposition. Both aspects must be explicitly considered in a unified formulation of the effects of group conditions on the formation and change of judgments.

The Role of the Stimulus-Situation

It is obviously not possible to divorce the quality and course of the group forces which act upon the individual from the specific stimulus-conditions. Of necessity the structure of the situation molds the group forces and determines their direction as well as their strength. Indeed,

Table 3   Errors of Critical Subjects with Unanimous Majorities of Different Size.

Size of Majority	Control	1	2	3	4	8	10–15
N	37	10	15	10	10	50	12
Mean Number of Errors	0.08	0.38	1.53	4.0	4.20	3.84	3.75
Range of Errors	0–2	0–1	0–5	1–12	0–11	0–11	0–10

this was the reason that we took pains in the investigations described above to center the issue between the individual and the group around an elementary matter of fact. And there can be no doubt that the resulting reactions were directly a function of the contradiction between the observed relations and the majority position. These general considerations are sufficient to establish the need to vary the stimulus-conditions and to observe their effect on the resulting group forces.

Accordingly we have studied the effect of increasing and decreasing the discrepancy between the correct relation and the position of the majority, going beyond the basic experiment which contained discrepancies of a relatively moderate order. Our technique permits the easy variation of this factor, since we can vary at will the deviation of the majority from the correct relation. At this point we can only summarize the trend of the results which is entirely clear. The degree of independence increases with the distance of the majority from correctness. However, even glaring discrepancies (of the order of 3–6″) did not produce independence in all. While independence increases with the magnitude of contradiction a certain proportion of individuals continues to yield under extreme conditions.

We have also varied systematically the structural clarity of the task, employing judgments based on mental standards. In agreement with other investigators, we find that the majority effect grows stronger as the situation diminishes in clarity. Concurrently, however, the disturbance of the subjects and the conflict-quality of the situation decrease markedly. We consider it of significance that the majority achieves its most pronounced effect when it acts most painlessly.

Summary

We have investigated the effects upon individuals of majority opinions when the latter were seen to be in a direction contrary to fact. By means of a simple technique we produced a radical divergence between a majority and a minority, and observed the ways in which individuals coped with the resulting difficulty. Despite the stress of the given conditions, a substantial proportion of individuals retained their independence throughout. At the same time a substantial minority yielded, modifying their judgments in accordance with the majority. Independence and yielding are a joint function of the following major factors: (1) The character of the stimulus situation. Variations in structural clarity have a decisive effect: with diminishing clarity of the stimulus-conditions the majority effect increases. (2) The character of the group forces. Individuals are highly sensitive to the structural qualities of group opposition. In particular, we demonstrated the great importance of the factor of unanimity. Also, the majority effect is a function of the size of group opposition. (3) The character of the individual. There were wide and, indeed, striking differences among individuals within the same experimental situation.

EXERCISES AND DISCUSSION TOPICS FOR CHAPTER 9

Exercises

1. Being yourself, or selecting a character from the simulation, choose five reference groups which you consider important for that person. Find out what the norms are for these reference groups. Discover points of conflict between the norms of the various reference groups and how these conflicts are resolved. (e.g. middle-class Protestant female minority group teacher.)
2. People have common reference groups. Being yourself or a character in the simulation, get together with people who are in one or more of your reference groups. Find the differences among members of a common reference group. Discuss how the behavior in a common reference group is affected by membership in other reference groups.

Discussion Topics

People belong to some reference groups by biology or culture (women, Chinese). What happens when these people begin membership in a newer reference group? (liberated women, Chinese–Americans). Discuss how people can assimilate two or more reference groups into a single consistent role.

Talk about who sets norms in reference groups (e.g. acknowledged leaders, traditions, etc.). What are the primary values of different reference groups? Discuss Kohn's article; how do these values influence the behavior of people in groups? How does this affect behavior in the Psych City community?

Apply Asch's article and technique to group dynamics as seen in the simulation and real communities. Discuss ways in which group pressure can be counteracted.

CHAPTER 10

Social Power

Roles assigned to participants vary in the amount of social power they have at their disposal. The mayor of Psych City generally would have more power at his disposal than would someone playing a minority group student or a white parent. This distribution of power can be altered over time by the formation of appropriate coalitions. An extreme example would be the case where all participants band together in opposition to the mayor altering the power balance in their favor. In addition there are various kinds of power that can be exercised in social interaction. French and Raven (1959) describe four basic types of social power:

1. reward and coercive power,
2. referent power,
3. expert power,
4. legitimate power.

REWARD AND COERCIVE POWER

Reward power is based on the perception that an individual can provide some sort of reward for the participant. In Psych City this may mean the person may be able to use his influence to further his own aims in some manner. Coercive power indicates the ability of a participant to exercise some form of punishment over other members. He may be able to block attainment of a goal for instance, or make goal attainment costly in terms of time or effort. Exactly where this kind of power lies will become increasingly apparent as the simulation develops.

REFERENT POWER

Referent power is less likely to be apparent in Psych City than reward power, but still may become a factor. This kind of power emerges from reward power and can be described as the desire to be like another person. That is, after observing someone exercising reward power, it may seem like a good idea to adopt his behavior patterns for yourself. Essentially, this amounts to emulating a successful model and becoming somewhat like him.

EXPERT POWER

This type of power is based on the possession of some sort of special knowledge. In the simulation situation, one person may have knowledge not generally available to the group. Exercising this knowledge in the appropriate situation may give him an advantage over the other members. Assume, for example, that the group decides to run meetings according to Robert's Rules of Order. Comprehensive knowledge of these rules may provide a tactical advantage to the member or group who possesses it.

LEGITIMATE POWER

The fourth type of power, legitimate power, is based upon the norms of the group and usually is held by someone occupying a high position in the group. The role of mayor in Psych City is an example. This role is typically accorded certain powers such as the regulation of meetings. This power can be taken away through group pressure or alteration of the group norms.

There are then, four basic types of power which may appear in the Psych City simulation. The success of your role in the simulation may depend upon how well you recognize and utilize these forms of power. None of these forms of power are unlimited. Typically one uses power at some cost to himself. A person who possesses some degree of legitimate power may lose it if he attempts to exercise it too often. The mayor, for example, may attempt to control proceedings to such an extent that an uprising is provoked and his power reduced. Expert power may often be used only once or twice before it becomes public knowledge and therefore loses its effectiveness. The successful participant in Psych City may be one who learns when and how to exercise the power at his disposal.

MACHINES AND BOSSES*

Thomas R. Dye

To understand American politics, one must not only have knowledge of the public candidates and officeholders; one must also comprehend the intricate, pervasive, and awesome operations of the political organizations and machines which make it possible for these public figures to achieve prominence. These dynamic, often invisible groups exert an influence on community affairs which is probably unmatched by any other single group. While there is some evidence that the old-style machines, such as Tammany Hall, are losing their power, it is inevitable that they will be replaced with new forms of political advocacy, such as the organization created by George McGovern and his followers.

In this selection, Mr. Dye describes some of the functions which political bosses and machines have served.

Machine politics may be going out of style, but something resembling machine politics still exists in Chicago, Pittsburgh, Philadelphia, and a number of other cities. Party organizations in most cities tend to be better organized, more cohesive, and better disciplined than state or national party organizations. Tightly disciplined party organizations, held together and motivated by a desire for tangible benefits rather than by principle or ideology, and staffed by professional politicians emerged in the nation's large cities early in the 19th century. The machine style of city politics has historical importance: between the Civil War and the New Deal, every big city had a machine at one time or another, and it is sometimes easier to understand the character of city politics today by knowing what went on in years past. But a more important reason for examining the machine style of politics is to understand the style of political organization and activity that employs personal and material inducements to control behavior. These kinds of inducements will always be important in politics, and the big city machine serves the prototype of a style of politics, in which ideologies and issues are secondary and personal friendships, favors, jobs, and material rewards are primary.

The political machine was essentially a large brokerage organization. It was a business organization, devoid of ideologies and issues, whose business it was to get votes and control elections, by trading off social services, patronage, and petty favors to the urban masses, particularly the

*Thomas R. Dye, *Politics in States and Communities*, Copyright © 1969. Reprinted by permission of Prentice-Hall, Inc., Englewood Cliffs, N.J.

poor and the recent immigrants. To get the money to pay for these social services and favors, it traded off city contracts, protection, and privileges to business interests, which paid off in cash. Like other brokerage organizations, a great many middle men came between the cash paid for a franchise for a trolley line or a construction contract and a Christmas turkey sent by the ward chairman to the Widow O'Leary. But the machine worked. It performed many important and social functions for the city.[1]

First of all, it personalized government. With keen social intuition, the machine recognized the voter as a man, generally living in a neighborhood, who had specific personal problems and wants. The machine politician avoided abstract and remote public issues or ideologies, and concentrated instead on the personal problems and needs of his constituents. Lincoln Steffens once quoted a Boston ward leader:

> I think that there's got to be in every ward somebody that any bloke can come to—no matter what he's done—and get help. Help, you understand; none of your law and justice, but help.[2]

The machine provided individual attention and recognition. As Tammany Hall boss, George Washington Plunkitt, the philosopher king of old style machine politics, explained:

> I know every man, woman, and child in the 15th district, except them that's been born this summer—and I know some of them too. I know what they like and what they don't like, what they are strong at and what they are weak in, and I reach them by approachin' at the right side. For instance, here's how I gather in the young men. I hear of a young feller that's proud of his voice, thinks that he can sing fine. I ask him to come around to Washington Hall and join our Glee Club. Then there's the feller that makes a name as a waltzer on his block, the young feller that's handy with his dukes—I rope them all in by givin' them opportunities to show themselves off. I don't trouble them with political arguments. I just study human nature and act accordin'.[3]

The machine also performed functions of a welfare agency:

> What tells in holdin' your grip on your district is to go right down among the poor families and help them in the different ways they need help. I've got a regular system for this. If there's a fire in Ninth, Tenth, or Eleventh Avenue, for example, any hour of the day or night, I'm usually there with some of my election district captains as soon as the fire engines. If a family is burned out I don't ask whether they are Republicans or

[1]See Robert K. Merton, *Social Theory and Social Structure* (Glencoe: Free Press, 1957), pp. 71–81.

[2]Lincoln Steffens, *Autobiography* (New York: Harcourt, Brace & World, Inc., 1931), p. 618; also cited by Merton, *op. cit.*, p. 74.

[3]William L. Riordan, *Plunkitt of Tammany Hall* (New York: McClure Phillips & Co., 1905), p. 46.

Democrats, and I don't refer them to the Charity Organization Society, which would investigate their case in a month or two and decide they were worthy of help about the time they are dead from starvation. I just get quarters for them, buy clothes for them if their clothes were burned up, and fix them up till they get things runnin' again. It's philanthropy, but it's politics, too — mighty good politics. Who can tell how many votes one of these fires bring me? The poor are the most grateful people in the world, and let me tell you, they have more friends in their neighborhoods than the rich have in theirs.[4]

The machine also functioned as an employment agency. In the absence of government unemployment insurance or a federal employment service, patronage was an effective political tool, particularly in hard times. Not only were city jobs at the disposal of the machine, but the machine also had its business contacts:

Another thing, I can always get a job for a deservin' man. I make it a point to keep on the track of jobs, and it seldom happens that I don't have a few up my sleeve ready for use. I know every big employer in the district and in the whole city, for that matter, and they ain't in the habit of sayin' no to me when I ask them for a job.[5]

Banfield and Wilson argue effectively that it was not so much the petty favors and patronage that won votes among urban dwellers, so much as the sense of friendship and humanity that characterized the "machine" and its "boss."[6] The free turkeys and bushels of coal were really only tokens of this friendship. As Jane Addams, the famous settlement house worker, explained: "On the whole, the gifts and favors were taken quite simply as evidence of genuine loving kindness. The alderman is really elected because he is a good friend and neighbor. He is corrupt, of course, but he is not elected because he is corrupt, but rather in spite of it. His standard suits his constituents. He exemplifies and exaggerates the popular type of a good man. He has attained what his constituents secretly long for."[7]

The machine also played an important role in educating decent immigrants and assimilating them into American life.[8] Machine politics provided a means of upward social mobility for ethnic group members, which was not open to them in businesses or professions. City machines sometimes met immigrants at dockside and led them in groups through

[4]*Ibid.*, p. 52.
[5]*Ibid.*, p. 53.
[6]Edward C. Banfield and James Q. Wilson, *City Politics* (Cambridge: Harvard — M.I.T. Press, 1963), chap. 9.
[7]Jane Addams, *Democracy and Social Ethics* (New York: 1902), p. 254; also cited by Banfield and Wilson, *op. cit.*, p. 118.
[8]See Elmer E. Cornwell, Jr., "Bosses, Machines, and Ethnic Groups," *Annals of the American Academy of Political and Social Science* (May, 1964), pp. 27–39.

naturalization and voter registration procedures. Machines did not keep out people with "funny" sounding names, but instead went out of its way to put these names on ballots. Politics, became a way "up" for the bright sons of Irish and Italian immigrants.

Finally, for the businessman, particularly public utilities and construction companies with government contracts, the machine provided the necessary franchises, rights of way, contracts, and privileges. As Lincoln Steffens wrote: "You cannot build or operate a railroad, or a street railway, gas, water, or power company, develop and operate a mine, or cut forests or timber on a large scale, or run any privileged business, without corrupting or joining in the corruption of government."[9] The machine also provided the essential protection from police interference, which is required by illicit businesses, particularly gambling. In short, the machine helped to centralize power in large cities. It could "get things done at city hall."

Political analysts frequently remark that the day of the political machine has passed, and that big city political organizations have radically altered their style of operation. Federal and state welfare agencies now provide the basic welfare services that the bosses used to provide. Large scale immigration has stopped, and there are fewer people requiring the kinds of services once provided by the machine. Patronage jobs do not look as attractive in an affluent economy, and today civil service examinations cover most governmental jobs anyhow. In many ways the urban machine served the very rich and the very poor. The middle class was excluded, and much of the opposition to the machine came from the middle class. As the middle class grew in American society (today white collar workers outnumber blue collar workers), opposition to the machine has grown in every city. Middle class voters supported reform movements and good government crusades, which often succeeded in replacing the machine with professional city managers, civil service, reorganized city government, and city administrations pledged to eliminate corruption and exercise economy and efficiency in government.

Big city party organizations continue to thrive, although in a somewhat modified form. Party organizations such as those led by Mayor Richard J. Daley in Chicago, William Green in Philadelphia, David Lawrence in Pittsburgh, and Carmine DeSapio in New York all survived through the 1960's because they continued to perform important political and social functions in their communities. In a system of "fragmented" government

[9]Lincoln Steffens, *Autobiography*, p. 168.

in the nation's large cities, these party organizations continue to play an important part in organizing power: that is to say, in "getting things done at city hall."[10] A centralized, well disciplined party organization helps to overcome the dispersion of power one finds in a normal structure of a big city government, with its maze of authorities, boards, commissions, agencies, and separately elected officials.

Mayor Richard J. Daley of Chicago is perhaps the closest thing to the old style political boss still operating in the nation's large cities. In Chicago, few others understand so well the labyrinths of formal and informal power, the complex structure of federal, state, and local government and public opinion in Chicago as the mayor. Daley has served three four-year terms as mayor of Chicago beginning in 1955; he remains the captain of his old 11th ward Democratic committee; and he is chairman of the Cook County Democratic committee. He picks candidates' slates, runs the patronage machinery, and works his will on nearly all of the 50 submissive aldermen who comprise Chicago's city council. Illinois Democratic governors must be responsive to his wishes and Chicago's nine member delegation to the US House of Representatives also acts promptly on Daley's recommendations. The Cook County Democratic delegation to the Illinois legislature is firmly in his hands.

Chicago has had bosses before. There was "Big Bill" Thompson (1915–23, 1927–31), a Republican who left a safe deposit box stuffed with $1.5 million in cash when he died. There was a Democrat Ed Kelley (1933–47), who used his powers mostly to throw public projects to his personal and political pal, contractor Pat Nash. Chicago has also had reform mayors; one of these was Democrat Martin Kennelley (1947–55), whose good intentions were frustrated by a lack of political acumen and who was unseated by Daley in 1955.

Daley, a Roman Catholic, was born in the impoverished Bridgeport district of Chicago near the stockyards. He sold newspapers on the street as a boy and worked in the stockyards. He worked his way up to clerk in the stockyards office and then went at night to the law school at DePauw University. He was appointed secretary to the city council at 25, and has remained on the public payroll for the next 40 years. He still lives with his large family in his old city neighborhood. In 1936, when a state legislator from Daley's district died, Democratic boss Ed Kelley and ward leader Jake Arvey gave the job to Daley, who gradually worked his way

---

[10]For an excellent description of the functions of Mayor Daley's political organization in Chicago, see Edward C. Banfield, *Political Influence* (Glencoe: Free Press, 1961).

up in the Kelley–Arvey machine. When Adlai Stevenson became the Governor of Illinois in 1949 he rewarded the Chicago machine by making Daley the State Revenue Director. But more important to Daley's political power, he was also made county clerk for Cook County, which placed him in charge of all the voting machinery in the county and many patronage jobs. Daley's old teacher, Boss Jake Arvey, always felt that a boss should be a "behind-the-scenes operator" and should not run for public office himself, but Daley broke with his old boss Arvey to run for mayor against a Republican reform candidate, who charged scandal and corruption in Chicago in the Democratic government. Daley replied: "If I am elected I will embrace mercy, love, charity, and walk humbly with my God." When he was elected, one commentator observed: "Chicago ain't ready for reform!" From his base in Chicago, Daley quickly made himself the unchallenged leader of Illinois Democrats. Adlai Stevenson was not a "machine" Illinois Democrat, and Daley always remained somewhat cool towards Stevenson, but was a staunch supporter of Senator John F. Kennedy. Daley was a key supporter and consultant in Kennedy's race for the presidential nomination. On election day, 1960, Daley's machine in Chicago gave Kennedy a margin of 450,000 votes, giving the crucial state of Illinois to Kennedy, who lost the rest of the state so badly that his statewide edge was only 9000 votes. Daley was unworried about later charges of voting irregularities in Chicago.

Like other big city mayors, Daley's biggest problem today is race relations. Chicago's Negroes compose nearly a third of the city's population and half of the public school pupils. Daley remains close to many older Negro leaders whose support he has always courted, but he is not very close to younger, more militant Negro leaders like Negro comedian Dick Gregory of Chicago. Many younger Negroes refer to Daley's urban renewal and slum clearance programs as "Negro removal." Many white residents of Chicago have become upset by what they consider Daley's "concessions" to Negroes. Yet Daley is the classic style of the political broker, who continues to try to arrange compromises and win support from both Negroes and whites.

Unlike older bosses, Daley has maintained a progressive image. He has not tolerated much corruption in office, and he has kept a tight rein on gambling, prostitution, and organized crime. He brought in the nation's leading criminologist, University of California Professor Orlando W. Wilson, to clean up and revitalize the city police force, which he did, although he was later criticized by Negro leaders because of his strict enforcement policies. Daley also inaugurated many reforms, including an executive budget for the city, an extended merit system, a new zoning and housing code, and many other organizational improvements. Although a big city Democrat, Daley earnestly solicited the support of prominent businessmen for city projects. He has sought and won a great deal of newspaper support and has even appealed with success to civic leaders and good government associations.

As a political broker, Daley is seldom the initiator of public policy. His approach to policy questions is more like that of an arbitrator between competing interests. When political controversies develop, Daley often waits at the sidelines without committing himself, in the hope that public opinion will soon "crystallize" behind a particular course of action. Once the community is behind a project — and this determination Daley makes himself after lengthy consultations with his political advisors — he then awards his stamp of approval. This suggests that in policy matters many political "bosses" are not so much bosses as referees among interested individuals and groups. The boss is really "apolitical" when it comes to policy matters. He is really more concerned with resolving conflict and maintaining his position and organization than he is with the outcome of public policy decisions.

Machine politics will remain with us as long as there is an unmet need to personalize the operations of government, and as long as individuals need services that the formal machinery of government cannot provide. Machine politics will remain as long as people place little or no value on their vote, or more precisely, as long as they place a lower value on their vote than they do on the things a machine can offer them in exchange for it. Voters who are indifferent to issues and candidates, and there are still many of these, and who put little value on their vote can be easily induced to trade it for the small favors that the party organization can offer. And urban party organizations continue to perform important welfare duties, employment services, and petty favors. A recent survey of precinct politicians in a New Jersey county revealed the following list of services:[11]

1. Help poor people to get to work;
2. Help deserving people to get jobs on a highway crew, police force, or fire department or in state positions;
3. Show people how to get their social security benefits, welfare, and unemployment compensation;

[11]Richard T. Frost, "Stability and Change in Local Politics," *Public Opinion Quarterly*, 25 (Summer, 1961) 231–32.

4. Help citizens with problems like rent gouging, unfair labor practices, zoning, or unfair assessments;
5. Help one's precinct to get a needed traffic light, more parking space, or more policemen;
6. Run clambakes or other get togethers for interested people even though no political campaign is involved;
7. Help people who are in difficulty with the law;
8. Help newcomers to this county to get adjusted and get places to live and work;
9. Work with some of the other party's people to reduce the friction and keep the campaign from getting too rough;
10. Help boys with military service problems with advice on the best way to serve.

It is unlikely that these kinds of services will ever go out of style completely. A certain amount of machine politics will be found in every city.

STEVENSON – TRAGEDY AND GREATNESS*

Hans J. Morgenthau

The essay by Mr. Morgenthau on Adlai Stevenson presents a political lifestyle which is in marked contrast to that of the bosses in Mr. Dye's article. The form of behavior which Mr. Stevenson expressed is rarely found in the higher circles of public life. Although his style was attractive to many people, there have been many questions raised about the efficacy of this style for survival in political life. One of the challenges we face is to promote more effective humanistic and noncoercive methods of social influence in our communities.

Adlai Stevenson has been praised and buried. His wit and eloquence have been duly noted; his honesty and his disappointments commented on. Yet these qualities do not explain the impact his death has made upon the people. After all, there have been other witty, eloquent, honest and disappointed candidates for the Presidency whom men have not mourned as they mourn Adlai Stevenson. What sets Adlai Stevenson apart from all the other seekers after high office of his time, successful or unsuccessful?

What is the gift which only he has brought to American life, which made the vanquished shine more brightly than the victor? The answer is both simple and complex: It is the quality of greatness tinged with tragedy. The man in the street felt that tragic greatness without being able to define its substance. Everybody knew that here was a unique political figure, different from all others and in an undefinable, almost mysterious sense superior to them. Everybody also sensed that this political figure, in all his uniqueness, was more like ourselves than the common run of politicians (this is what we mean when we say that he was "more human" than they) and that his tragic failure was in some way the tragedy of all of us writ large. Adlai Stevenson was indeed political Everyman. His promise was ours, and so was his failure, and the tears we shed for him we shed for ourselves.

Wherein did Adlai Stevenson's greatness consist? Wherein does any man's greatness consist? It consists in his ability to push the human potential for achievement in a particular respect to its outer limits, or beyond them if they are defined in terms of what can be expected in the ordinary course of events. Thus we speak of great painters and great writers, great liars and great lovers, great statesmen and great merchants, great saints and great crooks. We call them great because they have done what others may do well, indifferently or badly, with a measure of excellence that at least intimates perfection.

Adlai Stevenson was great in his relationship to power. He was not a great statesman because he did not have the chance to use power for the purposes of the state. He was not a great politician because he did not choose to be a politician. But he was a great seeker after power, and it was his very greatness in the pursuit of power that was, as we shall see, responsible for the tragedy of his failure.

In order to understand the substance of Stevenson's greatness, we must remind ourselves that there are two ways in which to be great in the pursuit of power. The search for power ordinarily entails, at least in a certain measure, the sacrifice of the intellectual and moral virtues. It is in the nature of the struggle for power that the competitors must deceive themselves as they deceive others. Those who have chosen power as the ultimate aim in life must use truth and virtue as means to their chosen end and discard them when they do not serve that end. The prototype of this power seeker is endowed with what Russell Kirk in a contemporary reference has called "a canine appetite for personal power." He is a Borgia or a Stalin, the Machiavellian prince, who will stop at nothing to gain and hold the power he seeks. He will sacrifice all other values for the sake of power. His greatness consists in that single-minded, ruthless pursuit of power, of which lesser – and better – men are incapable. They stop at some point on the road to power, distracted and restrained by the common virtues of intellect and ethics.

Man is capable of another kind of greatness in the pursuit of power, which owes less to Machiavelli than to Plato's postulate of the philosopher-king and to the Hebrew–Christian ideal of the wise and good ruler. That greatness consists not in the single-minded pursuit of power but in the ability to subordinate the pursuit of power to transcendent intellectual and moral values. Rather than being possessed by power, those men possess it; rather than being devoured by it, they tame it. History has indeed known few rulers of this kind. But they have, as far as I can see, all been secure in the possession of power, generally by virtue of the automatic character of monarchical succession. Those who had to fight for gaining and keeping power, which is of course the normal situation in a democracy, have generally been precluded in this ever-present concern from attaining that greatness. The best they have been able to achieve has been an uneasy *modus vivendi*, a compromise between the demands of power and the requirements of the intellectual and moral virtues, with power having an excellent chance of prevailing when the chips are down. Of those who could not take power for granted but had to fight for it, I know only one who has attained that greatness: Abraham Lincoln. And it is indeed impossible to think of the substance of Stevenson's greatness without reflecting on the greatness of Lincoln. What they have in common explains their greatness; in what they differ accounts for the triumph of the one and the failure of the other.

What Lincoln and Stevenson have in common is a high degree of freedom from illusion, to which politicians – as all men – are prey, about themselves, about their actions, and about the world. What took the place of these illusions was a lucid awareness, both intellectual and moral, of the nature of the political act, of their involvement in it, and of the consequences of that involvement for themselves and for the world. That awareness gave them the intellectual distinction and moral sensitivity, which set them apart from the common run of politicians. It gave their actions the appearance of indecisiveness and the reality of moral force. It accounts for their personal qualities of eloquence, wit and sadness.

Jump into the Dark

Lincoln and Stevenson knew both the moral risks and the practical hazards inseparable from the political act. They knew that to act politically was to take a jump into the dark. Innocent people would suffer, and the outcome was uncertain. Moral absolution could not be bought with good intentions nor could success be vouchsafed through ingenuity. The actor on the political stage takes his fate into his hands. Try as he may, he cannot escape the risks and hazards of his acts. If he is of the run of the mill, he will consult the flight of the birds, the constellation of the stars, or their modern equivalent, the public opinion polls, and receive the illusion of that certainty which the facts of experience refuse him. If he is great in the manner of Lincoln and Stevenson, he cannot help but face the risks and hazards of his acts, to weigh them against the risks and hazards of alternative acts, to shudder at what he must do — and do it as though those risks and hazards did not exist. He acts in awareness, and in spite of, these risks and hazards. Here is the measure of the heroic dimension of Lincoln's actions.

What the actor's mind knows, his action is ignorant of. It can afford to be determined and bold because the mind has done its task of knowing, weighing, and judging. It is for that very same reason that the act carries within itself the conviction of justice in the sense of being appropriate to the end to be achieved. What needs to be done will be done, but nothing more, is the message the act seems to convey. Here is the core of the moral force of Lincoln's policies.

That contrast and tension between what the actor knows and what he must do accounts for his eloquence, his wit and his sadness. In both Lincoln and Stevenson, eloquence is more than a mere matter of rhetoric and literary skill; wit is more than a mere matter of fleetness of brain and quickness of tongue; and sadness is more than a mere matter of mood and nerves. They are the qualities of souls that have been formed by their awareness of what the political act implies, and by the burden of having to act nevertheless.

Lincoln and Stevenson share the gift of eloquence and wit with other great political figures. One thinks of Bismarck, Churchill, and Adenauer. The quality of sadness is theirs alone. It is the function of an intellectual and moral sensitivity in the face of power which, so it seems, is peculiarly American. It gives immunity against that ultimate illusion to which even the intellectually aware and morally sensitive political actor is apt to succumb. His heroism makes him act; his intellect makes him explain himself; his wit makes him transcend the incongruities of his political existence at least in thought. And so he may delude himself into believing that now he has mastered the political world. Lincoln and Stevenson were incapable of that ultimate illusion. They knew that, when all is said and done, they were still faced, without remedy or escape, with the moral ambiguities and practical pitfalls of the political act. Knowing what they knew about themselves, their actions, and the world, they could not but be sad. Their sadness denotes the resigned acceptance of the moral and intellectual imperfections of the political world and of their precarious place within it.

It is hardly necessary to point out that these qualities of greatness are more fully developed in Lincoln than they are in Stevenson. They were not clearly visible before Lincoln entered the White House; it was the pain of great decisions that brought them to the fore. Thus they have a grave and somber aura which Stevenson's qualities are lacking. Stevenson's greatness was not the result of an ineluctable confrontation between personality and fate: The only great decision he had to face, it is true three times, was whether or not to seek the nomination. Rather it was the spontaneous expression of a great personality in intellectual anticipation of the fateful decisions he might have to make. Hence the peculiar quality of playfulness, of the aimless intellectual exercise, which is alien to Lincoln.

What is the relevance of this difference between Lincoln and Stevenson for the latter's failure to gain political power after his initial success in Illinois? The answer to that question is obscured and rendered speculative by the intrinsic hopelessness of the 1952 and 1956 campaigns and by his failure to win the nomination in 1960. But why did he pursue the aspiration, foredoomed to failure, of becoming Secretary of State? And why did he silently suffer for four and a half years the humiliation of being Ambassador to the United Nations? Can these questions be explained away as accidents of history? Or do these persistent failures point to a fatal flaw, a tragic defect in Stevenson's greatness, which barred his way to power, but which might not have barred him from making use of it had he been able to achieve it? I think indeed that there was such a flaw. In order to understand its nature, let us return for a moment to Lincoln.

Abraham Lincoln we have said, revealed his greatness only after he had reached the highest office. He made his way to that office as a politician competing with other politicians, seeking power in the manner of politicians, always tough and sometimes ruthless and devious. Lincoln made no bones about wanting power, and the people gave it to him. It was only after he had reached it that he also achieved that awareness of, and detachment from it in which we found the key to his greatness.

Stevenson showed his awareness of and detachment from power from the very outset. No doubt, he wanted power. When it eluded him in 1952, he said that he envied one man, the Governor of Illinois. When as Ambassador to the United Nations and nominal member of the cabinet he had the trappings of power without its substance, he complained about the "disadvantage in being anywhere other than the seat of power." He never forgave himself for his indecision in 1960. He wanted power, but he wanted it only with intellectual and moral reservations openly revealed. He wanted power, but not with that "canine appetite," with that single-minded animal ferocity which carried his competitors in the Democratic Party to success. He wanted power, but he did not want it badly enough. His was a civilized pursuit of power in a barely civilized political world. Yet the people want their politicians to be wholehearted and uncompli-cated in their pursuit of power. By being so, the politicians give a token that they can hold and use power when they have it. It was this distance between the core of Stevenson's person and the pursuit of power and the interplay between the two, articulated by him and sensed by the people, that fascinated the masses and gained him their admiration but not their confidence.

It was that very same distance that saved the defeated Stevenson from the disintegration which is the common lot of the frustrated seekers of great power. They hate or drink themselves to death. Stevenson in defeat could fall back upon that moral and intellectual core of his person that remained unaffected by the lust for power. He remained what he had been: eloquent, witty, and sad, but now he was so in a peculiarly purpose-less way. The desire for power, too, remained; yet surviving the possi-bility of its satisfaction, it became patently futile and carried within itself a measure of humiliation.

Stevenson wanted to be Secretary of State, and I suggested him in 1960 to the President-elect for that position; for I thought then, as I think now, that he was far better qualified than his competitors. But it should have been obvious to him—and to me—that politically the appointment was impossible; for the victor did not awe him that much and, more impor-tantly, he could not be expected to countenance the star of Foggy Bottom to shine brighter than the sun of the White House.

UN Ambassador

Stevenson's acceptance of the ambassadorship to the United Nations, to which I was opposed from the outset, and his unwillingness to relin-quish it reveal most poignantly the desperation of his pursuit of power. The services he rendered to the country in that position could have been performed as well by lesser men, and they do not compensate for the personal diminution he suffered as a mouthpiece for policies on which he had no influence and was but rarely consulted.

Had Stevenson been more unrestrained a seeker of power, he might have disintegrated in defeat. Had he been less addicted to the pursuit of power, he might have given it up in defeat altogether and become one of the great reflective men of the nation. He did neither. What could already be discerned in 1952, 1956, and 1960 now became almost pathetically obvious: the conflict between intellectual and moral awareness and the pursuit of power, spoiling both.

There, then, is the rub. The intellectual and moral component was too dominant in Stevenson's personality for the good of his political ambitions. It made Stevenson reveal his greatness prematurely. In a democracy, ordinariness, not greatness, gains power. Once a great man, such as Lincoln, has gained power under the cover of ordinariness, he can afford to bare his greatness to the multitude, but not before. Lincoln's greatness evolved from his ordinariness, buttressed by power. Stevenson's greatness was a gift of nature, not grown from the successful conquest of power, but anticipating it. Yet had Stevenson possessed that quality of ordinariness necessary for the democratic conquest of power, behind which his greatness could for the time being have been hidden, he would in all probability still have lost in 1952 and 1956 and the world might never have known how great a man he was. Thus all may have turned out for the best. Alas, poor Adlai. Such is the irony of your life.

ONE FLEW OVER THE CUCKOO'S NEST*
(excerpt)
Ken Kesey

In the two previous selections in this chapter we have seen examples of social power in the public political context. While power is most frequently associated with politics, the exercise of this force is certainly not limited to the governance arena. Mr. Ken Kesey describes the subtle and sophisticated process of acquiring and utilizing social power (primarily reward and coercive) in a closed institutional setting. The contrast between the stated or manifest goals of the institution (e.g. helping people) and the unspoken or latent goals (e.g. keeping the patients in their place) is vividly illustrated in this excerpt. Many readers of Kesey's book have commented on the similarities between the actual social structure and processes of the hospital he writes about and other institutions and communities in our society.

In the glass Station the Big Nurse has opened a package from a foreign address and is sucking into hypodermic needles the grass-and-milk liquid that came in vials in the package. One of the little nurses, a girl with one wandering eye that always keeps looking worried over her shoulder while the other one goes about its usual business, picks up the little tray of filled needles but doesn't carry them away just yet.

"What, Miss Ratched, is your opinion of this new patient? I mean, gee, he's good-looking and friendly and everything, but in my humble opinion he certainly takes *over*."

The Big Nurse tests a needle against her fingertip. "I'm afraid" — she stabs the needle down in the rubber-capped vial and lifts the plunger — "that is exactly what the new patient is planning: to take over. He is what we call a 'manipulator,' Miss Flinn, a man who will use everyone and everything to his own ends."

"Oh. But. I mean, in a mental hospital? What could his ends be?"

"Any number of things." She's calm, smiling, lost in the work of loading needles. "Comfort and an easy life, for instance; the feeling of power and respect, perhaps; monetary gain — perhaps all of these things. Sometimes a manipulator's own ends are simply the actual *disruption* of the ward for the sake of disruption. There are such people in our society. A manipulator can influence the other patients and disrupt them to such an extent that it may take months to get everything running smooth once more. With the present permissive philosophy in mental hospitals, it's easy for them to get away with it. Some years back it was quite different. I recall some years back we had a man, a Mr. Taber, on the ward, and he was an *intolerable* Ward Manipulator. For a while." She looks up from her work, needle half filled in front of her face like a little wand. Her eyes get far-off and pleased with the memory. "Mistur Tay-bur," she says.

"But, gee," the other nurse says, "what on earth would *make* a man want to do something like disrupt the ward for, Miss Ratched? What possible motive. . .?"

She cuts the little nurse off by jabbing the needle back into the vial's rubber top, fills it, jerks it out, and lays it on the tray. I watch her hand reach for another empty needle, watch it dart out, hinge over it, drop.

"You seem to forget, *Miss* Flinn, that this is an institution for the insane."

The Big Nurse tends to get real put out if something keeps her outfit from running like a smooth, accurate, precision-made machine. The slightest thing messy or out of kilter or in the way ties her into a little white knot of tight-smiled fury. She walks around with that same doll smile crimped between her chin and her nose and that same calm whir coming from her eyes, but down inside of her she's tense as steel. I know. I can feel it. And she don't relax a hair till she gets the nuisance attended to — what she calls "adjusted to surroundings."

Under her rule the ward Inside is almost completely adjusted to surroundings. But the thing is she can't be on the ward all the time. She's got to spend some time Outside. So she works with an eye to adjusting the Outside world too. Working alongside others like her who I call the "Combine," which is a huge organization that aims to adjust the Outside as well as she has the Inside, has made her a real veteran at adjusting things. She was already the Big Nurse in the old place when I came in from the Outside so long back, and she'd been dedicating herself to adjustment for God knows how long.

And I've watched her get more and more skillful over the years. Practice has steadied and strengthened her until now she wields a sure power that extends in all directions on hair-like wires too small for anybody's eye but mine: I see her sit in the center of this web of wires like a watchful robot, tend her network with mechanical insect skill, know every second which wire runs where and just what current to send up to get the results she wants. I was an electrician's assistant in training camp before the Army shipped me to Germany and I had some electronics in my year in college is how I learned about the way these things can be rigged.

What she dreams of there in the center of those wires is a world of precision efficiency and tidiness like a pocket watch with a glass back, a place where the schedule is unbreakable and all the patients who aren't Outside, obedient under her beam, are wheelchair Chronics with catheter tubes run direct from every pantleg to the sewer under the floor. Year by year she accumulates her ideal staff: doctors, all ages and types, come and rise up in front of her with ideas of their own about the way a ward should be run, some with backbone enough to stand behind their ideas, and she fixes these doctors with dry-ice eyes day in, day out, until they retreat with unnatural chills. "I tell you I don't know *what* it is," they tell the guy in charge of personnel. "Since I started on that ward with that woman I feel like my veins are running ammonia. I shiver all the time, my kids won't sit in my lap, my wife won't sleep with me. I *insist* on a transfer — neurology bin, the alky tank, pediatrics, I just don't *care!*"

She keeps this up for years. The doctors last three weeks, three months. Until she finally settles for a little man with a big wide forehead and wide jowly cheeks and squeezed narrow across his tiny eyes like he once wore glasses that were way too small, wore them for so long they crimped his face in the middle, so now he has glasses on a string to his collar button;

they teeter on the purple bridge of his little nose and they are always slipping one side or the other so he'll tip his head when he talks just to keep his glasses level. That's her doctor.

Her three daytime black boys she acquires after more years of testing and rejecting thousands. They come at her in a long black row of sulky, big-nosed masks, hating her and her chalk doll whiteness from the first look they get. She appraises them and their hate for a month or so, then lets them go because they don't hate enough. When she finally gets the three she wants — gets them one at a time over a number of years, weaving them into her plan and her network — she's damn positive they hate enough to be capable.

The first one she gets five years after I been on the ward, a twisted sinewy dwarf the color of cold asphalt. His mother was raped in Georgia while his papa stood by tied to the hot iron stove with plow traces, blood streaming into his shoes. The boy watched from a closet, five years old and squinting his eye to peep out the crack between the door and the jamb, and he never grew an inch after. Now his eyelids hang loose and thin from his brow like he's got a bat perched on the bridge of his nose. Eyelids like thin gray leather, he lifts them up just a bit whenever a new white man comes on the ward, peeks out from under them and studies the man up and down and nods just once like he's oh yes made positive certain of something he was already sure of. He wanted to carry a sock full of birdshot when he first came on the job, to work the patients into shape, but she told him they didn't do it that way anymore, made him leave the sap at home and taught him her own technique: taught him not to show his hate and to be calm and wait, wait for a little advantage, a little slack, then twist the rope and keep the pressure steady. All the time. That's the way you get them into shape, she taught him.

The other two black boys came two years later, coming to work only about a month apart and both looking so much alike I think she had a replica made of the one who came first. They were tall and sharp and bony and their faces are chipped into expressions that never change, like flint arrowheads. Their eyes come to points. If you brush against their hair it rasps the hide right off you.

All of them black as telephones. The blacker they are, she learned from that long dark row that came before them, the more time they are likely to devote to cleaning and scrubbing and keeping the ward in order. For instance, all three of these boys' uniforms are always spotless as snow. White and cold and stiff as her own.

All three wear starched snow-white pants and white shirts with metal snaps down one side and white shoes polished like ice, and the shoes have red rubber soles silent as mice up and down the hall. They never make any noise when they move. They materialize in different parts of the ward every time a patient figures to check himself in private or whisper some secret to another guy. A patient'll be in a corner all by himself, when all of a sudden there's a squeak and frost forms along his cheek, and he turns in that direction and there's a cold stone mask floating above him against the wall. He just sees the black face. No body. The walls are white as the white suits, polished clean as a refrigerator door, and the black face and hands seem to float against it like a ghost.

Years of training, and all three black boys tune in closer and closer with the Big Nurse's frequency. One by one they are able to disconnect the direct wires and operate on beams. She never gives orders out loud or leaves written instructions. Doesn't need to any more. They are in contact on a high-voltage wave length of hate, and the black boys are out there performing her bidding before she even thinks it.

So after the nurse gets her staff, efficiency locks the ward like a watchman's clock. Everything the guys think and say and do is all worked out months in advance, based on the little notes the nurse makes during the day. This is typed and fed into the machine I hear humming behind the steel door in the rear of the Nurses' Station. A number of Order Daily Cards are returned, punched with a pattern of little square holes. At the beginning of each day the properly dated card is inserted in a slot in the steel door and the walls hum up: Lights flash on in the dorm at six-thirty: the Acutes up out of bed quick as the black boys can prod them out, get them to work buffing the floor, emptying ash trays, polishing the scratch marks off the wall where one old fellow shorted out a day ago, went down in an awful twist of smoke and smell of burned rubber. The Wheelers swing dead log legs out on the floor and wait like seated statues for somebody to roll chairs in to them. The Vegetables piss the bed, activating an electric shock and buzzer, rolls them off on the tile where the black boys can hose them down and get them in clean greens . . . .

EXERCISES AND DISCUSSION TOPICS FOR CHAPTER 10

Exercises

1. Pick an institution (e.g. your school). Study and identify the sources of power (formal and informal) and how they operate. Pick a specific

issue which has recently come up. Show how different sources have used power to shape the issue in order to further their own interests (e.g. trustees, administrators, alumni, students).
2. Identify examples of four types of power in the simulation. Compare and contrast the styles involved in exercising these forms of influence.

Discussion Topics

Compare Stevenson's politics and the tactics of the machine mentioned in Dye's article. Discuss the differences between them regarding power and its use.

Formal and informal power structures exist in every community. Discuss some of the uses of informal power sources. Which are most important? How are these used in the community?

From your observations of public figures, talk about the relationship between personality styles and use of power.

Is there a basic drive for power? Discuss the needs power fulfills. Can something take the place of power in society? Discuss the different styles of leadership and the different uses and types of power.

Sometimes in interpersonal relationships one person is more dominant and one is more submissive. Discuss factors which account for this dominance and submissiveness. How could the relationship be equalized?

Often decisions are made based on nonexpert power. Discuss ways of making expert power more prominent and effective.

Some people think that the primary purpose of institutions is to perpetuate themselves. Kesey's article points out the discrepancy between the institution's stated goals and latent goals. Discuss how institutions might act to preserve their influence. Talk about ways to implement changes in institutions so that they will achieve their stated goals.

CHAPTER 11

Group Decision Making

A great deal of the work and problem solving done in the world is done in groups. Decisions made in and by groups are made on the basis of the individual goals, interests and emotions of the individual members. Each participant usually would like to maximize his own interests as much as possible and still come up with an adequate decision satisfactory to other participants. In Psych City a number of different kinds of groups may appear. The Town Meeting contains all participants attempting to solve a common problem. Many of these people have interests in common while others have interests in conflict. The goal of the group is to reach a solution to the community problem that satisfies most of the participants. Each individual member is at the same time trying to reach his own goals as defined by his role. Due to the differing interests of participants, only part of the process of reaching goals can be achieved in the Town Meeting. Subgroups based on common interests should form in order to advance those interests in the context of solving the community problem.

Working in subgroups to advance your own interests has a number of advantages over working alone. Ideas brought up in a group are subjected to more critical analysis than is typical of a single individual. It is generally easier to be critical of someone else's ideas than of your own. As a result, nonproductive ideas are more likely to be spotted and discarded. Another advantage of group problem solving is the increased likelihood that correct solutions or better ideas will appear. Since people differ in the kinds of abilities and knowledge they possess, working together makes it more likely that these will be present in the solution of a problem. A combination of these skills is often more effective than any one ability alone.

Groups can also divide up work and therefore function more efficiently than individuals in some cases. Finally, a larger number of ideas are likely to occur to a group as a whole than to one individual working alone.

Working in groups can have its disadvantages. A great deal of time can be wasted when groups fall into trivial discussions not concerned with the problem at hand. Often, especially in a large group, one person may have the best solution to a problem but be unable to make it heard since only one person can talk productively at one time. Some people may monopolize a meeting and the best ideas may never get a hearing. Simply waiting for an opening in the discussion may cause an idea to be lost through forgetting or distraction. Differences in power or status may cause poor ideas to get a better hearing or final acceptance than do better ideas. Groups also tend to produce pressures for uniformity of decisions due to each member's needs to be liked or agreed with. As a result, the group may end up deciding unanimously to accept a solution to the problem faced, which is inferior to one or more alternative solutions that might have been accepted if given a fair and impartial hearing.

A variety of technical procedures and decisions can improve a group's problem-solving ability and reduce the probability that the disadvantages of group problem solving will influence your group's performance. One thing that you can avoid is the tendency to let the problem-solving group become too large. Although including the maximum number of people in your subgroup may have particular political or tactical advantages within the simulation, it may not be practical if your task is to solve a specific problem. A group of four to six members is optimal for most situations; more may be added if the problem to be solved is one that seems complex or has a variety of subproblems. The small group should contain a good sampling of skills and ideas without a high probability that individual goals will be in conflict. Four to six people give you the flexibility needed to efficiently divide up tasks among members for fairly complex problems.

A popular technique used in solving problems is called brainstorming. This simply consists of having the members of the group suggest as many solutions to a problem as they can think of and at the same time forbidding any criticism of these ideas until everyone is through making suggestions. This allows an opportunity for even the most outlandish ideas to be expressed without fear of looking stupid. When all ideas are out, the group then proceeds to pick the one which seems most likely to be successful by debating the merits of each and eliminating the ones which do not appear reasonable. One drawback to this method, which must be guarded against, is the greater opportunity for each participant's own biases to appear as well as the tendency to lose sight of the original problem.

Conflict can be used to produce superior solutions to problems. By pitting one idea against another and examining the possibilities of each, one can often be seen as better than the other. It is important to remember here that the conflict should be entirely between the ideas themselves and not the attitudes, prejudices, or personalities of the people who propose the ideas. It is easy to end up swapping accusations concerning each other's motives rather than to make sensible progress in solving the problem at hand. A similar procedure involves reducing the group's ideas to the two which seem most productive and then debating the relative merits of these two, most likely solutions.

Often the best procedure in solving a problem is to first examine all the available facts; second, identify and define the problem; and finally, offer solutions to the problem. This helps prevent the possibility that the group will start off on the wrong foot by attempting to solve a false problem. Inspection of relevant facts, before anything else is done, may allow the group to see the situation much more clearly than they might have if they have rushed into solving a problem that had been defined for them. Once an accurate definition of the problem is made, solutions can be offered which might be different and more effective than would be the case if the problem was less clearly defined.

Some groups function more effectively if they appoint a leader. This is particularly true if the group tends to be large. You will notice the chaos that results in Psych City if the mayor fails to show up and no one takes his place. A leader can provide a situation in which minority views are heard more easily than can an undirected discussion. Leaders who have not decided on a solution beforehand are most likely to produce this kind of atmosphere. To the extent that diversity of views is useful to the solution of a problem, this type of leader will be an advantage to your group.

Finally, there are some advantages to letting everyone participate fully in the process of reaching a decision. You will find that the group's acceptance of a decision or solution will vary with the extent to which each member feels he had a part in influencing that decision. This process is easily seen in the day-to-day politics of the world outside Psych City. If your group's acceptance of your ideas will work to your advantage, it is important that other members at least feel they have had a part in the decision process.

Groups can be either more or less effective than individuals depending upon the composition of the group and the nature of the problem. You can best advance your own interests by joining the most useful subgroups and seeing that they function efficiently. The groups you choose will depend upon your assigned role and the goals that it implies.

ELECTION COVERAGE COMPUTED*
Art Buchwald

In his inimitable style Mr. Buchwald caricatures our overdependence on computers and our modern sophisticated methods of making the democratic system work. While we struggle to maintain the belief that machines serve men, there is an increasing body of evidence which suggests that technology is having a profound influence on the plans and decisions which we make.

How technology affects the decision-making process and what we can do to achieve a balance between technical and social progress are issues which we need to address in our attempt to cope with the problems of our community.

I was very impressed with the television coverage of the last elections. Not only was I treated to up-to-the-minute results of the contests, but each network tried to outdo itself in giving me an analysis of the returns and what they meant long before the final figures were in.

Every network had its own computer working for it and, by feeding the early results into the machine, gave us all a preview of what would surely happen later on. Here is how it seemed to go, at least to me.

"... And now let's see what is happening in the Midwest. Chuck, do you have anything to report?"

"Yes, Chet, something very interesting is happening here in the State of Congestion. The incumbent Governor Gruengruen is leading his opponent Ezekial Habit by 5,489,430 to 30. Now ordinarily this would make Governor Gruengruen the winner, but our computer shows that in 1946 Governor Gruengruen was leading by six million votes to twenty-five but lost out when two rural counties from upstate went for his opponent Long John Johns. So on the basis of the returns so far I would say Ezekial Habit will probably squeak through and get a one percent majority, which of course will be an upset."

I switched channels and got Walter, who was saying, "Do you have any news from the Far West, Sidney?"

*Reprinted by permission of the World Publishing Company from *I Chose Capitol Punishment* by Art Buchwald. Copyright © 1962, 1963 by Art Buchwald.

"Yes, Walter, I do. The Western picture looks cloudy at this moment and it's Touch and Go. Congressman Sam Touch has been fighting State Assemblyman Go in a very interesting race. Touch received 158,002 votes, and Go 158,001 votes, but we are still waiting for the Rocky Mountain districts to report. Touch is very strong in the mountain, as he goes skiing there every winter. We must keep in mind, however, Go goes fishing there in the summer, and at this stage it could be anybody's race."

"What does the computer say, Sidney?"

"Every time I ask it, it replies: 'Do you mind if I do the results from the East first?'"

"Well, we'll get back to you, Sidney. Now let's get an analysis on the over-all picture from Henry. How does it look to you, Henry?"

"There are some very exciting trends here, Walter. So far the computer has conceded the defeat of five Governors and four Senators in spite of the fact that the Governors and Senators refuse to concede themselves. Now I've just telephoned the candidates and asked them to concede gracefully to the computers but they refuse to give up. For example, Governor Wrinkles is winning in Fall State by one million votes, yet the computer tells us these votes do not mean anything. "Wrinkles is still holding on, though the election, according to the computer, will be won by his opponent, Coroner William Casey."

I turned to another channel and heard someone say, "Dave, I've just talked to the State of Agitation and there is a lot of excitement up there because Governor Gluckstern has just announced now that the returns are in he's going to divorce Mrs. Gluckstern. This is the fourth time he will serve as Governor. The computer predicted Governor Gluckstern's victory and also his divorce, but it hasn't predicted how much alimony he will have to pay. We'll have those figures for you in a moment."

A POLITICAL DECISION-MAKING MODEL*

Robert E. Agger, Daniel Goldrich, and Bert E. Swanson

Mr. Aggers *et al.* have provided a model which we may use to make sense of the complex series of interrelated events which occur in the process of transforming an idea or expressed need into public policy.

*From Robert E. Agger, Daniel Goldrich, and Bert E. Swanson, *The Rulers and the Ruled: Political Power and Impotence in American Communities.* Copyright © 1964 by John Wiley and Sons, Inc. Reprinted by permission.

This model may be applied toward understanding events which have occurred in your community or it may be used as a strategical tool to assist us in the development and implementation of policy. By separating the complete process of decision making into discrete sequential steps it is possible to plan your actions more effectively, using appropriate resources and avoiding unnecessary obstacles.

Political decision-making concerns the actions of men in the process of making choices. A process is a series of related events or acts over a period of time. Each act in a decision-making series of acts may itself be a choice or a decision. In order to understand this complex of decisions within decisions, it is useful to conceive of decision-making processes as consisting of six stages and one event:

(1) Policy formulation
(2) Policy deliberation
(3) Organization of political support
(4) Authoritative consideration
Event: Decisional outcome
(5) Promulgation of the decisional outcome
(6) Policy effectuation

The political decision-making process is political only in the sense that those engaged in action at any stage are acting consciously, in some measure, in reference to the scope of government. Any decision-making process, whether intrapersonal or interpersonal, and whether in a family, job, or other institutional setting, may be thought of as involving such stages.

Policy formulation occurs when someone thinks that a problem can be alleviated, solved, or prevented by a shift in the scope of government. The problem — or unsatisfied need — may or may not be perceived by others as a problem or as being appropriate for local government action. Even though there may be widespread satisfaction with many policy areas, the complexities of and the continuous changes in modern life make it likely that problems will arise somewhere to stimulate policy formulation directed toward a shift in the current scope of local government. The formulator, and those participating in any of the stages of political decision-making, may be a private citizen or a government official.

A policy formulation may originate outside the particular polity. For example, as a general policy, municipal ownership of facilities to distribute electric power was first formulated outside one of our communities; a general desegregation policy was first formulated outside another. But whether someone "borrows" a policy formulation from outside the community or whether a policy is of local origin, it must at some time become a preference of a person within the polity in order to become part of a community political decision-making process. A policy preference that is not deliberated once it is formed is a political decision-making process that has been started but is stillborn in the mind of the potential political participant. Policy formulation is a stage that is necessary but not sufficient to sustain the existence of a political decision-making process.

Policy deliberation is the stage following policy formulation. It may take the political-action form of talking, writing, listening, or reading. When a policy formulation — a policy preference for a shift in the net or internal scope of government — is transmitted by one actor to another, and interpersonal deliberation of the policy formulation occurs a political demand has been made in the policy. It is at this point that the consideration of other policies may generate counterdemands.

Overt action in this context does not necessarily mean publicized action. Indeed, the action may take place behind closed doors, and the most aggressive newspaper reporter or political researcher may never hear of it. What makes research on political relations possible is that, although such actions may be known only to a few people, a sufficient number of those actions may be identified to enable researchers to construct a relatively valid picture of political decision-making processes.

Policy deliberation therefore may be open or secret: it may be restricted to smoke-filled rooms; it may take place at public meetings of the City Council; or it may be a topic of conversation on street corners or in private clubs. As with policy formulation, it is a stage that may be pre-empted either by public officials or by private citizens; or it may be a joint function. Wherever it occurs and whoever participates, this necessary stage is sufficient to allow a political decision-making process to be considered extant.

The decision-making process is considered arrested if a policy proposal is formulated and deliberated but does not advance beyond policy deliberation to the organization-of-political-support stage. Political process may be arrested at this point because those who started it believe that organization in behalf of their demands would provoke counter organization and defeat; or they may even fear severe, illegitimate sanctions if they were to organize. Demands of this sort may be suppressed or repressed as a result of correct or incorrect estimates of others' policy preferences, or of accurate or unwarranted fears that opponents will apply severe, illegitimate sanctions if they push their demands. In any event, political decision-making processes may die in this stage.

Organization of political support refers to such actions as holding and attending meetings to plan political strategy, producing and distributing information, and otherwise mobilizing support for or against demands for shifts in the scope of government. In most communities there are occasions in political life when leaflets are printed, handbills and petitions circulated, mimeograph machines run, and doorbells rung; paid political advertisements are published or broadcast and notices posted. These activities are considered the hallmarks of big-city machine politics. But in the four research communities they all were used to some extent by individuals other than party leaders, precinct committeemen, and their partisan coteries.

The organization of political support does not always require the use of these methods. Necessary political support might be mobilized by a telephone call from a single policy formulator or a few words spoken to one or two officials. On the other hand, a political decision-making process may involve extensive appeals using the highly refined techniques of mass-communications propaganda and public relations.

The decisional process has become a political issue when a demand reaches the stage of organizing political support, and two or more groups oppose each other on an aspect of policy formulation. Issues may be characterized according to the number and the emotional intensity of the individuals who have become actively involved in the issue, the extent to which issues are open or covert, and the extent to which participants view policy questions as involving basic ideological principles.

At times, certain patterns of governmental functioning may become accepted as customary, and demands for change may then take on a moralistic quality. A person's basic political beliefs — the political doctrines or ideology to which he subscribes — his way of life, or his personal integrity may seem to be at stake. It must be remembered that not all political decision-making processes need be issues; the organization of political support may be characterized by consensus rather than conflict. We will examine empirically the role of ideology in the emergence or avoidance of issues in decision-making later in the book.

Authoritative consideration is the next stage of decision-making. A variety of techniques may be used to make decisional choices or to select one of a set of optional courses as the decisional outcome. A demand may be voted upon directly by the citizens; proposed constitutional changes and local charter amendments are decided in this way, as are measures that involve the issuance of special bonds and the levying of special taxes. Other major policy questions also may be decided by citizen votes. The initiative and referendum are two electoral devices designed to

give the citizenry a direct method for authoritatively approving or rejecting a policy.

On the other hand, a policy may be selected from several choices by
formal or informal balloting in small groups of active participants: a city
council may vote on a policy proposal without submitting it to the
electorate. A small group of private citizens may even make the final
decision either by voting down a policy proposal without giving officials
the option of voting on it, or by choosing an alternative that is the authoritative decisional outcome, in fact if not in theory. There are occasions
when government officials appear to act as independent lawmakers but
are really the agents of private citizens.

To control a decision-making process a group of private citizens must
control (1) the policy-formulation stage, (2) the policy-deliberation
stage, (3) the organizing-political-support stage, or all of these stages. If
a policy proposal that is unacceptable to a group of influential private
citizens manages to reach officials, the officials may allow these influential private citizens to select the policy and may not exercise their constitutional authority; or the officials may share in the selection of policies with
nonofficials. Constitutional, formal authority to choose among several outcomes in decision-making does not mean that the authorities will or can
so choose. Even the political status associated with constitutional authority
may prove a narrow base for the exercise of political influence, compared
to the political status of certain private citizens.

A new policy that effects a shift in the scope of government must be
transmitted to an appropriate local government agency for official action,
if that shift is to become part of the formal, authoritative code of the
policy. If the formulators of a particular policy are themselves government
officials, they still must transmit the policy — that is, place the policy on
the official agenda for formal consideration — in order for it to become part
of the decisions of record, the laws, ordinances, or administrative regulations of government.

But what of a policy proposal that is blocked, vetoed, or otherwise
defeated before it is transmitted to governmental authorities? Assume
that a private citizen or an official makes a policy suggestion or demand
to other private citizens or, informally, to other officials. Then suppose
that the proposed policy change is rejected, no action is taken, and the
existing rule remains unchanged, either through the action of these
private citizens or through informal action by the officials. Although the
suggested policy was never transmitted formally to a local agency,
political decision-making has occurred: the actual political decision has

been to affirm the existing policy. Political decision-making does not mean that existing rules and regulations must be revised or that political decisions may not be made outside the locus of an official government agency.

The objective of demands for shifts in the scope of government may be to see a change in the way government operates without a change in the law or a decision to maintain an existing law. Laws or ordinances, administrative regulations, and judicial decisions, much like constitutions or charters, are often open to a variety of interpretations. Thus, a demand for a shift in the scope of government can be a demand for altered patterns of action by government officials without a formal change in the law or ordinance, administrative regulation, or judicial decision. Inducing government officials to act informally in appropriate ways may be a wiser course of action than attempting to obtain an authoritative modification in the scope of government. Therefore, political decision-making may take place either outside the halls of government or informally within the government, with neither fanfare nor public proclamations.

So far, the word "authoritative" has been used in two distinct but related ways; one is a special case of the other. We [have] said that government has "authoritative supremacy, a monopoly of legitimate force." In the phrases *authoritative rule*, *authoritative code of the polity*, and *constitutional authority*, the word *authoritative* refers to the existence of a governmental policy, that is, of a rule regarding the way men should behave toward each other. The violation of such a policy can be expected to lead to punishments deriving from the monopoly of force possessed by all governments.

In this view, government exists and is "legitimate," even though its citizens despise it, so long as the citizens do not revolt and as long as they expect that force will probably be used to punish violators of policy. If such expectations do not exist, or if the expectations refer not to a legitimate government but to contending groups whose policy views conflict, so that any action might be met by punishment, government has broken down, and anarchy temporarily reigns. Constitutions, written or unwritten, and their subsidiary laws and customs are the plan of government as an institution in which those who govern have effective authority derived from their ability to sanction, using force if necessary. These officials may not express themselves before others do, but theirs is the last voice heard before sanctions are used in the pursuit of social control and public order. By the decision-making stage of authoritative consideration — the second sense of the word *authoritative* — we mean the stage of action by the political participants who have the final voice. These participants have the last word in selecting one or another of two or more outcomes as the policy that defines the scope of government for a succeeding time period.

All decision-making processes have *decisional outcomes*. If a particular aspect of the scope of government has been questioned and a decisional process has developed, regardless of the degree of consensus or conflict, the process will influence events thereafter, even though it is no longer extant. A decisional outcome is assessed by comparing the scope of government that existed and was questioned with the scope that exists at the point in time selected for identifying the outcome. This assessment may be done on the basis of a simple scale showing whether there has been change or not, or on the basis of a more complex set of parameters.

A decisional outcome involves purposeful behavior by participants, but does not require particular forms of choice-making. For example, it does not require a formal balloting procedure by either the electorate or their governmental representatives. The "authorities" in the second sense of the term *authoritative* are not necessarily government officials or the electorate acting as officials, as in the case of the "authorities" in the first sense. This is because authoritative consideration in a decision-making process is that stage wherein the participants select one or another of two or more ways in which local government is to function henceforth. Thus, participants in an authoritative consideration stage may be government officials, private citizens, or both. There may be no opportunity for government officials to reject the choice of private citizens of a particular decisional outcome, just as there may be no occasion for any but government officials to participate in selecting one of several outcomes. Private citizens may select an outcome that maintains the scope of government as is, thus obviating any need for a new law or ordinance. But whether a decisional outcome maintains or shifts the scope of government, the question of whether the participants are officials or citizens should be answered by empirical investigation rather than by definition.

An analyst must select a point in time to assess what outcomes have occurred in political decision-making. This point will be discussed further in connection with the concepts of political power and community power structures. The analyst might find that the stage of authoritative consideration has not been reached in one or another decision-making process. Thus, there may be decisional outcomes without authoritative consideration in a decision-making process because demands may not have reached the men who could act to shift the scope of government. When a change in a specific scope of government has become the subject of political demands in a decisional process, the analyst must determine whether the maintenance of the specific scope of government resulted from purposeful resistance by people capable of shifting the scope or from lack of access to people with such capabilities.[1] "Access" refers to the ability to reach the authorities, the men who can choose one or another pattern of local-government functioning as the decisional outcome in a decisional process. If there have been no demands for a shift in the scope of government, there has been no decisional process and, consequently, no authoritative consideration.[2] If demands have resulted in a shift in the scope of government, there has been authoritative consideration, even if a consensus has existed.

An authoritative-consideration stage may exist in a wide range of forms; it may be a distinct stage which succeeds the prior stages and has different participants from those in the prior stage; it may be a stage that partially overlaps earlier stages with some overlapping of personnel; or it may be a stage that is indistinguishable from other stages either temporally or by its participants. Decisional processes range from those with relatively well-developed and distinct stages to those with a single, composite stage that empirically encompasses the four analytic stages. In the decisional process that has a single, composite stage only one set of people—or one person in an instance of complete one-man rule—formulates policy, deliberates, organizes political support, and authoritatively considers the proposed shift in the scope of government at any one time. These participants may decide to adopt or reject a given policy formulation, thereby shifting or maintaining a particular scope of government. In relatively developed and distinct decisional stages, the participants in one stage may or may not be the same as the participants in other stages. Political role specialization may develop in reference to these stages, so that in one community, or in one policy area within a community, some men—"idea men"—specialize in policy formulation, others specialize in deliberative activities, others in the organization of political support, and still others may limit their participation to a final authoritative-consideration stage. Subspecialization in political roles within stages is also possible. For example, some people may specialize in doorbell-ringing and precinct

---

[1] Acts intended to influence others by creating or reinforcing satisfaction with an existing scope of government are not treated as demands, and, hence, are not by themselves components of decision-making processes. On the other hand, such demands may be seen as part of a special category of "general" decision-making processes.

[2] An analyst, alternatively, may maintain that neither political power nor a political decision-making process exists until an authoritative-consideration stage has been reached.

work, others in pamphleteering, and still others in financing during the organization-of-political-support stage. However, political roles in the decisional stages may be more general in other communities or in other decisional processes.

Promulgation of the decisional outcome is also a stage not necessarily reached in a particular decision-making process. If the participants think that an existing policy is the best policy and that it should not be modified, there may be no occasion for an authoritative proclamation of an outcome. If a shift in the scope of government takes place without a formal, public pronouncement, this stage may not be present. But another way of looking at it is that this stage is manifested in the affirmation of an existing policy or in a quiet, covert change of policy. In any event, the present analysis of the decision-making process is most concerned with the four prior stages.

Policy effectuation is the last stage in this model of a political decision-making process. Administrative rather than legislative officials are ordinarily, but not always, the authorities at this stage. The courts may also play important roles in interpreting and shaping a general-policy decision. Private citizens also may join with, or even dominate, public administrators in this stage of political decision-making.

Policy effectuation is included as a stage in the decision-making process not only because a decisional outcome must be applied to be "final" or because its application may substantially change the decisional outcome from what had been intended. Is it included primarily because it may result in reappraisal of the policy, thereby initiating another cycle in the decision-making process. In this sense even policy effectuation is not a final or terminal stage of decision-making.

For a long time the functions of public administrators were regarded by political scientists as distinct from the functions of politicians. Politicians made the general rules in politics, while administrators applied these general rules to specific cases. Recently, the conception of politics and administration as inextricably intertwined has become accepted. In our view a useful distinction ought still to be made between administrative and political decision-making. This distinction does not preclude administrators from active involvement in political decision-making, nor politicians from active participation in administrative decision-making.

Demands that local government shift its scope may be administrative or political. Decisional processes may be similarly categorized. These are terms for polar opposites on a continuum and are therefore matters of degree rather than of kind. An *administrative* demand or decision-making process is regarded by its maker or participants as involving relatively routine implementations of a prior, more generally applicable decision; it implicates relatively minor values of a relatively few people at any one time and has "technical" criteria available to guide the technically trained expert in selecting one or another outcome as *the* decision. A *political* demand or decision-making process is thought to involve either an unusual review of an existing decision or an entirely new decision; it implicates relatively major values of a relatively large number of people and has value judgments or preferences as the major factors in determining selection by "policy-makers" of one or another outcome as *the* decision.[3]

The administrator thus is "in" politics by definition, but whether he is involved in political or administrative decision-making, or both, is an open, empirical question. The politician is also "in" politics, and he may be involved as a participant in the making of administrative as well as political decisions.

The roles played by bureaucrats — "administrators" — in the political system tend to be shaped by the organization of each government and by the constitutional doctrines and practices in each polity. However, a casual examination of political systems at the local-community or nation-state level suggests that official and informal organizations of political systems may diverge as much from one another as do official and informal internal structures of administrative agencies.

Several important consequences follow from these distinctions between administrative and political decisions, based as they are on the psychology of participants. One is that a particular decisional process may be political in one community and administrative in another. Or a decisional process may in time move from the political to the administrative category and back within a single community. Civil servants, bureaucrats, or public administrators may be active participants in political decision-making under some conditions and active participants in administrative decision-making under others. . . .

Summarizing the features of the model of political decision-making we

[3]Under many conditions of modern political life, the constituent variables may cluster together. The degree to which decisional processes are regarded by participants as (variable 1) routine, as (variable 2) implementations of earlier decisions, as (variable 3) implicating relatively minor values, as (variable 4) directly affecting relatively few people, as (variable 5) subject primarily to technical criteria of choice among alternatives, and as (variable 6) properly "decided" by experts generally may be seen as congruent. However, as one example of another possible pattern, some decisional processes may be regarded as relatively routine but involving major values of many people. It might be fruitful to develop more complex multi-dimensional schemes for the classification of decisional processes rather than simply viewing them as on a single administrative-political dimension.

can say: a decision-making process exists when a political demand is made. A demand is a communicated policy formulation that envisages a shift in the scope of government. The decision-making process may become arrested at this point because those considering the demand are pessimistic about attaining the desired decisional outcome, because they fear the consequences that might ensue if they press their demands, because they are insufficiently motivated, or for other reasons. If counter-demands and counterorganization develop along with political support in behalf of demands, the process has become a political issue.

Decisional outcomes may result from arrested processes, from unopposed demands, from the resolution of a political issue, or as a consequence of effectively opposed and defeated demands which have not become issues. The decisional outcome may or may not be publicly promulgated. A political decision-making process may generate new policy formulations and demands or lead to new policy effectuation — administrative decision-making — that may then generate new political decision-making processes. In order to determine the outcomes of decisional processes, an analyst must specify the point in time at which he is interested in determining who has had the political power that accrues to those who contribute to decisional outcomes.

Government officials may or may not be the only political actors at any stage of a decision-making process. Theoretically, they may monopolize political action or they may never enter the political scene actively. However, in most American communities they probably do engage in political action and share power with private citizens. But this is something for empirical determination rather than assumption. Since decision-making is not necessarily monopolized by officials, observations must be made to assess the extent to which citizens of a community participate and have power in the making of political decision. . . .

EXERCISES AND DISCUSSION TOPICS FOR CHAPTER 11

Exercises

1. The Good Society Exercise, designed by William Coplin and Steve Apter, shows what happens in a society based on the principles of order and justice when the realities of that society do not measure up to its ideals. It is a simple exercise requiring only a few extra facilities. At best, it requires seven small rooms, a typewriter, and a ditto machine. Under less than optimal conditions, one or two large rooms could be used and verbal communications or a blackboard could be used in

place of a typewriter and the ditto machine. A *post hoc* discussion session is advisable with some kind of systematic and visual (blackboard) attempt to relate what happened in the game to the simulation and the real world. The moderator in this exercise is the exercise administrator. He delivers communications to the various groups and sets time limits; he does not participate in the actual exercise.

The Good Society*

You are about to participate in a society consisting of seven teams. Six of the teams consist of three players each and are called Groups (*A, B, C, D, E, F*). The other team consists of five players and is called the Central Authority. The *Groups* and the *Central Authority* behave in the Good Society according to the following statement of principle:

> This Society guarantees equal opportunity and equal rights to every member. It advocates the need for stability, change, and justice. Inequality is as enslaving as much as disorder. Order and justice must prevail.

In spite of this statement of principle, however, the "goods" of the Good Society as measured by Power Units are not distributed equally. Moreover, the ability to make changes in the Good Society are also not shared equally by the groups. The simulation exercise is designed to represent what happens in a society in which order and justice are its guidelines and the reality of the society does not measure up to those guidelines.

Change in the Good Society

Power Weights (the units used to measure the wealth and influence of each team in the society) and *Petition Weights* (the weight of each team in the signing of a petition) are distributed in the following manner among the seven teams of the Good Society.

Name of Team	Power Weights	Petition Weights
Central Authority	100	3
Group *A*	45	2
Group *B*	35	2
Group *C*	10	1
Group *D*	8	1
Group *E*	4	1
Group *F*	4	1
Total	206	11

*Portions of this article appear by permission of the Syracuse Metropolitan Review and the authors.

Changes in the distribution of power units as well as any other facet of life in the Good Society can occur in two ways:

1. A *Petition* can be signed by the teams representing at least six *Petition Weights* which call for any specific change.
2. A *war* can be fought between any team in the society in which the more powerful size (the larger number of *Power Weights*) gets all but one of the losing side's power weights.

While there can be no more than 206 *Power Weights* for the entire Society, there can be an unlimited number of *Petition Weights*.

Maintaining Order in the Good Society

The maintenance of order in the Good Society is the responsibility of all of its members. The *Central Authority* has a special role given the large number of *Power Units* at its disposal. It can engage in war against members that fail to live up to the principles of the Society and can attempt to get *Petitions* signed. At the same time, it is up to the six *Groups* to make sure that the *Central Authority* does not abuse its role. These *groups* can sign *Petitions* to limit the actions of the *Central Authority* and even to the point of redistributing their power.

Specific Rules and Procedures

The main ideas of the exercise are contained above. However certain procedures and rules must be followed.

1. Each Team will meet in assigned rooms. For Groups *A* through *E*, only one team player can visit other rooms for purposes of discussion. For the Central Authority, four team players can visit other rooms for purposes of discussion.
2. All decisions taken by the Groups must be unanimous decisions. All decisions taken by the Central Authority must be supported by three members.
3. In addition to personal discussions, communications can be sent through messages or can be distributed as part of the *Newsletter*. The *Communication Form* should be used for both types of communications. The *Newsletter* will contain announcements by Groups and the Central Authority as well as editorial statements by reporters. The *Newsletter* will officially announce the results of all Wars and Petitions.

4. Simulation Control (moderator) will distribute all communications and will answer all questions you might have. The exercise will be run for an undisclosed period of time.

5. A *Petition Form* will be used for purposes of peaceful change. Any group or the Central Authority can start the Petition. Once enough signatures of Teams to constitute six Petition Weights are achieved, the Petition should be submitted to Control. It goes into effect as soon as Control officially announces the Petition through the *Newsletter* and remains in effect until a different petition is signed to alter the original one. No petitions can go into effect between the first declaration of war and the results ten minutes later.

6. War occurs when one or more teams declares war against one or more other teams. A *War Form* is submitted to the Simulation Control. Control will inform the other teams. The attacked team will have ten minutes to counterattack. More than one team can attack and more than one can counterattack. The side with the largest number of *Power Units* will win the war and will get all but one of the other team's *Power Units*. If more than two groups attack and win, the power units won will be distributed in accordance with the relative *Power Units* of the winning teams. Any teams submitting a War Form may retract it before the ten minute time limit is up.

Below are samples of the three forms used in the exercise:

———————— Petition Form

Originator: Central Authority: Group A: B: C: D: E: F:
Circle One

Petition Statement:

Signatures of Members of:

Central Authority   ————————————————————————————

Petition Weights   ————————————————————————————

Group A (2)   ————————————————————————————

Group B (2)   ————————————————————————————

Group C (1)   ————————————————————————————

Group D (1)   ————————————————————————————

Group E (1)   ————————————————————————————

Group F (1)   ————————————————————————————

(All three for each group)

————————

Communications Form

Sender: Central Authority: Group A: B: C: D: E: F:
Receiver: Central Authority: Group A: B: C: D: E: F:
Circle everyone to receive the message
A total Circle means publication in the Newsletter

Message:

Signature of Sending Team's Participants

War Form

Attacker: Central Authority: Group A: B: C: D: E: F:
Target: Central Authority: Group A: B: C: D: E: F:
Circle Target(s)

Signatures of Attacking Team

---

2. Visit one or more sessions of a public governance meeting (City Council, Town Meeting, Board of Education, etc.) in your community. Discover the sources of decisions being made there.

Discussion Topics

Apply Agger's decision-making model to issues in the simulation and in your own community.

What are some factors which lead to decisions? Discuss the major barriers to decisions. How do they arise? What can be done in the simulation to facilitate group decision making?

CHAPTER 12

Individual Change

During the course of your participation in Psych City, you should be able to observe changes in the behaviors of some of the participants. Change is defined here in terms of behaviors within a situation which are different from those which occurred at an earlier time in a similar situation. In addition to observable changes in people's behaviors, there also may be changes in various participants which are not directly available to your observation. These are changes which take place within a specific person but which are not manifested in overt behavior. Changes of this sort may lead to behavior which, on the surface, is compatible with earlier behaviors but is, in fact, structurally or motivationally different.

The noted psychologist Herbert Kelman has described a similar distinction in the area of attitude change. He has identified three different processes: compliance, identification, and internalization. The first of these, compliance, indicates a situation where a person's ability to reward behavior he likes or punish behavior he dislikes. Suppose that your subgroup in Psych City needs additional votes in the Town Meeting in order to pass a resolution which will further your group's goals. You may be able to get these votes by agreeing to vote for a proposition needed by another group if they vote for your resolution (reward) or by threatening some action injurious to their interests (punishment) if they do not. This kind of bargaining can be a very effective method of controlling some of other people's behavior in the simulation.

The second kind of change is less likely to appear in Psych City. Identification describes the situation where a person tries to act like another person because he identifies with him and sees him as a desirable model.

229

In real life, everyone has seen people who try to emulate someone else across the whole range of human behavior from Martin Luther King, Jr., to Adolph Hitler. Identification is one way of playing your assigned role. Here you attempt to imagine what someone who actually occupies such a role is like and subsequently you behave in a way which you believe is consistent with that role.

Internalization is the process by which certain attitudes and related behaviors are accepted as correct or desirable in and of themselves. An extreme example of this kind of change is religious or political conversion. When such a change takes place it alters not only a single set of behaviors but affects other attitudes and behaviors. Internalized change can manifest itself in a broad variety of behavior changes, affecting many areas of a person's functioning. The extent to which this process generalizes to other areas of a person's functioning depends upon how central the area of change is to the core aspects of an individual's personality. This type of change is usually the most difficult to accomplish, consequently it is unlikely to take place in the simulation to any great extent.

There are a number of processes, then, which can be called individual, psychological change. Some of these are relatively easy to accomplish and these generally involve modifying specific bits of behavior through reward and punishment. Change of this type tends to be relatively specific to certain situations and is therefore less likely to have impact on other areas of a person's functioning. Specific behavior change is less likely to be maintained over longer periods of time and may disappear when the person who dispenses the rewards and punishments is not around to keep an eye on the situation. Since your participation in Psych City is a relatively short term, uninvolving affair in comparison with other aspects of your life, emphasis on this type of change is recommended. For practical, tactical reasons within the simulation, you will probably find that compliance is a sufficient criterion for change in other participants in order to accomplish your tasks.

Your experience outside Psych City is another matter entirely. For this reason, change other than that described by the term compliance will be discussed here. These are changes which more approximate Kelman's description of internalization and refer to changes which are more likely to endure over time and which should have greater impact on other behaviors. Enduring change, particularly in matters which are important to a person, can be considerably more difficult to accomplish.

Central to the concept of change not described by the reinforcement theorists are the terms consistency and equilibrium. As discussed in the section on communication, people seem to have a tendency to keep their perceptions and ideas consistent. When these are relatively consistent, the person is said to be in a state of equilibrium. When a person's attitudes or perceptions about someone or something are in conflict, that person is said to be in a state of disequilibrium, a state that is often uncomfortable. Consequently, people experiencing disequilibrium try to reduce inconsistencies to a tolerable level, not necessarily to eliminate them altogether. People vary in their tolerance for inconsistencies in any particular area and many psychologists today think that a certain degree of inconsistency may be experienced as pleasurable. Nevertheless, inconsistency in perceptions and cognitions and the resulting disequilibrium are a major source of motivation for psychological and behavioral change.

In daily experience with the world you tend to expect certain things from your environment. The mailman is expected to arrive at 10:30 a.m., Walter Cronkite comes on at seven and your boyfriend loves you. If the mailman does not arrive until noon this may be mildly disconcerting but if your boyfriend informs you that he was never particularly fond of you, the disequilibrium is more intense than implied by the term disconcerting. The effect of inconsistency varies with your interest in the area where the inconsistency takes place. For this reason change becomes difficult in areas where you are most involved. It may be difficult to misperceive what your boyfriend is trying to tell you but it is done surprisingly often. You may attribute his statement to temporary insanity or to falling in with bad companions. One way or another you can find ways to protect your own self-esteem.

In many situations, the tendency to guard against inconsistent information is helpful to a person. If we changed very easily it would be difficult to develop regular attitudes and behavior patterns which allow the construction of interpersonal expectancies that aid in our day-to-day functioning. Still, this kind of process often prevents people from adapting realistically to a changing world. It is breaking into this process that the authors of the readings in this section have in mind when they use the term "unfreezing." The internally consistent attitudes about a person or a situation need to be thrown into disequilibrium when new information indicates they are erroneous. The tendency to avoid this disequilibrium is what makes necessary, adaptive change difficult for the same reasons that it helps us to function in a complex environment.

Unfreezing is necessary before any change will take place. This may sometimes be accomplished by making a person aware of inconsistencies between his own attitudes and the real situation. This does not always work—that tendency toward consistency again. Sometimes unfreezing can be helped if you point out that someone the person respects and admires sees the situation as you do. This procedure is often used in advertising when an athlete or movie star endorses a product. Here the recipient of the persuasive message must choose between inconsistencies. The inconsistency between his perception of the person he admires and that person's attitude toward the issue in question may be sufficient to unfreeze the attitude. There are a variety of techniques available to accomplish unfreezing. Any specific technique must be considered in light of the specific situation. At any rate, this is only the first step in changing behavior based upon internalized processes.

After unfreezing is accomplished, the person in question has not yet changed his behavior, he is only open to possible change. It may still be easier for the person to return to his old attitudes and behavior in dealing with the situation. New information must be provided to change the person. The degree to which new information is taken in, used and retained can depend on how compatible it is with other similar attitudes the person has. If it is also necessary to modify these attitudes, the possibility of change is minimized. If the attitude in question is unrelated to other attitudes held or is relatively incompatible with them, change is proportionally easier. This problem is not likely to be a major one in Psych City. Most attitudes pertinent to the simulation will be short term and fairly peripheral to you in importance. For this reason they should be rather easy to change. The process of continually behaving in a manner consistent with your role assignment can conceivably affect your attitudes. Behaving in a fashion which is inconsistent with your real attitudes can bring about changes in those attitudes. In Psych City however, you have the psychological out of knowing that your behavior is a response to your teacher's expectations and therefore is not "real." Such changes are not unknown to Psych City participants however.

The third phase of change, after unfreezing and actual attitude change has taken place, is the process of refreezing. This is the making of the change a stable part of the person. Even after the change has taken place, demands elicited by the environment or from other attitudes can cause the change to evaporate and return to the original attitude. It is difficult to become a left-wing radical if all your friends are conservative Republicans. The pressure to get along with your friends or to function in your job may cancel out change. These pressures are not likely to go away. You may have noticed, if you have gone away to college, that your old friends are not quite as groovy as they were when you were in high school. You may find more pleasure in your new friends at college. Perhaps, you have changed some. Many people, after undergoing profound change in some of their attitudes may begin also to change their friends, to people who hold attitudes more like their own. The nature of this process will be discussed in the chapter on group change (Chapter 13).

THE ILLUSIONLESS MAN
AND THE VISIONARY MAID* (abridged)

Allen Wheelis

The theme of Mr. Wheelis's story may be summarized as a question: what happens when two people with totally opposite lifestyles enter into a long-term relationship? In the excerpts from this story which are published below we are offered a unique literary glimpse at the psychological impact which results from the interaction of clashing perceptual frameworks within a relationship of mutual attraction.

The coping mechanisms utilized by the two major characters represent styles of adaptation which are frequently practiced by many individuals. The changes and nonchanges they experience highlight the intensity with which human beings strive to meet their social needs while at the same time struggling to maintain their psychological defenses which they perceive to be self-protective.

Once upon a time there was a man who had no illusions about anything. While still in the crib he had learned that his mother was not always kind; at two he had given up fairies; witches and hobgoblins disappeared from his world at three; at four he knew that rabbits at Easter lay no eggs; and at five on a cold night in December, with a bitter little smile, he said goodbye to Santa Claus. At six when he started school, illusions flew from his life like feathers in a windstorm: he discovered that his father was not always brave or even honest, that Presidents are little men, that the Queen of England goes to the bathroom like everybody else, and that his first-grade teacher, a pretty round-faced young woman with dimples, did not know everything, as he had thought, but thought only of men and did not know much of anything. At eight he could read, and the printed word was a sorcerer at exorcising illusions — only he knew there were no

*Allen B. Wheelis, M. D. "The Illusionless Man and the Visionary Maid," A Story, from *The Illusionless Man*. Harper & Row, Paperback Edition, 1971, reprinted by permission of the author. (Originally published in *Commentary*, May 1964.)

sorcerers. The abyss of hell disappeared into the even larger abyss into which a clear vision was sweeping his beliefs. Happiness was of course a myth; love a fleeting attachment, a dream of enduring selflessness glued onto the instinct of a rabbit. At twelve he dispatched into the night sky his last unheard prayer. As a young man he realized that the most generous act is self-serving, the most disinterested inquiry serves interest; that lies are told by printed words, even by words carved in stone; that art begins with a small "a" like everything else, and that he could not escape the ruin of value by orchestrating a cry of despair into a song of lasting beauty; for beauty passes and deathless art is quite mortal. Of all those people who lose illusions he lost more than anyone else, taboo and prescription alike; and as everything became permitted nothing was left worthwhile.

He became a carpenter, but could see a house begin to decay in the course of building — perfect pyramid of white sand spreading out irretrievably in the grass, bricks chipping, doors sticking, the first tone of gray appearing on white lumber, the first film of rust on bright nails, the first leaf falling in the shining gutter. He became then a termite inspector, spent his days crawling in darkness under old houses, lived in a basement room and never raised the blinds, ate canned beans and frozen television dinners, let his hair grow and his beard. On Sundays he walked in the park, threw bread to the ducks — dry French bread, stone-hard, would stamp on it with his heel, gather up the pieces, and walk along the pond, throwing it out to the avid ducks paddling after him, thinking glumly that they would be just as hungry again tomorrow. His name was Henry.

One day in the park he met a girl who believed in everything. In the forest she still glimpsed fairies, heard them whisper; bunnies hopped for her at Easter, laid brilliant eggs; at Christmas hoofbeats shook the roof. She was disillusioned at times and would flounder, gasp desperately, like a fish in sand, but not for long; would quickly, sometimes instantly, find something new, and actually never gave up any illusion, but would lay it aside when necessary, forget it, and whenever it was needed, back it would come. Her name was Lorabelle, and when she saw a bearded young man in the park, alone among couples, stamping on the hard bread, tossing it irritably to the quacking ducks, she exploded into illusions about him like a Roman candle over a desert.

"You are a great and good man," she said.

"I'm petty and self-absorbed," he said.

"You're terribly unhappy."

"I'm morose . . . probably like it that way."

"You have suffered a great deal," she said. "I see it in your face."

"I've been diligent only in self-pity," he said, "have turned away from everything difficult, and what you see are the scars of old acne shining through my beard; I could never give up chocolate and nuts."

"You're very wise," she said.

"No, but intelligent."

They talked about love, beauty, feeling, value, life, work, death—and always she came back to love. They argued about everything, differed on everything, agreed on nothing, and so she fell in love with him. "This partakes of the infinite," she said.

But he, being an illusionless man, was only fond of her. "It partaketh mainly," he said, "of body chemistry," and passed his hand over her roundest curve.

"We have a unique affinity," she said. "You're the only man in the world for me." "We fit quite nicely," he said. "You are one of no more than five or six girls in the country for me." "It's a miracle we met," she said. "I just happened to be feeding the ducks." "No, not chance; I couldn't feel this way about anybody else."

"If you'd come down the other side of the hill," he said, "you'd be feeling this way right now about somebody else. And if I had fed squirrels instead of ducks I'd be playing with somebody else's curves."

"You're my dearest darling squirrel," she said, "and most of all you're my silly fuzzy duck, and I don't know why I bother to love you—why are you such a fool? who dropped you on your head?—come to bed!" On such a note of logic, always, their arguments ended.

She wanted a church wedding with a dress of white Alençon lace over cream satin, bridesmaids in pink, organ music, and lots of people to weep and be happy and throw rice. "You'll be so handsome in a morning coat," she said, brushing cobwebs off his shoulders, "oh and striped pants, too, and a gray silk cravat, and a white carnation. You'll be divine." "I'd look a proper fool," he said, "and I'm damned if I'll do it." "Oh please! It's only once." "Once a fool, voluntarily, is too often." "It's a sacrament." "It's a barbarism." "Symbols are important." "Then let's stand by the Washington Monument," he said, "and be honest about it."

"You make fun," she said, "but it's a holy ceremony, a solemn exchange of vows before man and God."

"God won't be there, honey; the women will be weeping for their own lost youth and innocence, the men wanting to have you in bed; and the priest standing slightly above us will be looking down your cleavage as his mouth goes dry; and the whole thing will be a primitive and preposterous attempt to invest copulation with dignity and permanence, to enforce responsibility for children by the authority of a myth no longer credible even to a child."

So . . . they were married in church; his hands were wet and his knees shook, he frowned and quaked; but looked divine, she said, in morning coat and striped pants; and she was serene and beautiful in Alençon lace; the organ pealed, weeping women watched with joy, vows were said, rice thrown, and then they were alone on the back seat of a taxi, her lips seeking his, murmuring, "I'm so happy, darling, so terribly happy. Now we'll be together always."

"In our community," he said, "and for our age and economic bracket, we have a 47.3 per cent chance of staying together for twenty years."

She found for them a white house on a hill in a field of red poppies and white daisies, with three tall maple trees. There they lived in sunlight and wind, and she began to fill their life with fragile feminine deceptions, worked tirelessly at them, and always there was something new. She concealed the monotony of eating by variety, never two meals the same, one morning French toast in the shape of their house, the next a boiled egg with smiling painted face and a tiny straw hat; cut flowers on the table, color and sweetness blooming from a Dutch vase, as if unrelated to manure; Italian posters on the wall as if they had traveled; starched white curtains at the windows, as if made of a brocade too rich and heavy to bend; morning glories covering the outhouse with royal purple. When he came home at night she would brush the cobwebs from his hair, make him bathe and shave and dress — to appear as if he had not worked in dirt. She made wonderful sauces, could cook anything to taste like something else, created a sense of purity by the whiteness of tablecloth, of delicacy by the thinness of crystal, would surround a steak with parsley as if it were not flesh but the bloom of a garden, supported her illusions with candlelight and fine wine, and smiled at him across the table with lips redder than real. In the bedroom candlelight again, and yet another nightgown to suggest a mysterious woman of unknown delights, and a heavy perfume, as if not sweat but sweetness came from her pores.

Being an illusionless man, he admitted that he liked these elegant mirages, found them pleasant, that it was good to sleep with her fine curves under his hand, her sweet smells in his nose, that he slept better now than when he lived alone. He became less gloomy, but not much.

One Sunday afternoon, walking hand in hand in sunshine through the poppies and daisies, he noticed her lips moving. "What are you saying?" he said. "Do you love me?" "I'm fond of you," he said; "love is an illusion." "Is there anybody else? I'm terribly jealous." "Jealousy is the illusion of complete possession." "Do other women attract you?" "Yes." "Some men are not like that." "Some men are liars," he said.

She became pregnant, bought baby clothes, tried out names, was always singing. "Please be happy," she said. "By 1980 the world population will . . ." "Oh be quiet!" she said.

She prepared a room for the baby, hung curtains, bought a crib, read books, became apprehensive. "Will he be all right? What do you think? Will he be a good baby? He doesn't have to be pretty, you know, that's not so important, but I'd like him to be intelligent. And will he have two eyes and the right number of fingers and toes? I want him to have everything he needs and nothing too much. What do you think?" "Some minor congenital aberrations are inevitable," he said; "the major malformations are less . . ." "Don't say such things," she said, "why do you scare me?"; "I was just . . ." "Oh . . . and will I know what to do?" she said, ". . . how to take care of him? What do you think? Will I be any good at it?"

One night he felt her lips moving in his hair. "Praying?" he said. "Yes." "What did you ask?" "That someday you will say you love me."

She felt weak, became sick; in bed she looked pale and scared. "Will the baby be all right?" she said. "Don't ever leave me. What are you thinking? Tell me." She began to bleed, was terrified, lay very still, but lost the baby anyway.

She was depressed then, her face motionless and dark. "I lost it because you don't love me," she said.

"There is no established correlation," he said, "between the alleged state of love, or lack of it, and the incidence of miscarriage."

"I'm not wanting statistics," she screamed.

"What then?"

"Nothing. Everything. It's not enough . . . just being fond." I hate fondness. What's the matter with you? It wouldn't have happened . . . I want to be loved!"

"You're being hysterical," he said, "and you're not finishing your sentences."

Suddenly, all at once, she looked at him with a level detached gaze and did not like what she saw. "You were right," she said; "you *are* petty and self-absorbed. What's worse, you have a legal mind and there's no poetry in you. You don't give me anything, don't even love me, you're *dull*. You were stuck in a hole in the ground when I found you, and if I hadn't pulled you out you'd be there still. There's no life in you. I give you everything and it's not enough, doesn't make any difference. You can't wait to die, want to bury yourself now and me with you. Well I'm not ready yet and I'm not going to put up with it any longer, and now I'm through with you and I want a divorce."

"You've lost your illusions about me," he said, "but not the having of illusions."

"While you," she said, "have lost your illusions about everything, and can't get over being sore about it."

". . . they'll focus now on someone else . . ."

"Oh I hope so!" she said; "I can hardly wait."

". . . you waste experience."

"And you waste life!"

He wouldn't give her a divorce, but that didn't matter; for she couldn't bear the thought of his moving back to that basement, and anyway, she told herself, he had to have someone to look after him; so they lived together still and she cooked for him when she was home and mended his clothes and darned his socks, and when he asked why, she said, with sweet revenge, "Because I'm fond of you, that's all. Just fond."

She got a job with a theater, typed scripts and programs, worked nights in the box office, let her hair grow into a long silken curtain curled up at the bottom below her shoulders, wore loose chiffon blouses with clown sleeves, trailed filmy scarves from her neck, and fell in love with an actor named Cyrus Anthony de Maronodeck. Her *a*'s broadened and she affected a way of turning her head with so sudden a movement that it could not go unnoticed; no longer did she walk in or out of a room, she strode.

"Cyrus is so *interesting!*" she said, "makes everything an adventure, concentrates energy and passion into a moment until it glows!" She struck a pose: "'When I die,' he says, 'I may be dead for a long time, but while I'm here I'll live it to the hilt.'" "A philosopher, too," Henry said.

One Sunday night Cyrus borrowed a thousand dollars from Lorabelle for his sick mother; and the following day it transpired that he had borrowed also the week-end receipts from the box office and had taken his leave of the company. For several days Lorabelle wouldn't believe it, waited for word from him, bit her fingernails — until he was apprehended in Laredo crossing the border with a blonde.

She worked next in a brokerage house operating an enormous and very intelligent machine which tapped and hummed and whirred and rotated, sent its carriage hopping up and down and side to side, performed seventeen mathematical calculations without ever a mistake, took pictures of everything and had illusions about nothing — but Lorabelle did, and presently fell in love with her boss, Mr. Alexander Orwell Mittelby, a sixty-year-old man who loved her with a great passion, she told Henry, but who was married and unfortunately could not get a divorce because his wife was a schizophrenic, had a private nurse in constant attendance; the shock of divorce, Mr. Mittelby had said, would kill her.

"Alex is unique," Lorabelle told Henry, "simply not like the rest of us . . . not at all. He has no interest in himself, has grown beyond that. I've never met a man so mature, so genuinely wise. 'All my personal goals lie in the past,' he told me; 'the only thing left is to seek the common good.' He has no patience with personal problems, complexes . . . that sort of thing . . . sees the romantic protest for what it is: adolescent complaining. Oh Henry, I wish you could know him. He faces life with so much courage—such a gallant careless courage. 'Despair is a luxury,' he says, 'and I can't afford it.'"

Lorabelle wore short tight skirts, high needle-like heels, jeweled glasses, and her hair bouffant; she read the *Wall Street Journal* and *Barron's Weekly*, studied the new tax legislation, spoke out for *laissez faire* in discussion groups, and at an Anti-World-Federalist dinner chanced to meet Mrs. Mittelby who was not schizophrenic at all but a plain shrewd woman with a wrinkled face, gray hair, and a very sharp tongue. Lorabelle stared at her with deepening shock. "My husband's secretaries," Mrs. Mittelby said, "always seem stunned by my sanity . . . then seek other employment."

. . . And so it continued through the days and weeks of their lives, year after year: Catholic Church, Christian Science, yoga; Al, Bob, and Peter; Paris, Rome, and Nairobi; technocracy, mysticism, hypnotism; short hair, long hair, and wig; and whenever she would say, in that rapturous tone of hers, "I realize now . . ." Henry would know she had abandoned one illusion and was already firmly entrapped by the next. They became poor on her pursuits, lived in a basement; her illusions became sillier, shabbier, until finally she was sending in box-tops from cereal packages. Crow's feet appeared around her eyes, white hair among the gold; her skin became dry and papery. But as she got older something about her stayed young: the springing up of hope, the intoxicating energy, the creation of a new dream from the ruin of the old. From the despair of disillusion always she would find her way back: to a bell-like laughter with the rising note of an unfinished story, to a lilt of voice like the leap of water before rapids, to a wild dancing grace of legs and hips like a horse before a jump, to the happy eyes so easily wet with sympathy or love. . . .

One afternoon Lorabelle came home in a rapturous mood. "Oh, Henry, I've met the most wonderful man! A graduate student of Far Eastern studies and . . . you know, sort of a mystic himself . . . such a spiritual quality . . . name is Semelrad Apfelbaum . . . gives seminars on Buddhism." "Sounds like the real thing all right," Henry said bitterly. After dinner Lorabelle put on a diaphanous dress of black chiffon with a flowing lavender scarf, a gold chain around her neck, a sapphire on her finger, perfume in her hair. "Where are you going?" Henry said. "To meet Semelrad," she said; "he's so wonderfully kind, and so generous . . . is going to tutor me privately till I catch up with the class." "You're not going anywhere," Henry said. "I'm not a child, Henry," Lorabelle said with dignity. "But you *are* — precisely," Henry said. Lorabelle reminded him that theirs was a relationship of equality, with the same rights, that she must live her own life, make her own decisions, her own mistakes if need be; and when this failed to convince him she tossed back her head, affected great hauteur, and marched out of the room. Henry caught her at the door, turned her over his knee, applied the flat of his hand to the bottom of his delight; and it was perhaps that same night — for she did not go out — that Lorabelle got pregnant, and this time didn't lose it: the baby was born on Christmas, blue eyes and golden hair and they named her Noel.

Henry built a house of solid brick in a meadow of sage and thyme, and there Noel played with flowers and crickets and butterflies and field mice. Most of the time she was a joy to her parents, and some of the time — when she was sick or unkind — she was a sorrow. Lorabelle loved the brick house, painted walls, hung pictures, and polished floors; on hands and knees with a bonnet on her head she dug in the earth and planted flowers, looked up at Henry through a wisp of hair with a happy smile; "We'll never move again," she said. But one day the state sent them away and took over their house to build a freeway. The steel ball crashed through the brick walls, bulldozers sheared away the flower beds, the great shovels swung in, and the house was gone. Henry and Lorabelle and Noel moved back to the city, lived in a tiny flat under a water tank that dripped continuously on the roof and sounded like rain.

Henry and Lorabelle loved each other most of the time, tried to love each other all of the time, to create a pure bond, but could not. It was marred by the viciousness, shocking to them, with which they hurt each other. Out of nothing they would create fights, would yell at each other, hate, withdraw finally in bitter silent armistice; then, after a few hours, or sometimes a few days, would come together again, with some final slashes and skirmishes, and try to work things out — to explain, protest, forgive, understand, forget, and above all to compromise. It was a terribly painful and always uncertain process; and even while it was under way Henry would think bleakly, "It won't last, will never last; we'll get through this one maybe, probably, then all will be well for a while – a few hours, days, weeks if we're lucky – then another fight over something – what? – not possible to know or predict, and certainly not to prevent . . . and then all this to go through again; and beyond that still another fight looming in the mist ahead, coming closer . . . and so on without end." But even while thinking of these things he still would try to work through the current trouble because, as he would say, "There isn't anything else." And sometimes there occurred to him, uneasily, beyond all this gloomy reflection, an even more sinister thought: that their fights were not only unavoidable but also, perhaps, necessary; for their passages of greatest tenderness followed hard upon their times of greatest bitterness, as if love could be renewed only by gusts of destruction.

Nor could Henry ever build a house that would last forever, no more than anyone else; but he built one finally that lasted quite a while, a white house on a hill with lilac and laurel and three tall trees, a maple, a cedar, and a hemlock. It was an ordinary house of ordinary wood and the termites caused some trouble and always it needed painting or a new roof or a faucet dripped or something else needed fixing, and he grew old and gray and finally quite stooped doing these things, but that was all right, he knew, because there wasn't anything else.

Noel grew up in this house – a dreamy, soft-spoken girl, becoming more and more beautiful – wore her long hair in pigtails, practiced the piano, sang in a high true voice, played in the meadow, caught butterflies among the lilac. At nineteen she fell in love with Falbuck Wheeling who wore a tattered brown leather jacket and roared in on a heavy motorcycle dispelling peace and birds and butterflies, bringing noise and fumes and a misery Henry felt but could not define. Falbuck had a hard bitter face, said little, would sit at the kitchen table sullen and uncomfortable, and Henry could never get him into conversation because whatever the subject – literature, government, justice – Falbuck would sit staring at him, silent and disbelieving, until finally with a few labored and nasty words he would assert some rottenness behind the facade; then, as if exhausted by this excursion into communication, he would get up, taking Noel as if he owned her, and roar away. Noel spent her days with him and soon her nights, wore jeans and an old army shirt with the tails hanging out, let her hair hang loose and tangled, smoked cigarettes in a long black holder. Henry and Lorabelle talked earnestly to this wild, changed girl, now hardly recognizable as their daughter, advised caution and delay, but to no avail: she married Falbuck and went to live with him in a tiny room over a motorcycle shop. Henry and Lorabelle were left alone in the house on the hill, in peace now, with butterflies and the sound of wind in the three trees, and wished she were back.

Every morning Henry took his tools and went to his work of building houses — saw the pyramid of white sand spreading out in the grass, the bricks chipping, the doors beginning to stick, the first tone of gray appearing on white lumber, the first leaf falling in the bright gutter — but kept on hammering and kept on sawing, joining boards and raising rafters; on week-ends he swept the driveway and mowed the grass, in the evenings fixed the leaking faucets, tried to straighten out the disagreements with Lorabelle; and in all that he did he could see himself striving toward a condition of beauty or truth or goodness or love that did not exist, but whereas earlier in his life he had always said, "It's an illusion" and turned away, now he said "There isn't anything else" and stayed with it; and though it cannot be said that they lived happily, exactly, and certainly not ever after, they did live. They lived — for a while — with ups and downs, good days and bad, and when it came time to die Lorabelle said, "Now we'll never be parted," and Henry smiled and kissed her and said to himself, "There isn't anything else," and they died.

POSITIVE PRINCIPLES*

Gordon W. Allport

In his classical work *The Nature of Prejudice*, Gordon Allport presented a comprehensive description of the psychological and sociological causes and manifestations of prejudice. In this passage, he summarizes some general principles, derived from social science research, which may be used as guidelines in attempting to reduce prejudiced behavior in our society. While these principles were written approximately two decades ago, many of them appear to be applicable to our current problems of bigotry and discrimination.

1. Since the problem is many-sided, there can be no sovereign formula. The wisest thing to do is to attack all fronts simultaneously. If no single attack has large effect, yet many small attacks from many directions

*Reprinted with permission. From Gordon W. Allport, *The Nature of Prejudice*. Reading, Mass.: Addison-Wesley, 1954, pp. 507–510.

can have large cumulative results. They may even give the total system a push that will lead to accelerated change until a new and more agreeable equilibrium is attained.

2. Meliorism should be our guide. People who talk in terms of the ultimate assimilation of all minority groups into one ethnic stock are speaking of a distant Utopia. To be sure, there would be no minority-group problems in a homogeneous society, but it seems probable that in the United States our loss would be greater than our gain. In any case, it is certain that artificial attempts to hasten assimilation will not succeed. We shall improve human relations only by learning to live with racial and cultural pluralism for a long time to come.

3. It is reasonable to expect that our efforts will have some unsettling effects. The attack on a system always has. Thus a person who has been exposed to the intercultural education, to tolerance propaganda, to role-playing, may show greater inconsistency of behavior than before. But from the point of view of attitude change, this state of "unstructuredness" is a necessary stage. A wedge has been driven. While the individual may be more uncomfortable than before, he has at least a chance of recentering his outlook in a more tolerable manner. Investigation shows that people who are aware of and ashamed of, their prejudices are well on the road to eliminating them.[4]

4. Occasionally there may be a "boomerang effect." Efforts may serve only to stiffen opposition in defense of existing attitudes, or offer people unintended support for their hostile opinions.[5] Such evidence as we have indicates that this effect is relatively slight. It also is a question whether the effect may not be temporary, for any strategy sufficiently effective to arouse defensiveness may at the same time plant seeds of misgiving.

5. From what we know of mass media, it seems wise not to expect marked results from this method alone. Relatively few people are in the precise stage of "unstructuredness," and in precisely the right frame of mind, to admit the message. Further, it seems well, on the basis of existing evidence, to focus mass propaganda on specific issues rather than upon vague appeals that may not be understood.

6. The teaching and publishing of scientifically sound information concerning the history and characteristics of groups, and about the nature of prejudice, certainly does no harm. Yet it is not the panacea that many educators like to believe. The outpouring of information probably has three benign effects: (a) It sustains the confidence of minorities to see an effort being made to blanket prejudice with truth. (b) It encourages and

reinforces tolerant people by integrating their attitudes with knowledge. (c) It tends to undermine the rationalization of bigots. Belief in the biological inferiority of the Negro, for example, is wavering under the impact of scientific fact; racist doctrines today are on the defensive. Erroneous ideas, Spinoza observed, lead to passion—for they are so confused that no one can use them as a basis for realistic adjustment. Correct and adequate ideas, by contrast, pave the way for a true assessment of life's problems. While not everyone will admit correct ideas when they are offered, it is well to make them available.

7. Action is ordinarily better than mere information. Programs do well therefore to involve the individual in some project, perhaps a community self-survey or a neighborhood festival. When he *does* something, he *becomes* something. The deeper the acquaintance and the more realistic the contacts, the better the results.

By working in the community, for example, the individual may learn that neither his self-esteem nor his attachments are actually threatened by Negro neighbors. He may learn that his own security as a citizen is strengthened when social conditions improve. While preaching and exhortation may play a part in the process, the lesson will not be learned at the verbal level alone. It will be learned in muscle, nerve, and gland best through participation.

8. None of our commonly used methods likely to work with bigots whose character structure is so inaccessible that it demands the exclusion of out-groups as a condition of life. Yet even for the rigid person there is left the possibility of individual therapy—an expensive method and one that is sure to be resisted; but in principle at least, we need not yet despair completely of the extreme case, especially if tackled young, perhaps at clinics of child guidance, or by wise teachers.

9. While there is no relevant research on the point, it seems likely that ridicule and humor help to prick the pomposity and irrational appeal of rabble-rousers. Laughter is a weapon against bigotry. It too often lies rusty while reformers grow unnecessarily solemn and heavy-handed.

10. Turning now to social programs (the social system), there is first of all considerable agreement that it is wiser to attack segregation and discrimination than to attack prejudice directly. For even if one dents the attitudes of the individual in isolation, he is still confronted by social norms that he cannot surmount. And until segregation is weakened, conditions will not exist that permit equal-status contacts in pursuit of common objectives.

11. It would seem intelligent to take advantage of the vulnerable points where social change is most likely to occur. As Saenger says, "Concentrate on the areas of least resistance." Gains in housing and economic opportunities are, on the whole, the easiest to achieve. Fortunately, it is these very gains that minorities most urgently desire.

12. Generally speaking, a *fait accompli* that fits in with our democratic creed is accepted with little more than an initial flurry of protest. Cities that introduce Negroes into public jobs find that the change soon ceases to attract attention. Sound legislation is similarly accepted. Official policies, once established, are hard to revoke. They set models that, once accepted, create habits and conditions favorable to their maintenance.

Administrators, more than they realize, have the power to establish desirable changes by executive order in industry, government, and schools. In 1848 a Negro applied for admission to Harvard College. There were loud protests. Edward Everett, then President, replied, "If this boy passes the examinations he will be admitted and, if the white students choose to withdraw, all the income of the college will be devoted to his education."[6] Needless to say, no one withdrew, and the opposition quickly subsided. The College lost neither income nor prestige, though both at first seemed threatened. Clean-cut administrative decisions that brook no further argument are accepted when such decisions are in keeping with voice of conscience.

13. The role of the militant reformer must not be forgotten. It is the noisy demands of crusading liberals that have been a decisive factor in many of the gains thus far made.

These conclusions represent some of the positive principles that derive from research and theory. They are not intended as a complete blueprint — such would be pretentious. The points represent rather certain wedges which if driven with skill might be expected to crack the crust of prejudice and discrimination.

Notes and References

4. Cf. G. W. Allport and B. M. Kramer. Some roots of prejudice. *Journal of Psychology*, 1946, **22**, 9–39.

5. C. I. Hovland, *et al.* Experiments in Mass Communication. Princeton: Univ. Press, 1949, 46–50.

6. Quoted by P. R. Frothingham. *Edward Everett, Orator and Statesman*. Boston: Houghton Mifflin, 1925, 299.

RESISTANCE TO CHANGE*

Goodwin Watson

In the Allport selection, we were introduced to guidelines which might be used in changing people's prejudiced attitudes and behavior. Mr. Watson acknowledges that any attempt to bring about significant changes will be met by resistance. He describes some of the major sources of resistance to innovation and presents some recommendations for reducing resistance when one is involved in the process of changing people and systems.

This article emphasizes the importance of taking into account reactions to change, as well as the actual change. In many communities where new programs are being instituted, adequate attention has not been given to the impact which innovations will have on the people who are affected by these changes.

All of the forces which contribute to stability in personality or in social systems can be perceived as resisting change. From the standpoint of an ambitious and energetic change agent, these energies are seen as obstructions. From a broader and more inclusive perspective the tendencies to achieve, to preserve, and to return to equilibrium are most salutary. They permit the duration of character, intelligent action, institutions, civilization and culture.

Lewin's (1951) concept of apparently static systems as in "quasi-stationary equilibrium" has directed attention to the importance of reducing resistance if change is to be accomplished with minimal stress. The more usual strategies of increasing pressures by persuasion and dissuasion raise tensions within the system. If the opposite strategy — that of neutralizing or transforming resistance — be adopted, the forces for change already present in the system-in-situation will suffice to produce movement. For example, administrators may try by exhortation to get teachers to pay more attention to individual differences among pupils. Or, they may analyze the factors which now prevent such attention (e.g. large classes, single textbooks, standard tests) and by removing these pressures release a very natural tendency for teachers to adapt to the different individual pupils.

During the life of a typical innovation or change-enterprise, perceived

*Reproduced by special permission from "Resistance to Change," Goodwin Watson (ed.), *Concepts for Social Change*, Cooperative Project for Educational Development Series, Vol. I (Washington, D.C.: National Training Laboratories, 1966).

resistance moves through a cycle. In the early stage, when only a few pioneer thinkers take the reform seriously, resistance appears massive and undifferentiated. "Everyone" knows better; "No one in his right mind" could advocate the change. Proponents are labelled crack-pots and visionaries. In the second stage, when the movement for change has begun to grow, the forces pro and con become identifiable. The position can be defined by its position in the social system and its power appraised. Direct conflict and a show-down mark the third stage, as resistance becomes mobilized to crush the upstart proposal. Enthusiastic supporters of a new idea have frequently underestimated the strength of their opponents. Those who see a favored change as good and needed, find it hard to believe the lengths to which opposition will go to squelch that innovation. This third stage is likely to mean life or death to the proposed reform. Survival is seen as depending on building up power to overcome the enemy. Actually, as Lewin's force-field analysis indicates, an easier and more stable victory can be won by lowering the potency of the opposing forces. The fourth stage, after the decisive battles, finds supporters of the change in power. The persisting resistance is, at this stage, seen as a stubborn, hide-bound, cantankerous nuisance. For a time, the danger of a counter-swing of the pendulum remains real. Any conspicuous failure of the reform may mobilize latent opposition which, jointed with the manifest reactionaries, could prove sufficient to shift the balance of power. Strategy in this fourth stage demands wisdom in dealing, not only with the overt opponents, but with the still dissonant elements within the majority which appears, on the whole, to have accepted the innovation. Many teachers of a "new math" today may be less than wholehearted about its value. In a fifth stage, the old adversaries are as few, and as alienated as were the advocates in the first stage. The strategic situation is now that new change-enterprises are appearing and the one-time fighters for the old innovation (e.g. junior high schools) are being seen as resisters of the emerging change. (Edwards, 1927.)

At each stage of the innovation, from its inception to its defense as status quo, wise strategy requires perceptive analysis of the nature of the resistance. For purposes of this study, we shall focus first on the forces of resistance as they operate within the individual personality. Then we shall inventory the forces most easily identified in the social system. This is, of course, an arbitrary separation, utilized to facilitate the recognition of factors. In reality, the forces of the social system operate within the individuals and those attributed to separate personalities combine to constitute systemic forces. The two work as one.

A. Resistance in Personality

1. Homeostasis

Some of the stabilizing forces within organisms have been described by Cannon (1932) as "homeostasis." The human body has built-in regulatory mechanisms for keeping fairly constant such physiological states as temperature or blood sugar. Exercise increases pulse rate, but "resistance" to this change presently brings the heart-beat back to normal. Appetites rise, are satisfied and the organism returns to its steady state. Raup (1925) generalized the reversion to *complacency* as the most basic characteristic of the psychological as well as the physiological behavior of man.

The conception of organisms as naturally complacent unless disturbed by intrusive stimuli has had to be modified in recent years because of contradictory evidence showing a hunger for stimulation. Years ago, W. I. Thomas proposed the "desire for new experience" as one of the four most basic wishes underlying human behavior. (Thomas, Znaniecki, 1918–20.) Observers of rats, dogs, and chimpanzees have noted an "exploratory motive" strong enough to counterbalance fear of the unknown (Hebb, 1958, p. 171). Experiments with perceptual isolation of human subjects showed that lying quietly awake in a comfortable bed, free from disturbing stimuli, soon became intolerable. People need to interact with a changing environment (Lilly, 1956).

Frequently, educational changes prove temporary. For a time, after sensitivity training, a school principal may be more open and receptive to suggestions from teachers. But with time, the forces which made him behave as he did before training, return him to his own more brusque and arbitrary manner.

2. Habit

Most learning theory has included the assumption that unless the situation changes noticeably, organisms will continue to respond in their accustomed way. At least one psychologist (Stephens, 1965) has argued that the *repetition* of a response – often used as a criterion for having "learned" it – offers no conceptual problem. The model resembles a machine which, unless something significant is altered, will continue to operate in a fixed fashion. There should be no need for repeated exercise or for a satisfying effect to "stamp in" the learned response; once the circuit is connected it should operate until rearranged. Once a habit is established, its operation often becomes satisfying to the organism. Gordon

Allport (1937) has introduced the term "functional autonomy" to refer to the fact that activities first undertaken as a means to some culminating satisfaction often become intrinsically gratifying. The man accustomed after dinner to his chair, pipe and newspaper may resist any change in the details of his routine. The term "bus man's holiday" reflects the fact that men sometimes enjoy continuing in free time an activity which has been part of their required work. The concept of functional autonomy is probably too inclusive. Not all activities which are often repeated take on the character of drives. We have no wholly correct basis for predicting which habits will show most intrinsic resistance to change.

Sometimes a new educational practice – e.g. a changed form of teacher's class record book or report card arouses much resistance. After it has been established, perhaps with some persuasion and coercion, it becomes as resistant to change as was its predecessor. The familiar is preferred.

3. *Primacy*

The way in which the organism first successfully copes with a situation sets a pattern which is unusually persistent. Early habits of speech may be recognized despite much effort in later life to change. A child who has several times heard a story told in certain words is likely to be annoyed if the key phrases are not repeated exactly when the story is retold. Part of the joy in familiar music is the accord between established expectations and the flow of melody and harmony. Dreams of adults are often located in the settings of childhood. Even in senility, the recent experiences fade first, and the earliest associations persist longest. All later concepts perforce build on some of the earliest generalizations.

It is often observed that teachers, despite in-service courses and supervisory efforts, continue to teach as they themselves were taught. Their image of a teacher was formed in childhood and whenever they hear or read anything about better teaching, this is assimilated to that early and persisting concept.

4. *Selective Perception and Retention*

Once an attitude has been set up, a person responds to other suggestions within the framework of his established outlook. Situations may be perceived as reinforcing the original attitude when they actually are dissonant. Thus, in one famous experiment, a common stereotype associating Negroes with carrying razors, led observers of a cartoon to think they had seen the razor in the hands of the Negro rather than the white man

(Allport, Postman, 1945). Experiments with materials designed to bring about changes in attitude revealed that subjects did not hear clearly, nor remember well, communications with which they disagreed (Watson, Hartman, 1939; Levine, Murphy, 1943). It is a common observation that people usually prefer news sources, whether in print or broadcast, with which they are already in agreement. (Klapper, 1960.) By reading or listening to what accords with their present views; by misunderstanding communications which, if correctly received, would not be consonant with pre-established attitudes; and by conveniently forgetting any learning which would lead to uncongenial conclusions, subjects successfully resist the possible impact of new evidence upon their earlier views. There are relatively few instances in which old prejudices have been changed by better information or persuasive arguments.

The thousands of teachers who are exposed in graduate courses to different philosophies of education from those the teachers are accustomed to employ may do very well at answering test questions about the new approach but they carefully segregate in their mind, the new as "theory which, of course, would not work in the practical situation."

5. *Dependence*

All human beings begin life dependent upon adults who incorporate ways of behaving that were established before the newcomer arrived on the scene. Parents sustain life in the helpless infant and provide major satisfactions. The inevitable outcome is conservative. Children tend to incorporate (imitate, introject) the values, attitudes and beliefs of those who care for them.

All teachers were once beginners in the lower grades. At that time, their teachers loomed large and influential, whether friendly or hostile. The little pupil had to conform. His later adoption of the kind of teaching he then experienced is as natural as his acceptance of a particular alphabet and number-system.

There may later, in adolescence, be outbursts of rebellion and moves toward independent thought. But the typical adult still agrees far more than he disagrees with his parents on such basic items as language, religion, politics, child-rearing, and what a school should do.

6. *Superego*

Freud (1922) conceived one of the basic personality functions as engaged in the enforcement of the moral standards acquired in childhood from authoritative adults. From the first "No! No!" said to the baby, on through all the socializing efforts of parents, a code of controls is internalized. When the Oedipus complex is resolved, the child sets standards for himself corresponding to his image of the perfect and omnipotent parent. Any violation of these demanding rules is punished with a severity, the energy of which is derived from the attachment to parents as this operated in the Oedipal period — age three to five.

Here, then, in the Superego, is a powerful agent serving tradition. The repressive constraints which operate — partly unconsciously — do not derive from the realities of life in the present or the preceding generation. The Superego of the child corresponds to the Superego of the parent, not to his rational conclusions based on experience. Each mother and father passes on a heritage of taboos which he, in his childhood, acquired from ages past. An individual needs considerable ego-strength to become able to cope realistically with changing life situations in disregard of the unrealistic, perfectionistic demands of his Superego.

There is reason to believe that people who choose occupations in which they try to inculcate higher standards in others (clergymen, teachers, law-enforcement) are persons with extra strong Superego components. They take pride in making severe demands on themselves and on others. They bitterly resist any change which they conceive to be a relaxation of the firmest discipline and the highest expectations of perfection in performance. The influx of less able students into secondary schools and colleges has created almost intolerable conflict in teachers who still require achievement at levels which few can attain.

7. Self-Distrust

As a consequence of the dependence of childhood and the stern authority of the tradition-oriented voice of the Superego, children quickly learn to distrust their own impulses. Each says, in effect, "What I would really want is bad! I should not want it!"

John Dewey in *Human Nature and Conduct* (1922) saw the possibility of human betterment in the liberation of the creative impulses of youth. "The young are not as yet subject to the full impact of established customs. Their life of impulsive activity is vivid, flexible, experimenting, curious." What Dewey did not say is that within each young person there are powerful forces condemning and repressing any impulses which do not correspond to the established routines, standards and the institutions of society as it is and has been. The Puritan view that the enjoyable is evil gets a firm hold on children. Every clash between their desires and what adults expect of them, adds an increment to each child's self-rejection: "They must be right; I must be naughty to have such terrible feelings." Thus guilt is mobilized to prevent action for change. Men conclude that they are not worthy of any better life. To be "good" is to accept the *status quo ante*. Agitators and rebels speak with the voice of the evil serpent and should not be heeded.

The author, during the depth of the economic depression, found that most of a sample of unemployed men did not lay the blame for their predicament on faulty social mechanisms. Rather, they internalized the responsibility. They said, "I ought to have stayed on in school"; or "It was my fault that I lost the job; I shouldn't have said what I did!"; or "I should have waited to get married and have a family." Only about one in five wanted to change the economic system; the majority blamed themselves only (Watson, 1941).

Innumerable pupils, parents, teachers and administrators have felt impulses to alter school procedures. Most of these have been stifled by a feeling which is suggested by the expression: "Who am I to suggest changes in what the wisdom of the past has established?"

8. *Insecurity and Regression*

A further obstacle to effective participation in social change is the tendency to seek security in the past. The golden age of childhood is a Paradise Lost. When life grows difficult and frustrating, individuals think with nostalgia about the happy days of the past.

The irony is that this frustration-regression sequence enters life at just the time when change would be most constructive. When old ways no longer produce the desired outcome, the sensible recourse would be to experiment with new approaches. But individuals are apt at such a time to cling even more desperately to the old and unproductive behavior patterns. They are dissatisfied with the situation, but the prospect of change arouses even more anxiety, so they seek somehow to find a road back to the old and (as they now see it) more peaceful way of life.

Demands for change in school organization and practice become acute as a result of such social changes as automation, rapid travel to other lands, or racial desegregation. The reaction of insecure teachers, administrators and parents, is, too often, to try to hold fast to the familiar or even to return to some tried-and-true fundamentals which typify the schools of the past. A candidate for State Superintendent of Schools in California based his successful campaign in the mid-1960's, on return to the old-fashioned. The fact that California had been changing more rapidly in population, occupations, etc. than had any other state, was one factor in the appeal of this program of reaction.

B. Resistance to Change in Social Systems

1. Conformity to Norms

Norms in social systems correspond to habits in individuals. They are customary and expected ways of behaving. Members of the organization demand of themselves and of other members conformity to the institutional norms. This is the behavior described by Whyte in *The Organization Man* (1956). It includes time schedules; modes of dress; forms of address to colleagues, superiors and subordinates; indications of company loyalty; personal ambition to rise; appropriate consumption; and forms of approved participation in recreation and community life. Teachers, even more than businessmen, have been expected to exemplify certain proper behaviors.

Norms make it possible for members of a system to work together. Each knows what he may expect in the other. The abnormal or anomic is disruptive.

Because norms are shared by many participants, they cannot easily change. Above all, the usual individual cannot change them. He can get himself rejected for deviate behavior, but the norm will persist. A laboratory experiment (Merei, 1949) showed that even a child with strong leadership qualities was required, nevertheless, to conform to the established play norms of a small group of kindergarten children. An excellent teacher who declined to submit the prescribed advance lesson plans for each week, did not alter the norm; he was fired.

When one person deviates noticeably from the group norm, a sequence of events may be expected. The group will direct an increasing amount of communication toward him, trying to alter his attitude. If this fails, one after another will abandon him as hopeless. Communication to him will decrease. He may be ignored or excluded. He no longer belongs (Festinger, Thibaut, 1951).

The famous experiments, led by Lewin during the war, on altering norms of eating, indicated that changes are better introduced by group-decision than by expecting individuals to pioneer a practice not being used by their associates (Lewin, 1952).

The evidence indicates that if norms are to be altered, this will have to occur throughout the entire operating system. The sad fate of experimental schools and colleges (Miles, 1964) indicates the power of the larger system to impose its norms even on units which have been set apart, for a time, to operate by different standards and expectations.

2. *Systematic and Cultural Coherence*

The Gestalt principle that parts take on characteristics because of their relationship within the whole, implies that it is difficult to change one part without affecting others. Innovations which are helpful in one area may have side-effects which are destructive in related regions. For example, a technical change which increased the efficiency of pieceworkers in a factory enabled them to earn more than supervisors were being paid, so the new technique had to be abandoned. Electronic data processing in another company altered the size and relative responsibilities of related departments, generating considerable resentment (Mann, Neff, 1961). Studying change in a city Y.M.C.A., Dimock and Sorenson (1955) concluded: "No part of institutional change is an 'island unto itself'; changes in program call for changes in every other part of the institution . . . . and advance in one sector cannot proceed far ahead of change in other sectors. For example, program groups cannot be changed without officer training . . . which in turn is contingent upon advisor training . . . which in turn depends upon staff reeducation. Similarly, changes in staff goals and ways of working are dependent upon administrative procedures, policies and budgets which in turn require changes in Boards and Committees." A parallel statement for school systems might indicate that a change in teacher-pupil relationships is likely to have repercussions on teacher-principal interaction, on parent-principal contacts, on pressure groups operating on the superintendent, on Board member chances for re-election, and perhaps on the relationship of the local system to state or Federal agencies. Any estimate of resistance which takes account only of the persons primarily and centrally concerned will be inadequate; the repercussions elsewhere may be even more influential in the survival of the innovation.

3. *Vested Interests*

The most obvious source of resistance is some threat to the economic or prestige interests of individuals. A school consolidation which eliminates some Board members and a principal is unlikely to receive their warm support, although such cases have occurred. The most common resistance to educational improvements which would cost money comes from organized or unorganized taxpayers. Mort (1941) found that desirable school innovations were most likely to be adopted by communities with high financial resources. Poverty has been—at least until the recent anti-poverty program—a block to educational experimenting. The writer (Watson, 1946) found likewise that Y.M.C.A.'s located in communities with high volume of retail sales per capita were more likely to adopt recommended new practices.

A "vested interest" may be in freedom to operate as one pleases, quite as truly as in money-income or title on the door. Centralizing control of school decisions is usually unwelcome to the persons who would otherwise be making decisions in local school neighborhoods or classrooms.

Concern for school taxes and for positions on school boards is likely to center in the upper classes of the community. They are the people who have most power and influence. Newspapers and broadcasting are more accessible to them than to the underprivileged. A few powerful political or financial interests can block programs desired by a large majority of ordinary citizens. The influence of upperclass families on school policies is vividly portrayed in Hollingshead's *Elmtown's Youth* (1949).

4. The Sacrosanct

Anthropologists have observed that, within any culture, some activities are easily changed; others are highly resistant to innovation. Generally, the technology is receptive to new ideas and procedures. The greatest resistance concerns matters which are connected with what is held to be sacred. Some women can become managers of business or presidents of colleges in our male-dominated society, but they find it almost impossible to become a priest, rabbi, a bishop or pope in a conservative denomination. Translations of Scriptures into the vernacular have met strong disapproval. The ritual reading of some verses from the Bible or the recitation of a prayer is held onto with far more fervor than is spent on retention of school texts or equipment. Traditional ceremonies are apt to persist despite doubts as to their educational impact. The closer any reform comes to touching some of the taboos or rituals in the community, the more likely it is to be resisted. Introduction of improved technology in underdeveloped countries runs into formidable obstacles if it seems to impinge on religious superstitions, beliefs or practices (Spicer, 1952).

Cultures resist almost as stubbornly, alterations which enter the realm of morals and ethics. Even when few live by the traditional code, it must still be defended as "ideal" (Linton, 1945). A well-recognized illustration is the expectation of sexual continence between puberty and marriage. Kinsey may find very few youths who practice it, but schools, churches and courts must operate as if the prescription were unquestionable.

There is a clear connection between the operation of the Superego in individuals and the taboos persisting in the culture. Both uphold impossibly high standards and react punitively to recognized infractions of the excessive demands.

5. Rejection of "Outsiders"

Most change comes into institutions from "outside." Griffiths studying change in school systems concluded, "The major impetus for change in organizations is from outside" (in Miles, 1964, p. 431).

Few psychological traits of human beings are so universal as that of suspicion and hostility toward strange outsiders. Kohler (1922) observed this kind of behavior among his chimpanzees on the Island of Tenerife many years ago. Wood (1934) has explored, across different cultures, the mixture of curiosity and antagonism toward foreigners. A typical attack on any new proposal is that it doesn't fit our local conditions. Struggles to improve labor and race relations have commonly been discounted as inspired by "outside agitators" or "atheistic Communists." Research, development and engineering units are familiar with the way in which a new project is hampered if it is seen as NIH (not invented here).

The history of experimental demonstration schools is that they were often observed but seldom replicated. "This is fine, but it wouldn't work in our system." Differences in class of children, financial support, equipment and tradition helped to rationalize the resistance. The genius of agricultural agents a century ago led them away from model farms run by state colleges and toward demonstration projects within the local neighborhood. Farmers accepted what was being done within their county when they could not import new practices from far away.

A major problem in introducing social change is to secure enough local initiative and participation so the enterprise will not be vulnerable as a foreign-importation.

Summary of Recommendations

Our observations on sources of resistance within persons and within institutions can be summarized in some concise principles. These are not absolute laws but are based on generalizations which are usually true and likely to be pertinent. The recommendations are here re-organized to fit three headings: (1) Who brings the change? (2) What kind of change succeeds? and (3) How is it best done?

A. *Who brings the change?*

1. Resistance will be less if administrators, teachers, Board members and community leaders feel that the project is their own — not one devised and operated by outsiders.
2. Resistance will be less if the project clearly has wholehearted support from top officials of the system.

B. *What kind of change?*

3. Resistance will be less if participants see the change as reducing rather than increasing their present burdens.
4. Resistance will be less if the project accords with values and ideals which have long been acknowledged by participants.
5. Resistance will be less if the program offers the kind of *new* experience which interests participants.
6. Resistance will be less if participants feel that their autonomy and their security is not threatened.

C. *Procedures in instituting change*

7. Resistance will be less if participants have joined in diagnostic efforts leading them to agree on what the basic problem is and to feel its importance.
8. Resistance will be less if the project is adopted by consensual group decision.
9. Resistance will be reduced if proponents are able to empathize with opponents; to recognize valid objections; and to take steps to relieve unnecessary fears.
10. Resistance will be reduced if it is recognized that innovations are likely to be misunderstood and misinterpreted, and if provision is made for feedback of perceptions of the project and for further clarification as needed.
11. Resistance will be reduced if participants experience acceptance, support, trust, and confidence in their relations with one another.

12. Resistance will be reduced if the project is kept open to revision and reconsideration if experience indicates that changes would be desirable.

References

Allport, G. W. *Personality: A Psychological Interpretation.* New York: Holt, Rinehart and Winston, Inc., 1937.

Allport, G. W. and L. J. Postman. The basic psychology of rumor. *Transactions of N.Y. Academy of Sciences*, Series II, 1945, **8**: 61–81.

Cannon, W. B. *Wisdom of the Body.* New York: W. W. Norton & Company, Inc., 1932.

Dewey, John. *Human Nature and Conduct.* New York: Holt, Rinehart and Winston, Inc., 1922.

Dimock, H. S. and Roy Sorenson. *Designing Education in Values: A Case Study in Institutional Change.* New York, Association Press, 1955.

Edwards, L. P. *The Natural History of Revolution.* Chicago: University of Chicago Press, 1927.

Festinger, Leon and John Thibaut. Interpersonal communication in small groups. *J. Abn. Soc. Psychol.*, 1951, **46**: 92–99.

Freud, Sigmund. *Beyond the Pleasure Principle.* London: Hogarth Press, Ltd., 1922.

Hebb, D. O. *A Textbook of Psychology.* Philadelphia: W. B. Saunders Company, 1958.

Hollingshead, A. B. *Elmtown's Youth.* New York: John Wiley & Sons, Inc., 1949.

Klapper, Joseph T. *Effects of Mass Communication,* New York: The Free Press, 1960.

Kohler, Wolfgang. Zur Psychologie des Shimpanzen. *Psychol. Forsehung*, 1922, **1**: 1–45.

Levine, M. M. and G. Murphy. The learning and forgetting of controversial material. *J. Abn. Soc. Psychol.*, 1943, **38**: 507–517.

Lewin, Kurt. *Field Theory in Social Science.* New York: Harper & Row, Publishers, 1951.

Lewin, Kurt. Group decision and social change. In G. E. Swanson, T. M. Newcomb, and E. L. Hartley, *Readings in Social Psychology.* New York: Holt, Rinehart and Winston, Inc., 1952, pp. 463–473.

Linton, Ralph. *The Cultural Background of Personality.* New York: Appleton-Century-Crofts, 1945.

Mann, F. C. and F. W. Neff. *Managing Major Change in Organizations.* Ann Arbor, Mich.: Foundation for Research on Human Behavior, 1961.

Merei, F. Group leadership and institutionalization. *Human Rela.*, 1949, **2**: 23–39.

Miles, M. B. (Ed.) *Innovation in Education.* New York: Bureau of Publications, Teachers College, Columbia University, 1964.

Mort, Paul R. and F. G. Cornell. *American Schools in Transition.* New York: Bureau of Publications, Teachers College, Columbia University, 1941.

Raup, R. B. *Complacency: The Foundation of Human Behavior.* New York: Crowell-Collier and Macmillan, Inc., 1925.

Spicer, E. H. *Human Problems in Technological Change.* New York: Russell Sage and Winston, Inc., 1952.

Stephens, J. A. *The Psychology of Classroom Learning.* New York: Holt, Rinehart and Winston, Inc., 1965.

Watson, Goodwin. *A Comparison of "adaptable" versus "laggard" Y.M.C.A.'s* New York: Association Press, 1946.

Watson, Goodwin. What Makes Radicals? *Common Sense*, 1941, **10**: 7–9.

Watson, W. S., Jr. and G. W. Hartman. The rigidity of a basic attitudinal frame. *J. Abn. Socl. Psychol.*, 1939, **34**: 314–335.
Whyte, William H., Jr. *The Organization Man*. New York: Simon and Schuster, Inc., 1956.
Wood, M. M. *The Stranger*, New York: Columbia University Press, 1934.

EXERCISES AND DISCUSSION TOPICS FOR CHAPTER 12

Exercises

1. Write the changes you have observed in your own attitudes percep-tions and behavior as a result of your participation in the simulation. Try to determine why these particular changes have occurred.
2. Write your attitudes toward the issue you have been dealing with in the simulation. Compare this with your attitudes at the beginning of the simulation. Note the changes (if any) that have occurred.
3. Identify some of the major agents of change in your community (church, school, etc.). Study how each contributes to individual change. What process of influence do each employ?

Discussion Topics

Which of Allport's positive principles have been operating in the simulation? How could these positive principles be applied to the real world?

Discuss factors which contribute to resistance to change. How do they operate? How do you remove barriers to individual change?

Social scientists have been debating whether it is more effective to change attitudes first or change behavior first. Discuss your opinions about which method is more effective in producing changes in individuals.

What are some examples of individual change that you have observed in the simulation?

CHAPTER 13

Group and Community Change

Effecting change in groups is not all that different from effecting change in individuals. Walton, in his article, p. 274, discusses two tactics of group change: those based on power and those based on interpersonal relations. The tactics using power can be fairly well equated to individual change based on reward and punishment while the tactic involving interpersonal relations is similar to the tactics of internalization or attitude change.

The use of power can be reduced to the ability of one party to reward or punish another party. If you have not the ability to punish someone for behavior you do not like or to reward him for behavior you do like, you really do not have much power over him. Power here should be defined very broadly. It may include liking or disliking someone. If you are trying out for fullback on the football team, it helps if the coach does not have a violent dislike for you. Similarly, your girlfriend's love is a powerful reward if she bestows it upon you, a powerful punishment if she does not. What is true for individuals is often true for groups, since groups are aggregates of individual people.

There is a likelihood of more variation in groups than in any single individual. A group of twenty people can conceivably have twenty different attitudes toward the same issue. This is not likely for issues about which the group members have a common concern; they would tend to gravitate to other groups. Nevertheless, there still may be quite a variety of individual attitudes in a single group; witness the Democratic party. Some groups in Psych City, composed of people with similar roles, may be expected to exhibit similar attitudes and consequent behaviors. In this case, what is rewarding or punishing for one member ought to be so for others. To the extent that groups are composed of unlike roles, the rewards and punishments for that group are likely to be less homogeneous. This is a problem in changing groups that is less evident when considering individual change.

What most groups of people do have in common is similarity of goals. Most of the groups in the simulation are formed to achieve an end which is important to each individual to some degree. Therefore, rewards and punishments should be directed toward helping or hindering the achievement of the common goals. If a group of minority group members in the simulation have the goal of increased busing, you can reward the group, as a whole, if you can help them achieve more busing in Psych City. In exchange, you should be able to get them to behave in a manner which helps you move closer to the goals implied by your role. Your power to do this lies in the power invested in your role and your ability to persuade and gain allies who have power.

The second kind of group change is that of attitude change. If a group in the simulation is behaving in a way which frustrates your attempts to accomplish something, you may be able to change that behavior if you are able to persuade a majority of that group that their attitudes are wrong. Suppose you are a white parent who is opposed to busing students. If you can persuade a group of minority group member parents that integration is not good for their children or that busing does more damage than segregation, you have a good chance of reducing their noxious behavior. Admittedly this is an extreme example. Try another. Say a group of white radicals has allied themselves with the minority group parents. You then convince these radicals that the minority group members are in league with the liberal power structure (which the radicals hate) and that teaching sex education will inevitably lead to tension and revolt which will destroy the Establishment; you may have a chance to break up the radical–minority group coalition. You will be able to find more realistic cases within the simulation. The important point is that the consistency-inconsistency formula can hold for groups as well as for individuals.

A third technique is to propose a goal which will unite some group with your own. All the participants in the simulation can come together if all decide that increasing welfare payments is good for all concerned. This particular outcome is unlikely because of the differences among characters. There are similar less ambitious alternatives however. It is your job to figure them out. Opposing groups can be united if both see a common goal. Some recent coalitions between blacks and lower-class white workers bear this out.

Another perspective on group change is given by Benne and Birnbaum in their article, p. 293. This is an analysis of the social forces bearing on any change situation. It is called force field analysis and involves reducing forces which impede progress toward a goal and bolstering forces which facilitate attainment of the goal. The ease with which you gain your objective depends upon the degree to which you are able to get your obstructors to stop obstructing and your allies to increase their aid. This may seem rather obvious but it is relatively rare that groups in conflict are able to sit back and take an objective view of the situation. An objective view involves taking a realistic look at the helping and opposing forces and deciding which ones can be minimized or maximized. Your efforts can then be directed toward changing those forces which are actually amenable to change. A white parents group may decide that it is unrealistic to try to change the behavior of a black parents group but may be able to change the white radicals. The radicals, may in turn decide nothing can be done about a segregationist group but the city council which supports them may be swayed by the right kind of political pressure.

Walton, in his article, p. 274, discusses tactics of change; Benne and Birnbaum, in their article, p. 293, focus on where to apply those tactics. Both viewpoints utilize the concept of equilibrium in some fashion. In force field analysis, you apply your tactics to change situational pressures and thus create disequilibrium in the situations similar to the way disequilibrium is induced in an individual. The induction of disequilibrium in the form of attitude change is, in turn, an aspect of a particular tactic for group change. This can be pulled together if you look at groups (and people) as systems or parts of systems. An individual person can be seen as a system of perceptions and attitudes which are related to each other. If you change one or more of these attitudes, you may effect change in other attitudes within the person. Similarly, people can be seen as elements of a group. These people are related to each other in a variety of ways and changing one or more of these individual people may effect change in the group as a whole. This is particularly true if the person(s) changed is one who is important to the group.

Finally, groups themselves can be seen as elements of a larger group, the society. As with people, groups relate to each other in many ways. Change in one or more groups can mean change in the society, especially when these are important groups. This is community psychology. It is a discipline which considers change and its effects at every point, from the single individual to the society as a whole. It involves first an understanding of the individual elements. Second, and possibly more important, it involves understanding how these elements (whether people or groups) relate to other aspects of the whole. Thirdly, community psychology is concerned with how change takes place among and within the elements as well as within the social whole, and how change can be implemented in a way which benefits not only society but its individual members — you!

CHAOS OVER SCHOOL BUSING*

U.S. News and World Report

In this selection, we are given a view of how two communities have actually reacted to the introduction of a large-scale social innovation: school busing. The article describes not only the scope of the problem, and the proposed plan of action, but also the reactions of some represen- tative citizens from these two cities.

The complexities of the problem and diversity of opinion regarding the appropriate manner in which to deal with it, as reported in this article, are indicative of how difficult it is to plan for an entire community. In your role as a participant in the simulation, you are viewing the problem from a single perspective. Imagine how difficult it would be to empathize with the needs and beliefs of many factions, and at the same time, con- struct a single workable plan which will adequately handle all phases of the problem.

Two cities — Charlotte, N.C., and Los Angeles, Calif. — are becoming major testing grounds of busing as a way to integrate schools.

Both cities have been commanded by courts to achieve in their schools racial mixes that cannot be obtained without massive use of such busing.

Many thousands of youngsters will be forced to ride long distances to attend schools outside their neighborhoods. The cost will run into millions of dollars.

Opposition is rising among parents — both black and white.

Local school officials are wondering how they will get the money to finance the busing. And, they say, that money could be spent much more profitably on improving education than on busing.

Far more than local problems is involved. Other cities, all across the country, are looking at what is happening to Charlotte and Los Angeles — wondering if it will happen to them, too.

High officials in the Federal Government are concerned.

*Reprinted from "U.S. News and World Report," March 16, 1970.

The U.S. Secretary of Health, Education and Welfare, Robert H. Finch, has spoken out strongly on the subject.

Courts, he said, "are moving in the wrong direction" by ordering such programs of integration.

In an interview with Metromedia Radio News on February 27, Mr. Finch was asked about the problem that big cities face in improving educational techniques for Negroes. He answered:

"All of these major metropolitan districts — North, South, East or West — need extra help, dollar help, for more facilities, for higher pay for teachers.

"This is the only way you're going to solve this. You don't solve it by busing — I mean by hiring more buses."

"*Unrealistic.*" Mr. Finch cited specifically the recent court orders in Charlotte and Los Angeles. He described those orders as "totally unrealistic."

"That's not the best use of your resources," he said. And he added:

"But beyond that, it's not the best educational experience, because to haul young children for an hour or more — across long distances, as you have, particularly in the Los Angeles situation — means they can't get any tutoring after school, the parents have great difficulty getting to the teacher to talk about their child.

"They (the pupils) can't take part in athletic events or dramatic events or extracurricular events — and it's not good educational policy. So I feel very strongly that these decisions are moving in the wrong direction."

For on-the-scene accounts, "U.S. News and World Report" sent members of its staff into the Charlotte and Los Angeles school districts. They talked to parents and officials.

Following are their reports — a tale of two cities.

A Southern City — Troubled, Angry, Divided

Charlotte, N.C.

The biggest busing-for-integration program in the entire South was ordered by a federal court to begin here on April 1.

It would compel at least 13,000 youngsters to ride buses far across town to attend school. Total travel time, for many pupils, would exceed three hours a day — up to four hours, for some.

Costs, as estimated by school officials, would be $3.8 millions at the start — including the purchase of 526 buses — and at least $500,000 a year hereafter.

The aim is to produce a racial mix of about 71 per cent white pupils and 29 per cent black pupils in each of the 107 public schools in the Charlotte–Mecklenburg School District.

That district includes not only the city of Charlotte but also surrounding Mecklenburg County. So, much of the busing would be between the inner city and the suburbs.

People vs. people   Since the integration order was issued on February 5 by U.S. District Judge James B. McMillan, Charlotte has become a troubled and angry city, divided bitterly between those people for and those against the busing.

Opponents, led by the Concerned Parents Association, have been the most vociferous. Groups of parents meet almost nightly to plan ways of preventing the execution of the busing plan. There have been mass demonstrations and picketing. Leaders on both sides of the controversy have reported telephoned threats against their lives.

At a stormy public meeting on February 24, cheers greeted this statement by the school board's attorney, William J. Waggoner: "Judge McMillan went too far in ordering busing to accomplish racial balance."

The school board then voted, 6 to 2, to appeal the ruling. And on March 5 it won a temporary delay of the busing while the Fourth U.S. Circuit Court of Appeals reviews the case.

Next: a boycott?   If the board's legal appeal fails eventually to block the busing, leaders of the Concerned Parents Association vow that they will undertake a boycott of the schools.

More than 23,000 Charlotte residents have signed petitions pledging not to send their children to classes, once busing begins.

"I'm willing to go to jail if I have to," says Dr. Jack V. Scott, vice president of the parents' group.

Cost is one factor in the opposition to busing.

"You can buy an awful lot of education for the 3 million dollars these new buses will cost," says Sam S. McNinch III, one of the antibusing majority on the school board. He contends that it would be a far better use of the money to "go into our existing schools and correct the inequities."

School authorities say they don't know how they can raise the money required. The State of North Carolina has a law forbidding the use of State funds for busing to achieve racial mixing.

Money, however, is only a part of the problem.

The tired child   Parents resent removal of their children from the nearby neighborhood schools. They fear the bus rides to distant schools through congested traffic, with the attendant risks of accidents and delays by traffic jams.

Many parents are afraid youngsters will arrive at school worn out and unfit for study. School officials point out that a substantial number of children will be unable to take part in extracurricular activities because so much of their time will be taken up riding buses.

"I don't want to be bused," says 15-year-old Oscar Moore, an eighth-grader at Coulwood Junior High School.

"I already leave home at 7:30 and get out of school at 3:15 in the afternoon. If we're bused, I won't be able to take part in athletics. There will only be time to study and go to bed."

Mrs. Emma Harrison, a Negro housewife, is one of those against busing, She told a member of the staff of "U.S. News and World Report":

"My little boy, Rudolph, is in the sixth grade at Double Oaks School. I can see the school from my window. Now they want him to be moved to a school 9 miles away. It's going to bring hardship on lots of little children."

The plan was drawn up—with the aid of computers—by a court-appointed consultant from Providence, R.I., after Judge McMillan rejected the local board's plan, which was based on geographic attendance zones.

A judge's reasons   Judge McMillan ruled that assigning pupils to "neighborhood" schools is "racially discriminatory" in a city of 275,000 population where Negroes "have become concentrated almost entirely in one quadrant" of the city. He said:

"The quality of public education should not depend on the economic or racial accident of the neighborhood in which a child's parents have chosen to live—or find they must live—nor on the color of his skin.". . .

So the judge ordered that no school should be permitted to have a predominantly black student body and that pupils of all grades should be assigned in such a way that "as nearly as practicable the various schools at various grade levels have about the same proportion of black and white pupils."

That proportion, he said, should be approximately the same as in the total school population of the district—71 whites to 29 blacks.

"Paired" schools   The plan that was devised for elementary schools works this way:

*Ten predominantly black schools in the inner city of Charlotte are "paired" with 24 predominantly white schools at the edges of the city or in suburbs.

*Black children are to be bused from the inner-city schools to the predominantly white schools and white children bused to the inner-city schools.

The average distance of each bus ride between a pair of these schools is estimated at about 15 miles and the average travel time at 1 hour and 10 minutes each way.

In addition, each child first must reach his neighborhood school, where he will board the transfer bus. Then, after being returned to his neighborhood school in the afternoon, he must still make his way back home.

For each of thousands of students, a bus or other transportation is required just to reach his neighborhood school from home. So the result, parents complain, can be a total of up to four hours riding to and from school.

Some additional busing may become necessary when new integration plans for junior and senior high schools go into effect on May 4.

Parents who approve   There are numerous parents in Charlotte who are willing to accept this busing in the belief that its advantages outweigh its disadvantages.

"I've never seen any trauma arising from a child riding a bus, or any kind of evil from a child riding a bus," says Mrs. Julia Maulden, a member of the school board who favors the busing. "But I have seen evil from segregation."

Leaders of the National Association for the Advancement of Colored People, who took part in the suit that brought the busing order, argue that the effect will be to improve the quality of education for Negroes.

Walter McDaniel, a member of the Interested Citizens Association, predominantly Negro, says this:

"It's time that this city decided to commit itself to total integration of all its citizens. If it takes busing to bring about racial integration, it's time to bus."

One effect of the controversy has been to speed the growth of private schools in this area. At present, there are 20 such schools, enrolling more than 3,600 students. Plans have been announced recently to create two new private schools, and several others are reported in the planning stages.

10 years of desegregation   All this is occurring in a city which has prided itself on moderation in race relations.

Desegregation was begun here, on a small scale, more than a decade ago. And most Charlotte residents thought that they had complied with the law by last autumn.

Then, with a combination of "neighborhood" school assignments and "free choice" of schools by students, about 83 per cent of the county's 85,000 students were attending schools that contained at least some children of both races.

Judge McMillan has ruled, however, that this is not enough.

As for the expense of the busing that may be required to achieve that integration, Judge McMillan said:

"Cost is not a valid legal reason for continued denial of constitutional rights."

A Western City — Pattern for North?

Los Angeles

What's happening here is watched as a sign of what lies ahead for many big cities outside the South.

Los Angeles has been ordered by a State court to undertake the biggest and most expensive program of school integration ever attempted in the United States.

If that order sticks, massive busing will be required here — and similar demands are almost sure to follow in many big cities of the North.

The results could be sweeping changes — and soaring costs — in the American system of public-school education.

The sheer numbers involved in the Los Angeles case are staggering. To produce the racial mix demanded by Judge Alfred Gitelson, about 240,000 youngsters would have to be loaded into buses each morning, driven as far as 25 miles across this traffic-choked city, and then be bused home again after school.

A fleet of 2,200 new 91-passenger school buses would be needed.

Cost to this already overtaxed school system is estimated by interim School Superintendent Robert E. Kelly at 40 millions the first year, and about 180 millions over the next eight years.

This money would have to be diverted from existing educational programs, Mr. Kelly says, and he warns that the result would be the "virtual destruction" of the school district.

Local and State Officials — and many parents — are fighting to block the busing before its scheduled beginning next September. An appeal from Judge Gitelson's ruling is planned. It could go all the way to the U.S. Supreme Court.

Thus, out of this case may come the first High Court ruling on the legality – or illegality – of the so-called *de facto* segregation that is found in the North. And Northern school boards may learn what, if anything, they must do about such segregation.

The case of Los Angeles is different from that of Charlotte because:

*Charlotte schools formerly were segregated by law – *de jure* – as were all Southern schools. The Supreme Court in 1954 clearly outlawed that kind of segregation, and the U.S. courts are charged with seeing that it is eliminated.

*The kind of segregation found in Los Angeles, however, was not created by law. School officials claim that it is *de facto* segregation, the results of blacks living in one area, whites in another and all children attending the schools in their neighborhoods.

The Supreme Court never has held that such segregation is unconstitutional.

Judge Gitelson, however, ruled that Los Angeles school officials, by their policies, have at least "perpetuated, if not created, segregation." He held it is a constitutional duty of the officials to take positive measures to integrate the races in schools.

Ratios: lopsided   There is no question that schools in the huge Los Angeles School District display lopsided racial ratios.

Jefferson High School, for example, has 2,381 Negroes out of a total enrollment of 2,417. Monroe High School, in the San Fernando Valley, has 3,968 whites in an enrollment of 4,202.

The Los Angeles Unified School District is unique in many ways. For one thing, it is larger than the city itself, including both incorporated and unincorporated towns outside the city limits.

Distances are great. The district extends roughly 60 miles from its northern to its southern limit, and almost 40 miles east to west. Its total area is 711 square miles.

Negroes are concentrated mostly in the south-central part of the district. To get the court-ordered racial mix in schools of that black area, it is quite possible that youngsters would have to be bused from the all-white San Fernando schools – a trip of some 20 miles on the crowded Golden State Freeway.

Another thing unique about the Los Angeles Unified School District is the variety of racial and ethnic groups that it contains. Of 653,000 pupils in the district, about 52 per cent are classified as white, 23.5 per cent as Negro, and 4 per cent as Oriental or American Indian. There is another ethnic group – those with Spanish surnames, mostly of Mexican descent.

They make up about 20 per cent of the school enrollment.
All except the whites are classified as minority groups.

School formula   In his attempt to get a representative mixture of these groups, the judge laid down these rules:

*No school in the district may have a minority enrollment that is more than 15 per cent above or below the district's over-all minority enrollment.

*If this 15 per cent formula proves unworkable in some cases, it may be adjusted somewhat.

*Under no circumstances, however, may any school have a minority enrollment that is less than 10 per cent or more than 50 per cent of the total.

It is this formula that compels such massive use of buses. And it is the busing requirement that is stirring the public anger.

Los Angeles Mayor Sam Yorty says he is against the idea that students should be "involuntarily forced to go long distances to accomplish a social purpose without obtaining the consent of the people." He calls this "a very dangerous thing."

The mayor predicts, too, that similar demands for busing are going to be made elsewhere around the country, with results that are "literally going to tear some of our cities apart."

Compulsory busing, Mr. Yorty warns, is "so explosive that it could polarize public opinion to the point of setting the nation against itself."

California Governor Ronald Reagan has ordered his legal staff to "take all possible action" to assist the Los Angeles board of education in its fight against the busing order.

"It will be the continuing policy of this administration to vigorously oppose—by all legal means—the forced busing of California school children," the Governor said.

Such forced busing, he warns, will "shatter the concept of the neighborhood school as a cornerstone of our educational system."

Mr. Reagan stresses that the cost of the massive operation would siphon off money needed for new classrooms, books and other instruction aids. The expense of just the first year of busing, it is estimated, would pay for the hiring of 4,200 new teachers.

Under such circumstances, the Governor says, forced busing is "utterly ridiculous" as well as of "questionable legality."

Many parents are equally unhappy with the busing order. Mexican Americans point out that their children would be taken from schools where teachers speak Spanish and put into schools where administrators and teachers lack experience with Latin-American pupils.

One Los Angeles mother, Mrs. Joan Leicht, said: "It's about time the Federal Government and others start concentrating on education instead of treating children like cattle."

One consequence of the busing, she predicted, would be a decline in parent participation in school activities: "You can't take part in such things if you have to drive across the city to the school where they take your children."

"I can't see spending kids' time and taxpayers' money to support busing and still not come up with any better education," said Ralph R. Welter, head of a highschool advisory committee.

A black father complains that "black youngsters risk losing their identity if they are bused out of their own neighborhoods." He suggests the money could be better spent by providing "incentive pay" to bring better teachers into the schools in black communities.

From Mrs. Claire Dolan, a Negro mother of five, came this comment:

"I'd rather they bused good teachers down here to Watts (a Negro area) than bus my kids away. If I were a white parent, and they were busing my kids to a substandard school, I wouldn't want them to be bused.

"At best, busing is a poor substitute for what we really need—a complete shake-up in the school system so that a kid can get a quality education no matter where he lives."

What is developing here is a test of busing for integration in the North, just as Charlotte is providing a test for the South.

Copyright 1970 U.S. News and World Report, Inc.

THE VERTICAL NEGRO PLAN*

Harry Golden

Mr. Golden has that rare ability to provoke laughter and serious thought with the same material. His observations and proposals related to social problems sometimes seem to be totally absurd. But, in recognizing the absurdity of his solution, one may also come to see the objectively ridiculous nature of the problem and some of the nonsolutions which are proposed in order to allow us to avoid confronting the actual problem.

Many of us would probably reject the solutions put forth in this essay. However, we might be well advised to harness some of the creative

*Reprinted by permission of The World Publishing Company from *Only in America* by Harry Golden. Copyright© 1958, 1957, 1956, 1955, 1954, 1953, 1951, 1949, 1948, 1944 by Harry Golden.

energy, employed by Mr. Golden, and apply it toward developing new strategies for solving community problems. Our current plans are noticeably lacking in imagination and creativity.

Those who love North Carolina will jump at the chance to share in the great responsibility confronting our Governor and the State Legislature. A special session of the Legislature (July 25–28, 1956) passed a series of amendments to the State Constitution. These proposals submitted by the Governor and his Advisory Education Committee included the following:

(A) The elimination of the compulsory attendance law, "to prevent any child from being forced to attend a school with a child of another race."

(B) The establishment of "Education Expense Grants" for education in a private school, "in the case of a child assigned to a public school attended by a child of another race."

(C) A "uniform system of local option" whereby a majority of the folks in a school district may suspend or close a school if the situation becomes "intolerable."

But suppose a Negro child applies for this "Education Expense Grant" and says he wants to go to the private school too? There are fourteen Supreme Court decisions involving the use of public funds; there are only two "decisions" involving the elimination of racial discrimination in the public schools.

The Governor has said that critics of these proposals have not offered any constructive advice or alternatives. Permit me, therefore, to offer an idea for the consideration of the members of the regular sessions. A careful study of my plan, I believe, will show that it will save millions of dollars in tax funds and eliminate forever the danger to our public education system. Before I outline my plan, I would like to give you a little background.

One of the factors involved in our tremendous industrial growth and economic prosperity is the fact that the South, voluntarily, has all but eliminated VERTICAL SEGREGATION. The tremendous buying power of the twelve million Negroes in the South has been based wholly on the absence of racial segregation. The white and Negro stand at the same grocery and supermarket counters; deposit money at the same bank teller's window; pay phone and light bills to the same clerk; walk through the same dime and department stores, and stand at the same drugstore counters.

It is only when the Negro "sets" that the fur begins to fly.

Now, since we are not even thinking about restoring VERTICAL SEGREGATION, I think my plan would not only comply with the Supreme Court decisions, but would maintain "sitting-down" segregation. Now here is the GOLDEN VERTICAL NEGRO PLAN. Instead of all those complicated proposals, all the next session needs to do is pass one small amendment which would provide *only* desks in all the public schools of our state — *no seats*.

The desks should be those standing-up jobs, like the old-fashioned bookkeeping desk. Since no one in the South pays the slightest attention to a VERTICAL NEGRO, this will completely solve our problem. And it is not such a terrible inconvenience for young people to stand up during their classroom studies. In fact, this may be a blessing in disguise. They are not learning to read sitting down, anyway; maybe standing up will help. This will save more millions of dollars in the cost of our remedial English course when the kids enter college. In whatever direction you look with the GOLDEN VERTICAL NEGRO PLAN, you save millions of dollars, to say nothing of eliminating forever any danger to our public education system upon which rests the destiny, hopes, and happiness of this society.

My WHITE BABY PLAN offers another possible solution to the segregation problem — this time in a field other than education.

Here is an actual case history of the "White Baby Plan to End Racial Segregation":

Some months ago there was a revival of the Laurence Olivier movie, *Hamlet*, and several Negro schoolteachers were eager to see it. One Saturday afternoon they asked some white friends to lend them two of their little children, a three-year-old girl and a six-year-old boy, and, holding these white children by the hands, they obtained tickets from the movie-house cashier without a moment's hesitation. They were in like Flynn.

This would also solve the baby-sitting problem for thousands and thousands of white working mothers. There can be a mutual exchange of references, then the people can sort of pool their children at a central point in each neighborhood, and every time a Negro wants to go to the movies all she need do is pick up a white child — and go.

Eventually the Negro community can set up a factory and manufacture white babies made of plastic, and when they want to go to the opera or to a concert, all they need do is carry that plastic doll in their arms. The dolls, of course, should all have blond curls and blue eyes, which would go even further; it would give the Negro woman and her husband priority over the whites for the very best seats in the house.

While I still have faith in the WHITE BABY PLAN, my final proposal may prove to be the most practical of all.

Only after a successful test was I ready to announce formally the GOLDEN "OUT-OF-ORDER" PLAN.

I tried my plan in a city of North Carolina, where the Negroes represent 39 per cent of the population.

I prevailed upon the manager of a department store to shut the water off in his "white" water fountain and put up a sign, "Out-of-Order." For the first day or two the whites were hesitant, but little by little they began to drink out of the water fountain belonging to the "coloreds" — and by the end of the third week everybody was drinking the "segregated" water; with not a single solitary complaint to date.

I believe the test is of such sociological significance that the Governor should appoint a special committee of two members of the House and two Senators to investigate the GOLDEN "OUT-OF-ORDER" PLAN. We kept daily reports on the use of the unsegregated water fountain which should be of great value to this committee. This may be the answer to the necessary uplifting of the white morale. It is possible that the whites may accept desegregation if they are assured that the facilities are still "separate," albeit "Out-of-Order."

As I see it now, the key to my Plan is to keep the "Out-of-Order" sign up for at least two years. We must do this thing gradually.

TWO STRATEGIES OF SOCIAL CHANGE AND THEIR DILEMMAS*

Richard E. Walton

One of the ironic tragedies in our society is that the proponents of social change often direct more of their energy into fighting among each other than they do trying to solve the social problems they all acknowledge. Much of this bickering revolves around the philosophical and practical issues of strategy. The arguments frequently become so pervasive that it is difficult to retain an awareness of the original situation with which they were concerned.

*Reproduced by special permission. From Richard E. Walton, "Two Strategies of Social Change and Their Dilemmas," *The Journal of Applied Behavioral Science*, I, No. 2 (1965), 167–179. National Training Laboratory, Washington, D.C. Used by permission of author and publisher.

While it would be presumptuous to attempt to resolve this dilemma, it may be helpful to examine some of the assets and liabilities of the various approaches to social change. In this article, Mr. Walton describes and compares two strategies of social change: the exercise of power and the enhancement of interpersonal relations.

The type of intergroup setting which is of primary concern here is described by the following assumptions. First, assume a desire on the part of one group to change the allocation of scarce resources between two groups — these could be status, political power, economic advantage or opportunity, geographic occupancy, and so on. Alternately, assume incompatible preferences regarding social institutions — such as the Berlin Wall, racial segregation, union shop. Second, assume that although the leaders of the groups recognize these areas of conflict they also want to establish a more cooperative set of attitudes between the groups. Third, assume further that there is neither law nor a compulsory arbitration mechanism which can accomplish the desired change or settle the conflict of interest.

Some of our most pressing problems of social change fit these assumptions almost completely and others meet them to a lesser degree. In international relations, for instance, the important substantive conflicts between the United States and the Soviet Union are accompanied by a general desire for more favorable internation attitudes. Moreover, in the present polarized world where the stakes of change can be enormously high, no international legal machinery is available to settle the important issues.

In race relations, the civil rights movement of the last decade has sought social change at times and in places where legal machinery could not be brought to bear to establish and enforce humane treatment for Negroes, to say nothing about equalizing their right to vote, to use public accommodations, to find housing, to apply for jobs, and so forth. At the same time, the majority of Negro and white leaders have commented upon the necessity for improved intergroup attitudes.

In labor-management relations, also, there are important substantive issues, such as hours, wages, and working conditions, which are neither specified by law nor amenable to resolution by appeal to a higher order of common values. Often these differences are accompanied by a genuine and mutual desire for harmonious intergroup relations.

How does the leadership of a group behave in these situations when they seek a change in the status quo? What actions are instrumental to the change effort?

Two groups of social scientists — viewing the same general situation —

offer quite different explanations and advice. One change strategy is advanced by game theorists, diplomatic strategists, and students of revolutions. Their focus is on the building of a power base and the strategic manipulation of power. Another strategy is urged by many social psychologists and by many persons involved in human relations laboratory training. This approach involves overtures of love and trust and gestures of good will, all intended to result in attitude change and concomitant behavior change.

Tactics of the Power Strategy

In recent years there has been an attempt to explicate the rational tactics of power and strategic choice (Schelling, 1960; Rapoport, 1960; Boulding, 1962; Walton & McKersie, 1965). The work in this area suggests that the fixed sum games — those situations in which what one person gains the other loses — require the following tactical operations.

First, in order to establish a basis for negotiation with the other and improve the probable outcome for itself, a group must build its power vis-à-vis the other. Group A can increase its relative power by making group B more dependent upon it and by decreasing its own (A's) dependence upon B. Often the change is sought by groups with a relative power disadvantage. To command attention and establish a basis for a *quid pro quo*, they must threaten the other with harm, loss, inconvenience, or embarrassment. These threats in international relations range from nuclear war to unilateral cancellation of an official state visit. In civil rights they involve notoriety, demonstrations, consumer boycotts, and sit-ins, lie-ins, and the like. In labor relations they include wildcat strikes, authorized stoppages, unfavorable publicity campaigns. These tactics create a basis for negotiation only if the threats are credible. One important technique for increasing their credibility is to fulfill a given threat once or repeatedly, as required.

A second set of tactical operations is required in order for a group to make maximum use of its potential power. These include biasing the rival group's perceptions of the strength of the underlying preference functions. A leader of group A attempts to overstate his group's needs or preferences for various degrees of achievement of its stated objective. Also, leader A depreciates the importance to B of B's objectives. These operations require the skillful management of ambiguity and uncertainty. They involve manipulating communication opportunities such that B perceives A as being maximally (even if irrationally) committed to a course of action and that the leader of group B does not have a comparable opportunity to commit himself to a different set of actions.

An abundance of illustrative material from international relations is available for each of these tactical operations—for example, the Cuban missile episode, Berlin crises, and the crises over Suez, the Congo, and Vietnam. Leaders of various civil rights groups have behaved in similar ways. Illustrative encounters are those in Montgomerey (school-bus boycotts over public accommodations); Pittsburgh (consumer boycotts over employment); Chicago (lie-ins and demonstrations over de facto segregation in schools); Birmingham (demonstrations over public accommodations); Mississippi ("invading" the state in the interest of voter registration and freedom schools). Analyses of the negotiations in any of the major trade union strikes—such as those in steel in 1959, in rails in 1963, and in autos in 1964—would reveal labor-management behavior which conformed to the tactical operations of the power strategy.

Tactics of the Attitude Change Strategy

Theoretical and empirical work in recent years has identified the conditions and actions which result in change in intergroup relationships (Naess, 1957; Janis & Katz, 1959; Osgood, 1959; Kelman, 1962; Berkowitz, 1962; Sherif, 1962; Deutsch, 1962; Gibb, 1964; Walton & McKersie, 1965). The areas of agreement in these writings may be summarized in terms of the tactics of attitude change.

Increasing the level of attraction and trust between persons or groups involves the following types of operations, considering the leader of group A as the acting party: minimizing the perceived differences between the groups' goals and between characteristics of members of the two groups; communications to B advocating peace; refraining from any actions which might harm members of the rival group (inconvenience, harass, embarrass, or violate them in any way); minimizing or eliminating B's perception of potential threats from A; emphasizing the degree of mutual dependence between the groups, accepting or enhancing the status of the representative of the rival group; ensuring that contacts between groups are on the basis of equal status; attempting to involve many members in intergroup contact; attempting to achieve a high degree of empathy with respect to the motives, expectations, and attitudes of members of group B; adopting a consistent posture of trust toward the other group; being open about A's own plans and intentions; creating a network of social relations involving many mutual associations with third parties.

There is tension between the ideas which underlie the two change strategies outlined above. However, the two groups of social scientists who are associated with these respective change strategies tend to handle this tension either by ignoring it or by depreciating the assumptions, ideas, and tactics of the other. It is true that both systems of ideas treat certain realities of the total social field; and, admittedly, it is possible for one to center one's attention on those particular situations where his ideas by themselves are appropriate and upon those particular aspects of a more complex situation where his ideas apply. The practitioner himself cannot do this. He must deal with the total reality. The leader of a group who is advocating and seeking change directly experiences the tension between these two persuasive systems of ideas.

Social scientists can become more relevant and therefore more helpful to the practitioner if they, too, confront these tensions between ideas, these dilemmas in action programs.

It is important to identify still a third distinct process of change, namely, problem solving. This process can be used whenever the basic nature of the issue is one where there is the potential that arrangements can be invented or created allowing both parties to gain or where one party can gain without the other's sacrificing anything of value to himself. In other words, integrative solutions are logically possible (Blake, 1959). However, this alternative of problem solving is not applicable in the specific intergroup situations assumed here: The substantive conflicts are ones which by the nature of the issues and the parties' basic preferences can be resolved only by dominance-submission or some compromise outcome.

Leadership Dilemmas in Pursuing Both Power and Attitude Change Strategies

If—as we have assumed here—a leader of group A has the objective both of obtaining important concessions from B and of reducing intergroup hostility, he would prefer to pursue simultaneously both change strategies discussed above. But in many respects the strategies place contradictory tactical demands on a leader, forcing him to choose between these strategies or to find some basis on which to integrate the two in some broader strategy of change. Several of the contradictions, dilemmas, and choice points in the tactics of social change are discussed below.

Overstatement of Objectives Versus Deemphasizing Differences

On the one hand, it is often tactical to the power strategy to overstate one's ultimate goals or immediate objectives — in effect, exaggerating the differences between the two groups. The strategy of attitude change, on the other hand, would deemphasize differences. Thus, the U.S. references to the status of Berlin which overstate our pertinent preferences, needs, and requirements may improve our position in bargaining for new terms there; but these statements run the risk of convincing the Soviet Union that our differences run even deeper than they do and that there is less basis for conciliation and trust than they had believed.

Stereotyping: Internal Cohesion Versus Accurate Differentiation

Stereotyping members of the rival group, focusing on their faults, impugning their motives, questioning their rationality, challenging their competence — these are often employed by leaders and members of the first group to build internal cohesion and willingness to make necessary sacrifices. For example, these tendencies occurred in a moderate form as the Mississippi Summer Project prepared their field staff and student volunteers for their work in "hostile" Mississippi. The tendency to attribute negative attributes to members of the rival group may have aided in the implementation of the almost pure power strategy which characterized this particular project, but this tendency would have been a clear liability in another civil rights project where the objectives include achieving attitude change.

Emphasis on Power to Coerce Versus Trust

If group A increases B's dependence upon A, this may enhance A's power to obtain substantive concessions, but it will not elicit more positive feelings. In fact, it can be argued that the trust-building process requires that A would communicate about A's dependence upon B. A labor union may enhance its power position by making management more aware of the company's vulnerability to a strike. But the same union might elicit more trust if it were to indicate instead how much the union must count upon management.

Information: Ambiguity Versus Predictability

Whereas ambiguity and uncertainty are often tactical to the power strategy, openness and predictability are essential to the attitude change strategy. Similarly, the first strategy is facilitated when there is limited and disciplined interaction; the second, when there is a more extensive and more open contact pattern. Thus, the power strategy dictates that we restrict the flow of information and people between the Soviet Union and the United States and that the limited contacts be formal and structured and that the agenda of these contacts be quite guarded. Attitude change strategy on the other hand, calls for freedom of travel, a variety of settings for international contact, and spontaneity and openness in these interchanges.

Threat Versus Conciliation

Review of the tactical operations of the two strategies reveals another important choice point in dual or mixed strategies, namely, What should be the role of threat of harm? When A is primarily pursuing an attitude change strategy, he communicates peaceful plans, he reduces perceived threat to B, and he refrains from actions that harm B. However, to pursue a power strategy in the interest of obtaining substantive gains, A engages in quite different tactics.

Even instances of uncontrolled aggression out of frustration can build bargaining power for the frustrated group and serve as an implicit threat of more aggression if substantive gains are not forthcoming. The Harlem riots in the summer of 1964 illustrate this point. Although it was generally said at the time that these outbursts hurt the civil rights movement (i.e., "had set the movement back several years"), many changes which accommodated the Negroes' demands and needs were soon made in the budgets, plans, and organization of several commissions and departments of New York City. One column headline in the *New York Times*, July 1964, the week following the riots, read "City Accelerates Fight on Poverty: $223,225 Grant Made Amid Reference to Racial Riots." A casual content analysis of items in the news after the riots in Harlem, Rochester, Philadelphia, and elsewhere suggests that there were both substantive gains and attitudinal losses. Notwithstanding the fact that all responsible civil rights leaders deplored the wanton destruction of property and the indiscriminate defiance of legal authorities, their bargaining power was nevertheless strengthened in certain respects.

Hostility Management: Impact Versus Catharsis

This dilemma is related to the preceding one but can present a somewhat more subtle problem for group leadership. Both change strategies involve the purposeful management of hostile feelings. In the power strategy the expression of hostile feelings is managed in a way which creates optimal impact on the other group, communicating strength of interest in the issue or making a threat credible.

The attitude change strategy also involves the expression of hostile feelings, but in a way which creates an optimal impact on the expressing group. Hostility expression is managed in a way which allows catharsis and the reevaluation of one's own group's feelings, but with minimum impact on the other group. Otherwise the hostility level will tend to be maintained or increased.

Coalition Versus Inclusion

One final dilemma relates to the question of whether A tries to involve third parties or publics in a coalition *against* B or in a social group *with* B. Building bargaining power in the interest of substantive change may require A to isolate B and attempt to generate disapproval of B. This has been an important aspect of the strategy of the civil rights movement in the last decade. The movement has tried to identify and isolate those officials and power groups in the South who oppose integration and those national officials in the Republican Party who are unsympathetic with certain legislative and enforcement objectives. This has created a forced choice situation for the moderates and for the uncertain.

However, a strategy of attitude change involves creating a network of social relations among A, B, and others. Applied to the civil rights movement, an emphasis on attitude change would actively encourage dialogue, understanding, and mutual influence among (a) groups in the movement, (b) the middle-of-the-roaders, and (c) the segregationists and other right-wing groups.

Coping with the Dilemmas

How do those who seek both substantive changes opposed by another group and improvements in intergroup attitudes cope with these dilemmas?

If the group's leader sequences the emphasis placed upon these two objectives and their accompanying strategies, this does somewhat ameliorate the tension between the two sets of activities. In international negotiations between the East and the West, both sides have used a freeze-thaw approach. One may first engage in new initiatives intended to make substantive gains or to create a power base for the future, and then make peace overtures. As long as the cycle is not too short in duration and the initiatives and overtures are seen as genuine, a leader can engage in both sets of behaviors and still have them be credible. In race relations, a particular campaign may involve a street demonstration phase (power building) and a negotiation phase (a mixture of power bargaining and relationship building).

Another technique is to have the contradictory strategies implemented by different persons or subgroups. In international relations, power tactics occur in the confrontations between the United States and the Soviet Union in the United Nations General Assembly and Security Council, but their attitude change efforts are implemented by different groups involved in such activities as cultural exchange programs. In race relations, a similar distinction can be made between the programs of CORE and SNCC on the one hand and NAACP and the Urban League on the other. This technique makes it apparent that mixed or dual strategies can be pursued more readily by an organization than by a person, and more readily by a movement than by an organization.

When the relationship between strategies is fully understood by the leader, he can select power tactics which have least negative impact on attitudes and choose attitudinal structuring activities which detract least from the power strategy.

Whether or not the activities are sequenced or assigned to different persons within a group, an important way of coping with these dilemmas is to choose actions which minimize them. Recognition of the tactical requirements of both strategies results in eliminating provocative acts which elicit negative attitudes and add nothing to the power strategy — for example, impeccable dress and demeanor in many civil rights demonstrations or the self-imposed norm of volunteers of the Mississippi Summer Project to avoid mixed racial couples' appearing in public even though eventual acceptance of such a pattern was one of the goals of the movement.

When the relationship between strategies is fully understood by the leader, he can select power tactics which have least negative impact on attitudes and choose attitudinal structuring activities which detract least from the power strategy.

Nonviolence is an attempt to meet the requirements of both strategies, but as a tactic it falls short of achieving an optimal integration. This is true in part because the distinction made between violence and nonviolence is more meaningful to the acting group than to the target group. The distinction usually refers to whether or not there is a physical violation of members of the rival group. In fact, other violations may be experienced by them as equally devastating — such as violation of their traditions and other social norms (integrating schools), assaults on their power base (voting drives). In short, in some situations the only maneuvers which effectively increase bargaining power really do hurt.

Over-all Strategy Considerations

Although in many situations one must engage in the tactics of power only at some disadvantage in terms of achieving attitude change and vice versa, this is not always the case. Especially when one takes a longer-range viewpoint, one may discover that the substantive objectives of the power strategy are more likely to be realized at a later date if an improvement in intergroup attitudes is sought initially. The point is that attitude change may result in some lessening of the substantive conflict. If southern whites as a group were more accepting of Negroes (i.e., developed more favorable attitudes toward them for some independent reason), they would be less adamant on certain substantive issues — for example, segregated schools — and would, as a result, reduce the need for civil rights groups to utilize a power strategy. Moreover, in the case of many of the substantive gains which one may reach through the power strategy — an arms control agreement, a treaty on Berlin, an understanding reached regarding future employment practices affecting Negroes — the fulfillment of these arrangements is dependent upon the level of trust and confidence which exists in the relationship.

Similarly, a longer-range viewpoint may show that the objective of attitude change is more likely to be achieved at a later date if one engages in the power tactics initially. The substantive gains obtained by the power strategy almost always result in temporary setbacks in terms of the level of friendliness and trust between the groups; but in the somewhat longer run, the result may be better affective relations. Consider race relations. One reason why more positive attitudes may develop via the initial power strategy is that the commitment and self-respect which the Negroes usually demonstrate in pursuing the power strategy may engender respect on the part of the larger white community — after the initial heat of conflict has subsided.

Another indirect and eventual way that the power strategy can lead to more favorable attitudinal bonds is through the mechanism of dissonance reduction. If as a result of substantive gains a group must be treated differently (more equal), there is a tendency to regard them differently (more equal) in order to make one's beliefs and attitudes congruent with one's behavior.

There is a third reason why a power strategy designed to obtain substantive concessions may achieve attitude change as well, particularly for a group which is currently less privileged and exercises less power. This refers to an important precondition for achieving a stable and healthy intergroup relationship — equal status and power between groups. This suggests that as long as group A remains at a power disadvantage and there is a potential for achieving power parity, A's mix of power and attitude change tactics will include relatively more tactics. Thus, the power strategy for the civil rights groups during the last decade has dominated the attitude change strategy. This principle is also illustrated by the warlike actions of the Soviet Union during the period after World War II, when the United States alone possessed the atom bomb.

Whatever the existing balance of power, whenever B makes a move which would build its relative power, A will tend to act primarily in terms of the power strategy. This is illustrated by the United States' bargaining commitment moves when it discovered Soviet missiles in Cuba and when the Soviets attempted to make inroads in the Middle East and the Congo during the Suez and Congo crises respectively.

Implications

Recognition of these dilemmas is the first step toward developing a theory of social action which specifies the conditions under which one should conform to the tactical requirements of one strategy versus the other. But better theory is not enough. The agent of social change needs the behavioral skills required by simultaneously or sequentially mixed strategies. For example, international officials and civil rights leaders should be flexible enough to employ strategies of attitude change when a particular campaign reaches the negotiation phase.

What are the implications for training of leaders of groups advocating social change? Human relations training generally and laboratory learning in particular are geared to developing insights and skills central to the strategy of attitude change and are less relevant to the power strategy. I suggest that the conception of the problem of change should be broadened to incorporate – as necessary and legitimate – the power strategy.[1] We must understand what demands on leadership behavior are imposed by

[1]In the interest of sharpening the issues about our conception of the problem, I offer the following assertions regarding the role of bargaining, power, and violence in social change:

First, bargaining and bargaining tactics (including tactical deception, bluff, commitment, promises, threats, and threat fulfillment) are often necessary in social change situations where there are basic conflicts of interest. Moreover, many of these tactical operations are amoral in such situations.

Second, attempts to create cooperative relations between parties are more effective if there is some parity in their power. Power of a party derives from its capacity to influence some aspect of the fate of the other – either rewards or punishments. Often the only avenue open to a party with less relative power is to increase its capacity to harm (embarrass or inconvenience) the other. Moreover, it may be necessary for the party to engage in a series of maneuvers which are increasingly persuasive in communicating to the other party both a capacity and a willingness to use the power.

the power strategy of change both during the phase when power thinking necessarily dominates group leadership and the phase when preserving a power base is merely a consideration in designing an attitude change strategy. If these specialists deplore these power tactics simply because they violate their personal model of preferred social behavior, their advice which *is* appropriate and badly needed by the practitioner will be taken less seriously by him.

References

Berkowitz, L. *Aggression: A social psychological analysis.* New York: McGraw-Hill, Inc., 1962.

Blake, R. R. Psychology and the crisis of statesmanship. *Amer. Psychologist,* 1959, **14**, 87–94.

Boulding, K. *Conflict and defense: A general theory.* New York: Harper & Row, Publishers, 1962.

City accelerates fight on poverty. *New York Times,* July 28, 1964, p. 15.

Deutsch, M. A psychological basis for peace. In Q. Wright, W. M. Evan, & M. Deutsch (Eds.), *Preventing World War III: Some proposals.* New York: Simon and Schuster, Inc., 1962.

Gibb, J. R. Climate for trust formation. In L. P. Bradford, J. R. Gibb, & K. D. Benne (Eds.), *T-Group theory and laboratory method: Innovation in re-education.* New York: John Wiley & Sons, Inc., 1964.

Janis, I. L., & Katz, D. The reduction of intergroup hostility: Research problems and hypotheses. *J. conflict Resolution,* 1959, **3**, 85–100.

Kelman, H. C. Changing attitudes through international activities. *J. soc. Issues,* 1962, **18**, 68–87.

Naess, A. A systematization of Gandhian ethics of conflict resolution. *J. conflict Resolution,* 1957, **1**, 140–155.

Osgood, C. E. Suggestions for winning the real war with Communism. *J. conflict Resolution,* 1959, **3**, 295–325.

Rapoport, A. *Fights, games, and debates.* Ann Arbor: University of Michigan Press, 1960.

Schelling, T. *The strategy of conflict.* Cambridge, Mass: Harvard University Press, 1960.

Sherif, M. (Ed.). *Intergroup relations and leadership.* New York: John Wiley & Sons, Inc., 1962.

Walton, R. E. & McKersie, R. B. *A behavioral theory of labor negotiations.* New York: McGraw-Hill, Inc., 1965.

Third, where they are used, tactics of nonviolence are effective at least in part because the other group perceives this method as an alternative to violence. The option of violence is indirectly suggested *by advocating nonviolence.*

Fourth, there is experimental evidence that a cooperative bid by A is more effective in eliciting a cooperative response from B when it occurs against a series of noncooperative moves by A. Maybe this paradox also operates in some social situations creating an incentive for initial noncooperation.

"THE COST OF LIVING" FROM
IDIOTS FIRST*

Bernard Malamud

Too frequently we equate progress with improvement and assume that a change brings with it benefits for everyone. Unfortunately most innovations produce suffering for many individuals who happen to be in the path of progress. The many primitive tribes who have been exterminated while being introduced to civilization because of their lack of acquired immunity to the diseases of the Western world serve as a dramatic example of the dangerous side effects of progress. The preponderance of ulcers, heart attacks, pollution and drop-outs provide less dramatic but equally convincing evidence that the rapid changes we experience exact a price from the human beings for whom change is supposedly designed.

Bernard Malamud has written a story about a man and woman who are victims of progress. His story is a grim reminder of the dangers of blueprints and master plans which stress numbers and dollars at the expense of human dignity.

Winter had fled the city streets but Sam Tomashevsky's face, when he stumbled into the back room of his grocery store, was a blizzard. Sura, who was sitting at the round table eating bread and salted tomato, looked up in fright and the tomato turned a deeper red. She gulped the bite she had bitten and with pudgy fist socked her chest to make it go down. The gesture already was one of mourning for she knew from the wordless sight of him there was trouble.

"My God," Sam croaked.

She screamed, making him shudder, and he fell wearily into a chair. Sura was standing, enraged and frightened.

"Speak, for God's sake."

"Next door," Sam muttered.

"What happened next door?" — upping her voice.

"Comes a store!"

"What kind of a store?" The cry was piercing.

He waved his arms in rage. "A grocery comes next door."

"Oh." She bit her knuckle and sank down moaning. It could not have been worse.

They had, all winter, been haunted by the empty store. An Italian shoemaker had owned it for years and then a streamlined shoe-repair shop had opened up next block where they had three men in red smocks hammering away in the window and everyone stopped to look. Pellegrino's business had slackened off as if someone were shutting a faucet, and one day he had looked at his workbench and when everything stopped jumping, it loomed up ugly and empty. All morning he had sat motionless, but in the afternoon he put down the hammer he had been clutching and got his jacket and an old darkened Panama hat a customer had never called for when he used to do hat cleaning and blocking; then he went into the neighborhood, asking among his former customers for work they might want done. He collected two pairs of shoes, a man's brown and white ones for summertime and a fragile pair of ladies' dancing slippers. At the same time, Sam found his own soles and heels had been worn paper thin for being so many hours on his feet—he could feel the cold floor boards under him as he walked—and that made three pairs all together, which was what Mr. Pellegrino had that week—and another pair the week after. When the time came for him to pay next month's rent he sold everything to a junkman and bought candy to peddle with in the streets; but after a while no one saw the shoemaker any more, a stocky man with round eye-glasses and a bristling mustache, wearing a summer hat in wintertime.

When they tore up the counters and other fixtures and moved them out, when the store was empty except for the sink glowing in the rear, Sam would occasionally stand there at night, everyone on the block but him closed, peering into the window exuding darkness. Often, while gazing through the dusty plate glass, which gave him back the image of a grocer gazing out, he felt as he had when he was a boy in Kamenets-Podolskiy and going, three of them, to the river; they would, as they passed, swoop a frightened glance into a tall wooden house, eerily narrow, topped by a strange double-steepled roof, where there had once been a ghastly murder and now the place was haunted. Returning late, at times in early moonlight, they walked a distance away, speechless, listening to the ravenous silence of the house, room after room fallen into deeper stillness, and in the midmost a pit of churning quiet from which, if you thought about it, all evil erupted. And so it seemed in the dark recesses of the empty store, where so many shoes had been leathered and hammered into life, and so many people had left something of themselves in the coming and going, that even in emptiness the store contained some memory of their vanished presences, unspoken echoes in declining tiers, and that in a sense was what was so frightening. Afterwards when Sam went by the store, even in daylight he was afraid to look, and quickly walked past, as they had the haunted house when he was a boy.

But whenever he shut his eyes the empty store was stuck in his mind, a long black hole eternally revolving so that while he slept he was not asleep but within revolving: what if it should happen to me? What if after twenty-seven years of eroding toil (he should years ago have got out), what if after all of that, your own store, a place of business . . . after all the years, the years; the multitude of cans he had wiped off and packed away, the milk cases dragged in like rocks from the street before dawn in freeze or heat; insults, petty thievery, doling of credit to the impoverished by the poor; the peeling ceiling, fly-specked shelves, puffed cans, dirt, swollen veins; the back-breaking sixteen-hour day like a heavy hand slapping, upon awaking, the skull, pushing the head to bend the body's bones; the hours; the work, the years, my God, and where is my life now? Who will save me now, and where will I go, where? Often he had thought these thoughts, subdued after months; and the garish FOR RENT sign had yellowed and fallen in the window so how could any one know the place was to let? But they did. Today when he had all but laid the ghost of fear, a streamer in red cracked him across the eyes: National Grocery Will Open Another of Its Bargain Price Stores On These Premises, and the woe went into him and his heart bled.

At last Sam raised his head and told her, "I will go to the landlord next door."

Sura looked at him through puffy eyelids. "So what will you say?"

"I will talk to him."

Ordinarily she would have said, "Sam, don't be a fool," but she let him go.

Averting his head from the glare of the new red sign in the window, he entered the hall next door. As he labored up the steps the bleak light from the skylight fell on him and grew heavier as he ascended. He went unwillingly, not knowing what he would say to the landlord. Reaching the top floor he paused before the door at the jabbering in Italian of a woman bewailing her fate. Sam already had one foot on the top stair, ready to descend, when he heard the coffee advertisement and realized it had been a radio play. Now the radio was off, the hallway oppressively silent. He listened and at first heard no voices inside so he knocked without allowing himself to think any more. He was a little frightened and lived in suspense until the slow heavy steps of the landlord, who was also the barber across the street, reached the door, and it was — after some impatient fumbling with the lock — opened.

When the barber saw Sam in the hall he was disturbed, and Sam at once knew why he had not been in the store even once in the past two weeks. However, the barber became cordial and invited Sam to step into the kitchen where his wife and a stranger were seated at the table eating from piled-high plates of spaghetti.

"Thanks," said Sam shyly. "I just ate."

The barber came out into the hall, shutting the door behind him. He glanced vaguely down the stairway and then turned to Sam. His movements were unresolved. Since the death of his son in the war he had become absent-minded; and sometimes when he walked one had the impression he was dragging something.

"Is it true?" Sam asked in embarrassment, "What it says downstairs on the sign?"

"Sam," the barber began heavily. He stopped to wipe his mouth with the napkin he held in his hand and said, "Sam, you know this store I had no rent for it for seven months?"

"I know."

"I can't afford. I was waiting for maybe a liquor store or a hardware but I don't have no offers from them. Last month this chain store make me an offer and then I wait five weeks for something else. I had to take it, I couldn't help myself."

Shadows thickened in the growing darkness. In a sense Pellegrino was present, standing with them at the top of the stairs.

"When will they move in?" Sam sighed.

"Not till May."

The grocer was too faint to say anything. They stared at each other, not knowing what to suggest. But the barber forced a laugh and said the chain store wouldn't hurt Sam's business.

"Why not?"

"Because you carry different brands of goods and when the customers want those brands they go to you."

"Why should they go to me if my prices are higher?"

"A chain store brings more customers and they might like things that you got."

Sam felt ashamed. He didn't doubt the barber's sincerity but his stock was meager and he could not imagine chain store customers interested in what he had to sell.

Holding Sam by the arm, the barber told him in confidential tones of a friend who had a meat store next to an A&P Supermarket and was making out very well.

Sam tried hard to believe he would make out well but couldn't.
"So did you sign with them the lease yet?" he asked.
"Friday," said the barber.
"Friday?" Sam had a wild hope. "Maybe," he said, trying to hold it down. "maybe I could find you, before Friday, a new tenant?"
"What kind of a tenant?"
"A tenant," Sam said.
"What kind of store is he interested?"
Sam tried to think. "A shoe store," he said.
"Shoemaker?"
"No, a shoe store where they sell shoes."
The barber pondered it. At last he said if Sam could get a tenant he wouldn't sign the lease with the chain store.

As Sam descended the stairs the light from the top-floor bulb diminished on his shoulders but not the heaviness, for he had no one in mind to take the store.

However, before Friday he thought of two people. One was the red-haired salesman for a wholesale grocery jobber, who had lately been recounting his investments in new stores; but when Sam spoke to him on the phone he said he was only interested in high-income grocery stores, which was no solution to the problem. The other man he hesitated to call, because he didn't like him. That was I. Kaufman, a former dry goods merchant, with a wart under his left eyebrow. Kaufman had made some fortunate real estate deals and had become quite wealthy. Years ago he and Sam had stores next to one another on Marcy Avenue in Williamsburg. Sam took him for a lout and was not above saying so, for which Sura often ridiculed him, seeing how Kaufman had progressed and where Sam was. Yet they stayed on comparatively good terms, perhaps because the grocer never asked for favors. When Kaufman happened to be around in the Buick, he usually dropped in, which Sam increasingly disliked, for Kaufman gave advice without stint and Sura sandpapered it in when he had left.

Despite qualms he telephoned him. Kaufman was pontifically surprised and said yes he would see what he could do. On Friday morning the barber took the red sign out of the window so as not to prejudice a possible deal. When Kaufman marched in with his cane that forenoon, Sam, who for once, at Sura's request, had dispensed with his apron, explained to him they had thought of the empty store next door as perfect for a shoe store because the neighborhood had none and the rent was reasonable. And since Kaufman was always investing in one project or another they thought he might be interested in this. The barber came over from across the street and unlocked the door. Kaufman clomped into the empty store, appraised the structure of the place, tested the floor, peered through the barred window into the back yard, and squinting, totaled with moving lips how much shelving was necessary and at what cost. Then he asked the barber how much rent and the barber named a modest figure.

Kaufman nodded sagely and said nothing to either of them there, but back in the grocery store he vehemently berated Sam for wasting his time.

"I didn't want to make you ashamed in front of the goy," he said in anger, even his wart red, "but who do you think, if he is in his right mind, will open a shoe store in this stinky neighborhood?"

Before departing, he gave good advice the way a tube bloops toothpaste and ended by saying to Sam, "If a chain store grocery comes in you're finished. Get out of here before the birds pick the meat of your bones."

Then he drove off in his Buick. Sura was about to begin a commentary but Sam pounded his fist on the table and that ended it. That evening the barber pasted the red sign back on the window, for he had signed the lease.

Lying awake nights, Sam knew what was going on inside the store, though he never went near it. He could see carpenters sawing the sweet-smelling pine that willingly yielded to the sharp shining blade and became in tiers the shelves rising to the ceiling. The painters arrived, a long man and a short one he was positive he knew, their faces covered with paint drops. They thickly calcimined the ceiling and painted everything in bright colors, impractical for a grocery but pleasing to the eye. Electricians appeared with Fluorescent lamps which obliterated the yellow darkness of globed bulbs; and then the fixture men hauled down from their vans the long marble-top counters and a gleaming enameled refrigerator containing three windows, for cooking, medium, and best butter; and a case for frozen foods, creamy white, the latest thing. As he was admiring it all, he thought he turned to see if everyone was watching him, and when he had reassured himself and turned again to look through the window it had been whitened so he could see nothing more. He had to get up then to smoke a cigarette and was tempted to put on his pants and go in slippers quietly down the stairs to see if the window was really soaped. That it might be kept him back so he returned to bed, and being still unable to sleep, he worked until he had polished, with a bit of rag, a small hole in the center of the white window, and enlarged that till he could see everything clearly. The store was assembled now, spic and span, roomy, ready to receive the goods; it was a pleasure to come in. He whispered to himself this would be good if it was for me, but then the alarm banged in his ear and he had to get up and drag in the milk cases. At eight a.m. three enormous trucks rolled down the block and six young men in white duck jackets jumped off and packed the store in seven hours. All day Sam's heart beat so hard he sometimes fondled it with his hand as though trying to calm a wild bird that wanted to fly away.

When the chain store opened in the middle of May, with a horseshoe wreath of roses in the wondow, Sura counted up that night and proclaimed they were ten dollars short; which wasn't so bad, Sam said, till she reminded him ten times six was sixty. She openly wept, sobbing they must do *something*, driving Sam to a thorough wiping of the shelves with wet cloths she handed him, oiling the floor, and washing, inside and out, the front window, which she redecorated with white tissue paper from the five-and-ten. Then she told him to call the wholesaler, who read off this week's specials; and when they were delivered, Sam packed three cases of cans in a towering pyramid in the window. Only no one seemed to buy. They were fifty dollars short the next week and Sam thought if it stays like this we can exist, and he cut the price of beer, lettering with black crayon on wrapping paper a sign for the window that beer was reduced in price, selling fully five cases more that day, though Sura nagged what was the good of it if they made no profit — lost on paper bags — and the customers who came in for beer went next door for bread and canned goods? Yet Sam still hoped, but the next week they were seventy-two behind, and in two weeks a clean hundred. The chain store, with a manager and two clerks, was busy all day but with Sam there was never, any more, anything resembling a rush. Then he discovered that they carried, next door, every brand he had and many he hadn't, and he felt for the barber a furious anger.

That summer, usually better for his business, was bad, and the fall was worse. The store was so silent it got to be a piercing pleasure when someone opened the door. They sat long hours under the unshaded bulb in the rear, reading and rereading the newspaper and looking up hopefully when anyone passed by in the street, though trying not to look when they could tell he was going next door. Sam now kept open an hour longer, till midnight, although that wearied him greatly, but he was able, during the extra hour, to pick up a dollar or two among the housewives who had run out of milk or needed a last minute loaf of bread for school sandwiches. To cut expenses he put out one of the two lights in the window and a lamp in the store. He had the phone removed, bought his paper bags from peddlers, shaved every second day and, although he would not admit it, ate less.

Then in an unexpected burst of optimism he ordered eighteen cases of goods from the jobber and filled the empty sections of his shelves with low-priced items clearly marked, but as Sura said, who saw them if nobody came in? People he had seen every day for ten, fifteen, even twenty years, disappeared as if they had moved or died. Sometimes when he was delivering a small order somewhere, he saw a former customer who either quickly crossed the street, or ducked the other way and walked around the block. The barber, too, avoided him and he avoided the barber. Sam schemed to give short weight on loose items but couldn't bring himself to. He considered canvassing the neighborhood from house to house for orders he would personally deliver but then remembered Mr. Pellegrino and gave up the idea. Sura, who had all their married life, nagged him, now sat silent in the back. When Sam counted the receipts of the first week in December he knew he could no longer hope. The wind blew outside and the store was cold. He offered it for sale but no one would take it.

One morning Sura got up and slowly ripped her cheeks with her fingernails. Sam went across the street for a haircut. He had formerly had his hair cut once a month but now it had grown ten weeks and was thickly pelted at the back of the neck. The barber cut it with his eyes shut. Then Sam called an auctioneer who moved in with two lively assistants and a red auction flag that flapped and furled in the icy breeze as though it were a holiday. The money they got was not a quarter of the sum needed to pay the creditors. Sam and Sura closed the store and moved away. So long as he lived he would not return to the old neighborhood, afraid his store was standing empty, and he dreaded to look through the window.

CHANGE DOES NOT HAVE TO BE HAPHAZARD*

Kenneth D. Benne and Max Birnbaum

Institutional and community change are topics which have been given considerable attention. Social activists are constantly engaged in this process; academicians and intellectuals philosophize about modifying the structures within our society; and students are interested in all forms of social change. Yet there is only a limited body of practical literature available to assist those who wish to understand the mechanics of

*Kenneth D. Benne and Max Birnbaum, "Change Does Not Have To Be Haphazard," *The School Review*, published by the University of Chicago Press, LXVIII, No. 3. Used by permission of the authors and publisher, 1960, pp. 283–293.

creating change in formal settings. Messrs. Benne and Birnbaum provide a model of how to apply change strategies in an institutional environment. Their analyses and suggestions illustrate how social science principles may be incorporated into the development of a problem-solving methodology.

No institution or organization is exempt from change. Today the student who returns to his alma mater ten years after graduation can expect to find changes, not only in personnel, but also in personnel policies and teaching practices. The executive returning to the firm where he once worked, the nurse going back to her old hospital, the social worker visiting his agency — all can expect to find sweeping changes.

It is fairly easy to identify changes in institutional patterns after they have occurred. It is more difficult to analyze changes while they are going on and still more difficult to predict changes or to influence significantly the direction and the tempo of changes already under way. Yet, more and more, those who have managerial functions in organizations must analyze and predict impending changes and take deliberate action to shape change according to some criteria of retrogression or progress. The planning of change has become part of the responsibility of management in all contemporary institutions, whether the task of the institution is defined in terms of health, education, social welfare, industrial production, or religious indoctrination.

Whatever other equipment managers require in analyzing potentialities for change and in planning and directing change in institutional settings, they need some conceptual schema for thinking about change. This need stems from the profusion and variety of behaviors that accompany any process of change.

One useful model for thinking about change has been proposed by Kurt Lewin, who saw behavior in an institutional setting, not as a static habit or pattern but as a dynamic balance of forces working in opposite directions within the social-psychological space of the institution (1).

Take, for example, the production level of a work team in a factory. This level fluctuates within narrow limits above and below a certain number of units of production per day. Why does this pattern persist? Because, Lewin says, the forces that tend to raise the level of production are equal to the forces that tend to depress it. Among the forces tending to raise the level of production might be: (a) the pressures of supervisors on the work team to produce more; (b) the desire of at least some team members to attract favorable attention from supervisors in order to get ahead individually; (c) the desire of team members to earn more under the incentive plan of the plant. Such forces Lewin called "driving forces." Among the forces tending to lower the level of production might be: (a') a group standard in the production team against "rate busting" or "eager beavering" by individual workers; (b') resistance of team members to accepting training and supervision from management; (c') feelings by workers that the product they are producing is not important. Granted the goal of increased productivity, these forces are "restraining forces." The balance between the two sets of forces, which defines the established level of production. Lewin called a "quasi-stationary equilibrium." We may diagram this equilibrium. . . (See Fig. 1.)

According to Lewin, this type of thinking about patterns of institutionalized behavior applies not only to levels of production in industry but also to such patterns as levels of discrimination in communities; atmosphere of democracy or autocracy in social agencies; supervisor-teacher-pupil relationships in school systems; and formal or informal working relationships among levels of a hospital organization.

According to this way of looking at patterned behavior, change takes place when an imbalance occurs between the sum of the restraining forces and the sum of the driving forces. Such imbalance unfreezes the pattern: the level then changes until the opposing forces are again brought into equilibrium. An imbalance may occur through a change in the magnitude of any one force, through change in the direction of a force, or through the addition of a new force.

For examples of each of these ways of unfreezing a situation, let us look again at our original illustration. Suppose that the members of the work team join a new union, which sets out to get pay rises. In pressing for shifts in over-all wage policy, the union increases the suspicion of workers toward the motives of all management, including supervisors. This change

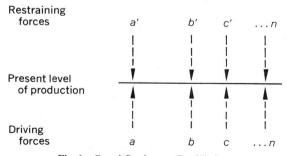

Fig. 1   Quasi-Stationary Equilibrium.

tends to increase the restraining force — let's say restraining force b'. As a result, the level of production moves down. As the level of production falls, supervisors increase their pressure toward greater production, and driving force a increases. This release of increased counterforce tends to bring the system into balance again at a level somewhere near the previous level. But the increase in magnitude of these opposed forces may also increase the tension under which people work. Under such conditions, even though the level of production does not go down very much, the situation becomes more psychologically explosive, less stable, and less predictable.

A war that demands more and more of the product that the work team is producing may convert the workers' feelings that they are not producing anything important — restraining force c' — to a feeling that their work is important and that they are not working hard enough. This response will occur provided, of course, that the workers are committed to the war effort. As the direction of force c' is reversed, the level of production will almost certainly rise to bring the behavior pattern back into a state of equilibrium at a higher level of productivity.

Suppose a new driving force is added in the shape of a supervisor who wins the trust and the respect of the work team. The new force results in a desire on the part of the work team to make the well-liked supervisor look good — or at least to keep him from looking bad — in relation to his colleagues and superiors. This force may operate to offset a generally unfavorable attitude toward management.

These examples suggest that in change there is an unfreezing of an existing equilibrium, a movement toward a new equilibrium, and the refreezing of the new equilibrium. Planned change must use situational forces to accomplish unfreezing, to influence the movement in generally desirable directions, and to rearrange the situation, not only to avoid return to the old level, but to stabilize the change or improvement.

This discussion suggests three major strategies for achieving change in any given pattern of behavior: the driving forces may be increased; the restraining forces may be decreased; these two strategies may be combined. In general, if the first strategy only is adopted, the tension in the system is likely to increase. More tension means more instability and more unpredictability and the likelihood of irrational rather than rational responses to attempts to induce change.

It is a well-known fact that change in an organization is often followed by a reaction toward the old pattern, a reaction that sets in when pressure for change is relaxed. After a curriculum survey, one school system put into effect several recommendations for improvement suggested by the survey. The action was taken under pressure from the board and the superintendent, but when they relaxed their vigilance, the old pattern crept back in.

This experience raises the problem of how to maintain a desirable change. Backsliding takes place for various reasons. Those affected by the changes may not have participated in the planning enough to internalize the changes that those in authority are seeking to induce; when the pressure of authority is relaxed, there is no pressure from those affected to maintain the change. Or, a change in one part of the social system may not have been accompanied by enough co-relative changes in overlapping parts and subsystems.

On the basis of this model of analysis, several principles of strategy for effecting institutional change may be formulated. We shall present the principles with illustrations of each.

To change a subsystem or any part of a subsystem, relevant aspects of the environment must also be changed.

The manager of the central office of a large school system wants to increase the efficiency of the secretarial forces by placing private secretaries in a pool. It is the manager's hope that the new arrangement will make for better utilization of the secretaries' time. In this situation at least two driving forces are obvious: fewer secretaries can serve a larger number of sub-executives; a substantial saving can be expected in office space and equipment. Among the restraining forces are the secretaries' resistance to a surrender of their personal relationship with a status person, a relationship implicit in the one-to-one secretary-boss relationship; the prospective dehumanization, as the secretaries see it, of their task; and a probable increase in work load. Acceptance of this change in role and relationship would require accompanying changes in other parts of the subsystem. Furthermore, before the private secretaries could wholeheartedly accept the change, their bosses as well as lower-status clerks and typists in the central office would have to accept the alteration in the secretarial role as one that did not necessarily imply an undesirable change in status. The secretaries' morale would surely be affected if secretaries in other parts of the school system, secretaries to principals in school buildings, for example, were not also assigned to a pool.

Thus to plan changes in one part of a subsystem, in this case in the central office of the school system, eventually involves consideration of changes in overlapping parts of the system—the clerical force, the people accustomed to private secretaries, and others as well. If these other changes are not effected, one can expect lowered morale, requests for transfers, and even resignations. Attempts to change any subsystem in a larger system must be preceded or accompanied by diagnosis of other subsystems that will be affected by the change.

To change behavior on any one level of a hierarchial organization, it is necessary to achieve complementary and reinforcing changes in organization levels above and below that level.

Shortly after World War II, commanders in the United States Army decided to attempt to change the role of the sergeancy. The sergeant was not to be the traditionally tough, driving leader of men but a supportive, counseling squad leader. The traditional view of the sergeant's role was held by enlisted men, below the rank of sergeant, as well as by second lieutenants, above the rank of sergeant.

Among the driving forces for change were the need to transform the prewar career army into a new peacetime military establishment composed largely of conscripts; the perceived need to reduce the gap between military life and civilian status; and the desire to avoid any excesses in the new army that might cause the electorate to urge a return to the prewar volunteer military establishment.

Among the immediate restraining forces were the traditional authoritarian role behaviors of the sergeancy, forged by wartime need and peacetime barracks service. These behaviors were in harmony with the needs of a military establishment that by its very nature is based on the notion of a clearly defined chain of command. Implicit in such a hierarchy are orders, not persuasion; unquestioning obedience, not critical questioning of decisions. Also serving as a powerful restraining force was the need for social distance between ranks in order to restrict friendly interaction between levels.

When attempts were made to change the sergeant's role, it was discovered that the second lieutenant's role, at the next higher level, also had to be altered. No longer could the second lieutenant use the authority of the chain-of-command system in precisely the same way as before. Just as the sergeant could no longer operate on the principle of unquestioning obedience to his orders, so the second lieutenant could no longer depend on the sergeant to pass orders downward unquestioningly. It was soon seen that, if the changed role of the sergeant was to be stabilized, the second lieutenant's role would have to be revised.

The role of the enlisted man also had to be altered significantly. Inculcated with the habit of responding unquestioningly to the commands of his superiors, especially the sergeant, the enlisted man found the new permissiveness somewhat disturbing. On the one hand, the enlisted man welcomed being treated more like a civilian and less like a soldier. On the other hand, he felt a need for an authoritative spokesman who represented the army unequivocally. The two needs created considerable conflict. An interesting side effect, which illustrates the need of the enlisted men for an authoritative spokesman for the army, was the development of greater authority in the rank of corporal, the rank between private and sergeant.

To recapitulate briefly, the attempts to change the role of the sergeancy led unavoidably to alterations in the roles of lieutenant, private, and corporal. Intelligent planning of change in the sergeancy would have required simultaneous planning for changes at the interrelated levels.

The place to begin change is at those points in the system where some stress and strain exist. Stress may give rise to dissatisfaction with the status quo and thus become a motivating factor for change in the system.

One school principal used the dissatisfaction expressed by teachers over noise in the corridors during passing periods to secure agreement to extra assignments to hall duty. But until the teachers felt this dissatisfaction, the principal could not secure their wholehearted agreement to the assignments.

Likewise, hospitals have recently witnessed a significant shift of functions from nurses to nurse's aides. A shortage of nurses and consequent overwork led the nurses to demand more assistance. For precisely the same reasons, teachers in Michigan schools were induced to experiment with teacher's aides.

The need for teachers to use the passing period as a rest period, the desire of the nurses to keep exclusive control over their professional relationships with the patient, and the resistance of teachers to sharing teaching functions with lay people — all these restraining forces gave way before dissatisfactions with the status quo. The dissatisfactions became driving forces sufficiently strong to overcome the restraining forces. Of course, the restraining forces do not disappear in the changed situation. They are still at work and will need to be handled as the changed arrangements become stabilized.

In diagnosing the possibility of change in a given institution, it is always necessary to assess the degree of stress and strain at points where change is sought. One should ordinarily avoid beginning change at the point of greatest stress.

Status relationships had become a major concern of staff members in a certain community agency. Because of lowered morale in the professional staff, the lay board decided to revamp lay-professional relationships. The observable form of behavior that led to the action of the board was the striving for recognition from the lay policy-making body by individual staff members. After a management survey, the channels of communication between the lay board and the professional staff were limited to communication between the staff head and the members of the lay board. The entire staff, except the chief executive, perceived this step as a personal rejection by the lay board and as a significant lowering of the status of staff members. The result was still lower morale. Because of faulty diagnosis the change created more problems than it solved.

The problem of status-striving and its adulteration of lay-professional relationships could have been approached more wisely. Definition of roles — lay and professional — could have been undertaken jointly by the executive and the staff in an effort to develop a more common perception of the situation and a higher professional *esprit de corps*. Lack of effective recognition symbols within the staff itself might have been dealt with first, and the touchy prestige symbol of staff communication with the lay board put aside for the time being.

If thoroughgoing changes in a hierarchial structure are desirable or necessary, change should ordinarily start with the policy-making body.

Desegregation has been facilitated in school systems where the school board first agreed to the change. The board's statement of policy supporting desegregation and its refusal to panic at the opposition have been crucial factors in acceptance of the change throughout the school system and eventually throughout the community. In localities where boards of education have not publicly agreed to the change, administrators' efforts to desegregate have been overcautious and halfhearted, and the slightest sign of opposition in the institution or the community has led to a strengthening rather than a weakening of resistance to desegregation. Sanction by the ruling body lends legitimacy to any institutional change, though, of course, "illegitimate" resistance must still be faced and dealt with as a reality in the situation.

Both the formal and the informal organization of an institution must be considered in planning any process of change.

Besides a formal structure, every social system has a network of cliques and informal groupings. These informal groupings often exert such strong restraining influence on institutional changes initiated by formal authority that, unless their power can be harnessed in support of a change, no enduring change is likely to occur. The informal groupings in a factory often have a strong influence on the members' rate of work, a stronger influence than the pressure by the foreman. Any worker who violates the production norms established by his peer group invites ostracism, a consequence few workers dare to face. Schools, too, have their informal groupings, membership in which is often more important to teachers than the approval of their supervisors. To involve these informal groups in the planning of changes requires ingenuity and sensitivity as well as flexibility on the part of an administrator.

The effectiveness of a planned change is often directly related to the degree to which members at all levels of an institutional hierarchy take part in the fact-finding and the diagnosing of needed changes and in the formulating and reality-testing of goals and programs of change.

Once the workers in an institution have agreed to share in investigating their work problems, a most significant state in overcoming restraining forces has been reached. This agreement should be followed by shared fact-finding by the group, usually with technical assistance from resources outside the particular social system. Participation by those affected by the change in fact-finding and interpretation increases the likelihood that new insights will be formed and that goals of change will be accepted. More accurate diagnosis results if the people to be changed are trained in fact-finding and fact-interpreting methods as part of the process of planning.

This article has been written from the standpoint that change in an institution or organization can be planned. Is this a reasonable view? Can change be deliberately planned in organizations and institutions as complex as school systems, hospitals, and armies? Do not many determinants of change operate without the awareness or knowledge of those involved?

It is true that most people are unaware of many factors that trigger processes of change in the situations in which they work. And most people are unaware of many factors that influence the direction of change. Many factors, even when known, are outside the power of people in an organization to control. For some forces that influence change in an organization stem from the wider society: new knowledge, new social requirements, new public demands force the management of a school system to alter the content and the methods of its instructional program. Some factors cannot be fully known in advance. Even when they are anticipated, the school cannot fully control them.

Some forces that work for change or resistance to change in an organization stem from the personalities of the leaders and the members of the organization. Some of these factors are unknown to the persons themselves and to those around them. Some personality factors, even when they are known, cannot be altered or reshaped, save perhaps by therapeutic processes beyond the resources of school teachers or administrators.

All this is true. Yet members and leaders of organizations, especially those whose positions call for planning and directing change, cannot evade responsibility for attempting to extend their awareness and their knowledge of what determines change. Nor can they evade responsibility for involving others in planning change. All concerned must learn to adjust to factors that cannot be altered or controlled, and to adapt and to alter those that can be. For as long as the dynamic forces of science, technology, and intercultural mixing are at work in the world, change in organizations is unavoidable. Freedom, in the sense of the extension of uncoerced and effective human choice, depends on the extension of man's power to bring processes of change, now often chaotic and unconsidered, under more planful and rational control (2).

References

1. Kenneth D. Benne and Bozidar Muntyan, *Human Relations in Curriculum Change*. (New York: Holt, Rinehart and Winston, Inc., 1951).
2. Ronald Lippitt, Jeanne Watson, and Bruce Westley, *Dynamics of Planned Change*. (New York: Harcourt, Brace & World, Inc., 1958).

EXERCISES AND DISCUSSION TOPICS FOR CHAPTER 13

Exercises

1. Isolate one change that has recently occurred in your community. Try to follow this change through all segments of the community. Discover how change affects everyone in a community.
2. Design the most effective way of handling an issue that you have dealt with in the simulation. Determine how, ideally, you would solve this problem in real life. Discover means used to bring people to agree on changes to be made in communities.

Discussion Topics

Discuss Walton's two strategies of change and how they have worked in the simulation and in other situations with which you are familiar. What is force field analysis. Using force field analysis, point out major obstacles and helping forces for change in the simulation for one issue (welfare, low-income housing, etc.).

Reactions to change are many and varied. Discuss these reactions and how communities can plan innovations so that adaption to change is made most readily without serious problems. How does your community solve its problems? Discuss different strategies used.

Observe the process of change during the simulation. Chart your group's progress through the various stages of the simulation.

CHAPTER 14

Evaluation of the Psych City Experience

One of the points stressed implicitly by the authors of the empirical research selections and explicitly by some of those who wrote about understanding and improving communities is that it is important to periodically assess the impact and value of your course of action in order to maximize your effectiveness. In the same way, it is crucial that you, as students of community behavior, attempt to examine your learning experience. This will help you to determine which parts of your experience have been successful and which have not. It will enable you to assign responsibility for facilitating or impeding learning to the proper source. Was the material stimulating or did you put in a lot of extra time (or both)? Were the exercises irrelevant or were you too involved in other activities to be able to devote sufficient time to this experience? These are samples of the types of questions you might ask.

Just as no one can *tell* you *how* to learn, no one can really *dictate* to you the *correct* means for evaluating yourself. The best we can do is offer some guidelines, present some alternative approaches, and encourage you to take advantage of those which seem useful and design your own assessment techniques where you find deficits in ours.

In the Introduction to this book (page xv) we presented four objectives which we hoped to approach. We would like to review these objectives and insert some comments regarding their assessment.

1   *To provide an opportunity for each participant to learn how another person might think, feel and behave by role playing the part of a particular character in a simulated community situation.*

304

Role playing can be a frustrating experience. In the simulation situation, where controversial material is being dealt with, many people, at first, feel impelled to present their own opinions rather than those of the character whom they are portraying. After overcoming this problem, some students are able to incorporate the thoughts and feelings of their character but find it difficult to express their reactions in the Town Meeting. Not until you can become behaviorally involved in the role is it possible to have an adequate understanding of what such a person experiences. The final stage in the development of your role is the consistent enactment of the role over an extended period of time. One indication of this level of functioning is contained in the statement of a student who participated in the Psych City simulation:

> When I spoke during the Town Meeting I was no longer aware of the distinction between myself and my role. I responded without thinking, as my character would.

It is impossible to measure the first objective by completely remaining within the context of the simulation. However, if this objective is to have enduring value it should also generalize to the "real" world. One method of assessing this generalization is to monitor your reactions to people you meet, especially those who are different from you. To what extent do you attempt to understand what their feelings and thoughts are? Are you making greater or fewer instant stereotypic judgments about these people? Do you see their behavior in terms of right or wrong or do you attempt to relate their behavior to their personal circumstances? While it is difficult to control for experiential factors other than Psych City which may have influenced you during this time period, the answers to these questions may assist you in exploring the impact of this learning experience on your own life.

2   *To encourage participants to increase their awareness of how and why decisions are made and actions are taken in community settings by having participants:*

   (a) *serve as participant observers in the simulation,*
   (b) *attend actual community meetings,*
   (c) *read relevant fiction and nonfiction material,*
   (d) *engage in prescribed exercises,*
   (e) *discuss all of these experiences.*

Most intensive learning experiences tend to influence the student for a long while after the formal program has ended. Often, learning leads to an

increased awareness of the complexities involved in community interactions. This is accompanied by the abandonment of some old ideas and
the adoption of new perceptions, many of which are only partially formed.
When this new information has been absorbed, but not yet integrated and
assimilated into the student's conceptual framework, the result is frequently confusion and uncertainty about how a community functions.

The dilemma which the student in this situation faces is how to discriminate between the unsettling feelings which accompany personal
growth and the confusion which comes from a poorly presented learning
experience.

3 *To assist participants in learning to relate psychological concepts and
research to community behavior by presenting experiential and academic
alternatives in an integrated manner.*

The crucial issue in evaluating this objective is the extent to which you
can proceed back and forth from the raw data of community experience to
the clarifying methods and principles of social science. Can you explain
or predict the behavior of the City Council any more effectively when you
apply a psychological model you have learned? Are you able to derive
some general principles of conflict resolution which are equally valid for
most intergroup rivalry situations? Do you feel better prepared to assess
the relative value of various theories in facilitating our efforts to cope with
social problems?

4 *To provide participants an opportunity to assess various methods of
learning about community behavior by having them experience these
alternatives and presenting them with material which describes methods
for assessing their experience.*

One of the overall goals of this experience has been to help students
learn how to learn. The benefit of developing new practical methods for
enhancing your level of awareness and problem-solving skills, goes far
beyond the immediate situation. It is our belief that one role which educators should play is to make their students less dependent upon them as
the students develop. Their job would then include a form of planned
obsolescence in its performance.

Some of the indicators which are associated with increased sophistica-
tion in regard to learning methods are: (1) more active as opposed to
passive participation by the learner; (2) greater flexibility and creativity
in the choice and utilization of resources; (3) more efficient use of time

and energy in accomplishing a learning task; (4) a greater tendency to combine several learning methods in fulfilling a single educational assignment; (5) an increased interest in the process of learning.

When you evaluate your experience, there is one general objective which you might keep in mind — *the goal of this experience is to allow you to explore the process of life in a modern community through the use of a controlled approximation of reality.* This implies that we must first recreate reality in order to understand it, before we build more ideal models of how we would like to see communities function. By retaining this concept we may minimize the problem experienced by others of judging our efforts to be unsuccessful because we have created in our simulation a community filled with confusion, conflict, hostility, and inefficiency. In fact, this is an accurate portrayal of some segments of life. If we wish to strengthen the counter qualities of order, harmony, understanding, love and productivity, we must acknowledge and comprehend the reality of the former state. If your community has not solved its problems to your satisfaction, it may signify that rather than having failed at your task, you may have successfully re-created reality.

THE PROBLEMS OF MEASUREMENT OF ROLE-PLAYING EXERCISES*

William L. Claiborn

In this article Mr. Claiborn points out the problems involved in assessing and evaluating role-playing experiences. He also presents some suggestions and techniques to help you to evaluate your Psych City experience.

Despite the increased popularity of group laboratory sessions involving simulated role-playing exercises, little has been done to provide systematic analysis of the effects of participation in such exercises (Gamson, 1969). Perhaps like many of the newer educational techniques, the proliferation of simulated exercises has stayed well ahead of the attempts by psychologists and educational specialists to develop adequate measurement devices and to evolve a set of techniques and strategies for effective evaluation. Probably the major reason why so little evaluation work has been accomplished is that it is very difficult to do. It requires (1) definition of goals and expected outcomes of the exercises, (2) definition of firm and

*Prepared especially for this book.

operationally useful criteria for success of the exercises, and (3) development and implementation of an effective measurement strategy. Each of
these problems will be discussed in turn in the following paragraphs.

Simulated role-playing exercises have been introduced for a wide
variety of purposes, in some occasions probably for no purpose at all
other than fascination in its novelty or a naïve notion of its inherent value.
Role-playing exercises find use in five major types of situations: academic
instruction, training programs, encounter and T-group sessions, psycho-
therapeutic settings, and entertainment. Each of these situations has
unique "purposes" which would determine the appropriate evaluation
strategies.

The first of these, academic instruction, seems perhaps to be an unusual
place for role-playing exercises to appear. Traditional forms of teaching,
including didactic lectures and formal discussion sections, are a far step
from the use of complex role-playing exercises producing high levels of
participant involvement. However, increasingly in the social sciences and
education such exercises are used as part of the normal instructional
sequence. Indeed, in some universities there are now courses which consist entirely of such programmed exercises. The purpose of role playing is
to enhance the learning of the specified academic content.

The second focus for occurrence of such role-playing exercises is in
training programs. Training programs often have specified objectives
which require providing participants with experience in situations with
the demands of the job for which they are being trained. Therefore, it is a
logical extension of training programs to include role playing which can
incorporate most of the advantages of actual situational learning and few
of the disadvantages. Such exercises allow the simulating of many conditions which would be difficult or impossible to produce under most circumstances. It allows the participant to practice his behavior in smaller,
analyzable segments. Since it is not real life, the consequences are
revocable; different behaviors can be sampled and their consequences
examined. In a short period of time, experiences which would normally
occur over the course of months or years, can be illustrated, experienced,
and analyzed. Obviously the major disadvantage to such role playing is
the very lack of reality which brings it most of its advantages. Particularly,
it is difficult to create the intensity and range of behaviors found in real-
world situations and sometimes it is difficult to engage the participants to
the degree required for realistic enactment.

With increasing frequency, such role-playing exercises are making their
appearance in encounter or T-group laboratory exercises. T-groups,

evolving out of the behavioral science revolution beginning in the late 1940s, attempt through experimentation with forms of direct person-to-person communication to deal with emotional and other aspects of communication. Exercises, then, are often designed to confront an individual or a group of individuals with the perspectives, attitudes, and relationships felt and experienced by other people. Such encounters may lead to increased, or improved, accuracy of perception of the feelings and attitudes of these participants. This kind of technique is used particularly to help managers experience their subordinates feelings and attitudes or to help police relate to community people or to help the wealthy and the powerful understand the poor and the powerless.

Fourth, role-enactment techniques are now being used in some form in the course of psychotherapy. It is assumed that the individuals participating in such exercises are in need of controlled, often highly emotional or sensitive experiential learning which permits the sampling of a variety of behaviors, without the danger and consequences of real-life experience. Patients and clients use the experiences to make therapeutic improvement.

Finally, with store bought games, newspaper or magazine games, people can for the sake of personal enjoyment or enlightenment, engage in exercises designed to place them in roles quite novel or unique to them. This use of role playing might be described as a form of self-education pursued for its own sake rather than from some other outside or externally defined purposes.

None of the situations in which role-playing exercises are found necessarily define specified changes or outcomes expected for participants. In particular, many theorists are unable to describe the desired outcomes of such exercises in other than vague and general terms. This leads us to the problem and definition of criteria. What is, in fact, the desired outcome? In a situation where the outcome is only poorly or vaguely specified, there is no way in which the enterprising researcher or student can check to see whether goals or criteria have been met. One consequence of this, not surprisingly, is that little research is done and often the completed research is criticized for its irrelevance to the assumed criterion.

There are four major classes of criteria that can, and are, occasionally used in attempting to evaluate such role-playing exercises. They are behavior change, verbal attitude changes, changes in personal satisfaction, and experiential changes. Behavior change, a concept used here to apply to complex social behaviors which include verbal behavior but are not limited to it, is often thought by psychologists as an extremely important, perhaps limited criterion of success. If exercises are valuable, they should show up directly in significant and meaningful changes of the participants' behavior. Unfortunately it is not always clear as to what behavior should actually be changed. For example, if a policeman participates in a role-playing exercise in which he is confronted with militant blacks in a tense situation involving an arrest, the useful, most effective police action is not readily apparent. There is no list of accepted good behaviors, there is no agreed upon strategy. One man's successful handling may be described by some criterion-setters as a good example of law and order, by another set of criterion-setters as an example of police brutality. Obviously then, before successful setting of behavioral criterion can occur, some public agreement must be made of the operations which define successful outcome. Another problem with using behavioral change as a criterion, is the difficulty in clearly limiting and specifying how the behavior is to be measured. More will be presented on this problem later.

The second criterion used for evaluating intensive role-playing exercises is that of attitude change. Since attitudes are usually assessed by questionnaires and other paper and pencil measures, we shall distinguish here between them and other behavior. While attitudes are generally assumed to be ultimately reflected in behavior, measuring attitude change is sometimes viewed as a short cut to measuring "real" change. Accepting the notion that attitude change is a criterion for success against which to evaluate participation requires determination of which attitudes should change and in which direction they should change. A simple notion, for example, that attitudes should become more positive probably is destined to failure since direct experience with people does not always make one's attitudes more favorable. In a study reported elsewhere, (Claiborn, 1971) following a role-playing experience, evaluative attitudes were shown to have changed toward more negative or less accepting direction. Role-playing experiences may lead to more accurate attitudes and assessments which in some cases may be positive, in other cases negative. Perhaps the exercises take some form of the pink out of the rose-colored glasses. In any case, it should be clear that when trying to assess and evaluate attitudes change as a criterion for measuring the effects of a role-playing exercise, the researcher needs to carefully specify both the kinds of attitude changes and the direction of these changes he expects.

A third type of criterion sometimes used in research and role playing is that of personal satisfaction. Usually pencil and paper measures are taken of an individual's feelings about himself, his adequacy, his adjustment, or his place in the world. The notion is that following such role-playing exercises the participant should increase his personal satisfaction, and have a more satisfactory self-concept. Several measures have been suggested for this purpose, but the points raised in the preceding discussion of attitude change are applicable here. It certainly is possible that an individual would learn more of his personal inadequacies than of his competencies; although often an individual learns that other people, as well as himself, have weaknesses, frailities, fears, and inadequacies. In some senses, this criterion is a private criterion rather than a public one, where the behavior changes and attitude changes are more observable, measurable, and definable. Personal satisfaction and self-concept change seem to be personal changes, not necessarily clearly reflected directly in outward behaviors.

The final category of criterion definition is an experiential one. The existential, experiential theorists often refuse to submit their criterion to operational definition and, in fact, say the experience in and of itself is valuable. Direct, observable outcomes are not to be expected. If that is the case, of course, the scientist need proceed no further and can rest assured that he has created an experience or encounter and has no need to worry about consequences. In some cases the people concerned with experiential criteria would say that the process is more important than the outcome and would focus research on examination of the nature of the interactions, perhaps attuning themselves to the intensity of the personal involvement of the participants. It should be clear that this category of criteria is the least amenable to traditional research models requiring operationalization of dependent variables.

In the development of any criterion, it is important to make logical or theoretical links between the exercise itself and the outcome measure. The development and specification of criteria should reflect theoretical or cognitive connections between the exercises, the experience, the learning and change, and the outcome measures. The set of constructs should be related in a nomological network. Research can provide a test for part of the theory. Having a theoretical structure provides a basis for understanding and evaluating the data obtained. Changes in a vacuum make no sense. If the results do not come out as predicted, the model provides concrete suggestions for altering or modifying strategies, making necessary or beneficial changes in the role-playing exercise.

Continuing use and support for role-playing exercises requires justification. In cost accounting terms, it is necessary to show that the money or resources expended in pursuit of the role-playing exercise produces greater benefits per unit cost than those produced by other methods. Since the outcome of the role playing is compared with the outcome of other alternatives, the criteria of comparison must be similar. It is not sufficient to set narrow criteria for success of a role-playing exercise and specify and even meet those criteria unless the changes can be further justified in terms of the initial goal and relative cost effectiveness. Different criteria for different change strategies prevents comparison.

To facilitate the collection of information on the effectiveness of role-playing exercise it is important to be able to make appropriate deductive and inductive statements about your data through the use of good experimental design. Problems and vagaries of experimental design, are well discussed elsewhere, (especially Campbell and Stanley, 1963). Generally, it is important to have an appropriate control against which to compare the participants in the exercise. This control is often in the form of a group whose members do not participate in the exercise. The use of control groups permits the experimenter to evaluate sources of distortion such as: experimenter bias, expectancy or placebo effects, and change over time. Specifically, subjects participating in a role-playing exercise may benefit, not from the specifics of the role-playing exercise, but from the general opportunity to participate and the resultant focused attention. Submitting to measurements is itself sometimes sufficient to produce cognitive or behavioral changes and, hence to indicate effects of the experience when, in fact, the participation in the role playing, *per se*, was not the source of the change. If the role-playing exercise extends over time, other historical events may intervene to change people's attitudes and behaviors. In order to control for the effects of history, a control against time is necessary.

Since it is impossible in all but the most elaborate of experimental designs to control for all the possible contaminants, it seems important that the researcher specify which of his hoped for conclusions are the most important and then endeavor to control for the likely confounding effects of that particular criterion. For example, if the experimenter wants to certify that the role-playing exercise is more effective than other forms of training, his appropriate comparisons would include other forms of training, it would not be sufficient to examine only the result of the role-playing exercise by itself. If the researcher wanted to show the effects of role playing independent of experimenter bias and placebo effect, the design should include provisions for the placebo controls, such as the use of single and double blind procedures, placebo treatment, etc.

The pretest, posttest method is a commonly used device to evaluate change from one point to another. The participants are pretested before the beginning of the exercise and posttested following it. Any changes between pre- and posttests are attributed to the participation. While some of the weaknesses of this design have already been mentioned, specific measurement problems do develop in measuring change (Harris, 1963). In any case, particular care should be used when setting up designs to measure change so as not to restrict or limit their usefulness.

It is usually said that some measurement is better than none. Generally that seems to be the case, as long as the data collected from the inadequate measurement are not for purposes for which they have no validity. Certainly any student of role-playing exercises would want to provide the best data in terms of defining criteria and experiment design that he could obtain. The limitations of resources, time, and interest, of course, will define what strategy is actually implemented.

Two major strategies for measuring the effects of a role-playing exercise are (1) pencil and paper measures, (2) behavioral measures. The pencil and paper measures can be divided into factual assessments and attitudinal questionnaires. The behavioral measures can be divided into situational test behaviors and nonreactive measures. Each will be discussed in turn.

One simple and direct way of getting at the effectiveness of a role-playing exercise is to ask a series of concrete, factual questions. Did the participants learn more about the facts of the situation in which they were involved? Did they know the names of the people? Do they know the important concepts? Do they know the relationships? Can they differentiate and distinguish among their own roles and the role behaviors of others? Most such questionnaires for assessing factual change can be developed on a face valid basis, much like an achievement test. That is, the operational definition of the goals can simply be the set of facts contained in the role-playing exercise much like a test measures facts contained in a textbook. Attitude measurement is a more complex task. Researchers have devised and perfected many sophisticated attitude measurement scales and devices. Three of the most common are "likert type" item scales, semantic differential and situational questionnaires, (Fishbein, 1967). The semantic differential requires subjects or participants to rate concepts on a series of usually bipolar adjectives such as hot-cold, good-bad, to assess emotional polarity of various concepts. Attitude, in this case, is viewed as being located in a dimensional semantic space. Situational questionnaires, on the other hand, simply try to specify probablistic situations and ask the participant what his behavior is likely to be. This is in a sense, a pencil and paper way of getting at behavioral observations. While pencil and paper measures are much easier to administer, they can be given to far larger numbers of people, and can have respectable reliability, they usually do not have intrinsic or predictive validity and they are second best measures. People say things that they do not do and do things they do not say.

One concern among attitude measurement people is that attitude change in itself may not be the important criterion. It may be, for example, more important that there is increased variability or differentiation of attitudes. The real world is complex and one way of measuring cognitive development is to evaluate the complexity with which one views his world. In the pencil and paper measures as discussed here, cognitive complexity could be reflected in greater variability in a posttest session than in the pretest session, rather than as a simple change in direction.

Among the behavioral measures the most obvious would consist of observing the person's behavior in situations similar to the training experience to see if his behavior changes. For example, the policeman can be watched while he goes through the arrest procedure involving a black militant. This behavior can be evaluated by supervisors or by some defined criterion (although the problems of conceptual definition of behavior criterion has been mentioned earlier). Obviously, it is going to be difficult to be in the observer's position at the time various behaviors occur and it is a relatively inefficient and expensive, time-consuming way of collecting evaluation data.

A final source of behavioral data is that found in nonreactive measures (Webb, Campbell, Schwartz, and Sechrest, 1966). While it is possible to establish test situations which are contrived, they often lack some of the elements of reality essential to the behavior in question. However, the use of nonreactive measures such as traces, public behavior and the like, can be particularly useful in evaluating the long-term effects of role-playing exercises. Examples include change in absence rates, staff turnover, public statements, written policies, or number of complaints filed. These and many other unobtrusive measures provide their data about the appropriate criterion behavior without disturbing or disrupting the participants. They are in fact *in situ* behavior samples which in some sense can become the criterion.

A research design to evaluate Psych City might look like the following (Claiborn, 1971): (A) Formalize and operationalize hypothesis, (B) Randomly assign students to participants and controls, (C) Pretest all students on attitude measures of interest, (D) Conduct Psych City, (E) Collect unobtrusive or other process data, (F) Posttest all students, (G) Collect any other criteria data, (H) Analyze data and report in terms of hypotheses. The choice in selection of such matters reflects the imagination of the researcher.

One important problem in setting up a measurement strategy is that, unfortunately, most of our concepts of behavior do not represent unified behavioral patterns. That is, if we have a concept of anger, the expression of anger is likely to be different and differentiated in various situations. If our theoretical model produces only gross predictions of change, such as the person would be less angry or more angry, it is going to be extremely difficult to define a set of situations which are necessary and sufficient to define the domain of activity encompassed under the term anger. A more successful or more likely successful approach to such research would involve concrete specification of goals and of changes in terms of the specific criterion measures rather than in terms of vague, nonspecific concepts.

The use of defined role-playing exercises provides a ready made opportunity for systematic intervention in data analysis by permitting easy replication, and direct control of important independent variables. Some of the difficulties and parts to be considered are outlined above, but studies with good hypotheses, design, and measures can yield meaningful results. The specifications of these variables are limited only by the creativity of the investigators.

References

Campbell, D. & Stanley, J. *Experimental and Quasi-Experimental Designs for Research.* Skokie, Illinois: Rand McNally, 1963.

Claiborn, W. The Effects of Role Playing Exercise on Role Perceptions. Unpublished manuscript, 1971.

Fishbein, M. (Ed.) *Readings in Attitude Theory and Measurement*, New York: Wiley, 1967.

Gamson, W. *SIMSOC Simulated Society.* New York: Free Press, 1969.

Harris, C. (Ed.) *Problems in Measurement Change.* Madison, Wisc.: University of Wisconsin Press, 1963.

Webb, E., Campbell, D., Schwartz, R., & Sechrest, L. *Unobtrusive Measures: Nonreactive Research in the Social Sciences.* Skokie, Illinois: Rand McNally, 1966.

EXERCISES AND DISCUSSION TOPICS FOR CHAPTER 14

Exercises

1. Write your own personal evaluation of the simulation. List positive and negative points. Provide evidence for your evaluation.
2. Design an evaluation for the simulation experience. Below is an example of an evaluation for the Psych City simulation. It might be used both before and after the simulation.

Instructions

In the following list are pairs of words. These pairs of words can be used to describe people, places, or things. In answering these questions, give answers based on what these words mean to you.

At the top of each page above each list, you will see a description of a person. This is the person which you are to describe. For example:

TODAY'S WEATHER

Now look at the first pair of words below. If you feel that TODAY'S WEATHER is very much like the word on the left, make your check mark to the left

hot ___X__ : ___ : ___ : ___ : ___ : ___ : ___ :   cold

If you feel TODAY'S WEATHER is very much like the word on the right, make your check mark on the right.

hot ___ : ___ : ___ : ___ : ___ : ___ : _X_ :   cold

If you feel TODAY'S WEATHER stands somewhere in the middle, make your mark somewhere in the middle.

hot ___ : ___ : ___ : _X_ : ___ : ___ : ___ :   cold

You can put your check mark anywhere along the line. You place it closer to one end of the line if that word is very much like what you are to describe.

Situation

The situation is that of a P.T.A. meeting. The Superintendent of Schools has just ordered the busing of students in order to comply with new state education guidelines for racial balancing of schools. A large number of interest groups are represented at this meeting. Among them are (1) a large group of irate white parents, (2) a smaller group of black militants opposed to integration plans, (3) many moderates both black and white, and (4) teachers of various opinions on the busing issue. The meeting is heated and confusing.

Below you will find description of four people who are at this meeting. For each individual, we would like your impression of how he sees the situation, how you see him, and how you see the situation yourself.

On the scale below, please indicate how you, *yourself*, would rate the above situation if you were present as an interested party, based on your *own* opinions.

pleasant	___ : ___ : ___ : ___ : ___ : ___ : ___ :	unpleasant
strong	___ : ___ : ___ : ___ : ___ : ___ : ___ :	weak
interesting	___ : ___ : ___ : ___ : ___ : ___ : ___ :	uninteresting
easy	___ : ___ : ___ : ___ : ___ : ___ : ___ :	hard
exciting	___ : ___ : ___ : ___ : ___ : ___ : ___ :	boring
good	___ : ___ : ___ : ___ : ___ : ___ : ___ :	bad

Person A:

Person *A* is a white parent. He is employed as an electrician and has two high-school-age children. The parents of Person *A* were born in Europe; he has a high school education, is a conservative Republican and is worried about the effect of school busing on his children.

1. Please indicate on the following scale how you think Person *A* would perceive the P.T.A. meeting described above.

pleasant	___ : ___ : ___ : ___ : ___ : ___ : ___ :	unpleasant
strong	___ : ___ : ___ : ___ : ___ : ___ : ___ :	weak
interesting	___ : ___ : ___ : ___ : ___ : ___ : ___ :	uninteresting
easy	___ : ___ : ___ : ___ : ___ : ___ : ___ :	hard
exciting	___ : ___ : ___ : ___ : ___ : ___ : ___ :	boring
good	___ : ___ : ___ : ___ : ___ : ___ : ___ :	bad

2. Please indicate on the following scale how you would rate the person described above (Person *A*).

pleasant	___ : ___ : ___ : ___ : ___ : ___ : ___ :	unpleasant
strong	___ : ___ : ___ : ___ : ___ : ___ : ___ :	weak
interesting	___ : ___ : ___ : ___ : ___ : ___ : ___ :	uninteresting
easy	___ : ___ : ___ : ___ : ___ : ___ : ___ :	hard
exciting	___ : ___ : ___ : ___ : ___ : ___ : ___ :	boring
good	___ : ___ : ___ : ___ : ___ : ___ : ___ :	bad

Person B

Person *B* is a black accountant who has a son of high school age. He is strongly in favor of integration and busing. For many years Person *B* has been active in the N.A.A.C.P. Politically, Person *B* is a liberal to left-wing Democrat.

1. Please indicate on the following scale how you think Person *B* would perceive the P.T.A. meeting described earlier.

pleasant	___:___:___:___:___:___:___:	unpleasant
strong	___:___:___:___:___:___:___:	weak
interesting	___:___:___:___:___:___:___:	uninteresting
easy	___:___:___:___:___:___:___:	hard
exciting	___:___:___:___:___:___:___:	boring
good	___:___:___:___:___:___:___:	bad

2. Please indicate on the following scale how you would rate the person described above (Person *B*).

pleasant	___:___:___:___:___:___:___:	unpleasant
strong	___:___:___:___:___:___:___:	weak
interesting	___:___:___:___:___:___:___:	uninteresting
easy	___:___:___:___:___:___:___:	hard
exciting	___:___:___:___:___:___:___:	boring
good	___:___:___:___:___:___:___:	bad

Person C

Person *C* is a member of the state education committee responsible for the new busing law. He is at this meeting to explain the law and answer questions. He is in full agreement with the law and is partially responsible for enforcing it.

1. Please indicate on the following scale how you think Person *C* would perceive the P.T.A. meeting described earlier.

pleasant	___:___:___:___:___:___:___:	unpleasant

strong   __:__:__:__:__:__:__: weak

interesting __:__:__:__:__:__:__: uninteresting

easy   __:__:__:__:__:__:__: hard

exciting   __:__:__:__:__:__:__: boring

good   __:__:__:__:__:__:__: bad

2. Please indicate on the following scale how you would rate the person described above (Person C).

pleasant   __:__:__:__:__:__:__: unpleasant

strong   __:__:__:__:__:__:__: weak

interesting __:__:__:__:__:__:__: uninteresting

easy   __:__:__:__:__:__:__: hard

exciting   __:__:__:__:__:__:__: boring

good   __:__:__:__:__:__:__: bad

Person D

Person D is the role you have been assigned to play in Psych City this semester. Think about that role.

1. Please indicate on the following scale how you think Person D (your role) would perceive the P.T.A. meeting.

pleasant   __:__:__:__:__:__:__: unpleasant

strong   __:__:__:__:__:__:__: weak

interesting __:__:__:__:__:__:__: uninteresting

easy   __:__:__:__:__:__:__: hard

exciting   __:__:__:__:__:__:__: boring

good   __:__:__:__:__:__:__: bad

2. Please indicate on the following scale how you would rate the person who is described in your assigned role (Person D).

pleasant   __:__:__:__:__:__:__: unpleasant

strong   __:__:__:__:__:__:__: weak

interesting	__:__:__:__:__:__:__:	uninteresting
easy	__:__:__:__:__:__:__:	hard
exciting	__:__:__:__:__:__:__:	boring
good	__:__:__:__:__:__:__:	bad

Finally, if you were the person chiefly responsible for the outcome of the P.T.A. meeting described, how would you handle it? What people, groups, ideas or information would you consider? What actions would you take to insure a successful meeting? What would be your most important goal as the person responsible? (Where possible, please give the reasons for your answers.)

Discussion Topics

Discuss the situational factors which could have made Psych City different for your group (if roles were assigned differently, if the time of the simulation was changed, etc.).

Talk about role playing as an educational tool. Is role playing relevant? It is useful in real-life situations?

What kinds of criteria might be useful in evaluating the outcome of Psych City? Try to specify a set of criteria, and how you would measure them.

Think of several unobtrusive measures that might be available for use in Psych City. How would you go about collecting this data? What would it mean?

References and Recommended Readings[1]

ROLE EXPECTANCIES AND INTERPERSONAL PERCEPTION
(Chapters 6 & 7)

Altrocchi, J. (1959). Dominance as a factor in interpersonal choice and perception. *Journal of abnormal and social psychology*, **59**, 303–307.

Anderson, N. H. and A. A. Barrios (1961). Primary effects in personality impression formation. *Journal of abnormal and social psychology*, **63**, 346–350.

Aronson, E. and D. Linder (1965). Gain and loss of self-esteem as determinants of interpersonal attractiveness. *Journal of experimental social psychology*, **1**, 156–172.

*Asch, S. E. (1946). Forming impressions of personality. *Journal of social psychology*, **41**, 258–290.

Backman, C. W. and P. F. Secord (1959). The effect of perceived liking on interpersonal attraction. *Human Relations*, **12**, 379–384.

Blossom, J. and A. H. Maslow (1957). Security of judges as a factor in impressions of warmth in others. *Journal of abnormal and social psychology*, **55**, 147–148.

Bruner, J. S. and L. Postman (1949). Perception, cognition and behavior. *Journal of personality*, **18**, 14–31.

Bruner, J. S. and R. Taguri (1954). The perception of people. In G. Lindsey (Ed.) *Handbook of Social Psychology*. Cambridge, Mass.: Addison-Wesley. Pp. 634–654.

Byrne, D. (1961). Interpersonal attraction and attitude similarity. *Journal of abnormal and social psychology*, **62**, 713–715.

*Cline, V. B. (1964). Interpersonal perception. In B. A. Maher (Ed.) *Progress in experimental personality research*, Vol. 1. New York: Academic Press. Pp. 221–284.

Crockett, W. H. (1965). Cognitive complexity and impression formation. In B. A. Maher (Ed.) *Progress in experimental personality research*, Vol. 2. New York: Academic Press.

[1]Starred (*) references are those particularly recommended as supplementary readings. These are generally books or review chapters covering a subject discussed in this book. Experimental articles which are especially relevant or illustrative are also starred.

322   Psych City: A Simulated Community

Davis, K. E. and E. E. Jones (1960). Changes in interpersonal perception as a means of reducing cognitive dissonance. *Journal of abnormal and social psychology*, **61**, 402–410.

DeSoto, C., J. L. Kuethe, and R. Wunderlick (1960). Social perception and self perception of high and low authoritarians. *Journal of social psychology*, **52**, 149–155.

Exline, R. (1963). Explorations in the process of person perception: visual interaction in relation to competition, sex, and need for affiliation. *Journal of personality*, **31**, 1–20.

Feshback, S. and R. D. Singer (1957). The effects of fear arousal and suppression of fear upon social perception. *Journal of abnormal and social psychology*, **55**, 283–288.

Gergen, K. J. and B. Wishnov (1965). Others self evaluations and interaction anticipation as determinants of self presentation. *Journal of personality and social psychology*, **2**, 348–358.

*Goffman, E. (1959). *The presentation of self in everyday life*. Garden City, N.Y.: Doubleday.

Gordon, C. and K. J. Gergen (Eds.) (1968). *The self in social interaction*, Vol. 1. New York: Wiley.

*Heider, F. (1958). *The psychology of interpersonal relations*. New York: Wiley.

Izard, C. E. (1960). Personality similarity and friendship. *Journal of personality and social psychology*, **61**, 47–51.

Jackson, D. N. (1962). The measurement of perceived personality trait relationships. In N. F. Washburne (Ed.) *Decisions, values and groups*, Vol. 2. New York: Pergamon Press. Pp. 177–188.

Jones, E. E. (1954). Authoritarianism as a determinant of first impression formation. *Journal of personality*, **23**, 107–127.

Jones, E. E. (1964). *Ingratiation: a social psychological analysis*. New York: Appelton-Century-Crofts.

*Jones, E. E. and K. E. Davis (1965). From acts to dispositions: the attribution process in person perception. In L. Berkowitz, (Ed.) *Advances in experimental social psychology*, Vol. 2. New York: Academic Press.

*Kelley, H. H. (1950). The warm-cold variable in first impressions of persons. *Journal of personality*, **18**, 431–439.

Kipris, D. M. (1961). Changes in self concepts in relation to perceptions of others. *Journal of personality*, **29**, 449–465.

Leventhal, H. and D. L. Singer (1964). Cognitive complexity, impression formation and impression change. *Journal of personality*, **32**, 210–226.

Levy, K. H. and M. L. Richter (1963). Impressions of groups as a function of the stimulus values of their individual members. *Journal of abnormal and social psychology*, **67**, 349–354.

Lindzey, G. and J. A. Urdan (1954). Personality and social choice. *Sociometry*, **17**, 47–63.

McDonald, R. L. (1965). Ego control patterns and attributions of hostility to self and others. *Journal of personality and social psychology*, **2**, 273–277.

*Pepitone, A. (1964). *Attraction and hostility*. New York: Atherton.

*Schacter, S. (1959). *The psychology of affiliation*. Stanford: Stanford University Press.

Scodel, A. and P. Mussen (1953). Social perceptions of authoritarians and non-authoritarians. *Journal of abnormal and social psychology*, **48**, 181–184.

Secord, P. F. and C. W. Backman (1964). *Social Psychology*. New York: McGraw-Hill.

Shrauger, S. and J. Altrocchi (1964). The personality of the perceiver as a factor in personality perception. *Psychological Bulletin*, **62**, 289–308.

Smith, A. J. (1957). Similarity of values and its relation to acceptance and the projection of similarity. *Journal of psychology*, **43**, 251–260.

COMMUNICATION (Chapter 8)

*Abelson, R. P., E. Aronson, W. J. McGuire, T. N. Newcomb, M. J. Rosenberg, and P. Tannenbaum (Eds.) (1969). *Theories of cognitive consistency: a sourcebook*. Chicago: Rand McNally.

*Back, K. W. (1951). Influence through social communication. *Journal of abnormal and social psychology*, **46**, 9–23.

Bavelas, A. (1951). Communication patterns in informal groups. (1968). In Cartwright, D. and A. Zander (Eds.) *Group Dynamics*. Chap. 37.

Bales, R. F. (1952). Some uniformities of behavior in small social systems. In G. E. Swanson, T. M. Newcomb and E. L. Hartley (Eds) *Readings in social psychology*. New York: Holt, Rinehart and Winston. Pp. 146–159.

Brehm, J. W. and A. R. Cohen (1962). *Explorations in cognitive dissonance*. New York: Wiley.

*Campbell, D. T. (1963). Social attitudes and other acquired behavioral dispositions. In S. Koch (Eds.) *Psychology: a study of a science*. New York: McGraw-Hill. Pp. 94–172.

*Chapanis, N. P. and A. Chapanis (1964). *Cognitive dissonance: five years later*. *Psychological Bulletin*, **61**, 1–22.

*Chein, I. (1948). Behavior theory and the behavior of attitudes: some critical comments. *Psychological Review*, **55**, 175–188.

Cohen, A. R. (1958). Upward communication in experimentally created hierarchies. *Human Relations*, **11**, 41–53.

*Feldman, S. (Ed.) (1966). *Cognitive consistency: motivational antecedents and behavioral consequences*. New York: Academic Press.

Festinger, L. (1950). Informal social communication. *Psychological Review*, **57**, 271–282.

*Festinger, L. (1957). *A theory of cognitive dissonance*. New York: Harper & Row.

Friedman, J. L. (1964). Involvement, discrepancy and change. *Journal of abnormal and social psychology*, **69**, 290–295.

Greenwald, A. G. (1966). Effects of prior commitment on behavior change after a persuasive communication. *Public Opinion Quarterly*, **29** (4), 595–601.

*Greenwald, A. G., T. Brock, and T. Ostrom (1968). *Psychological Foundations of Attitudes*. New York: Academic Press.

*Heider, F. (1958). The psychology of interpersonal relations. New York: Wiley.

Hovland, C. I. (Ed.) (1957). *The order of presentation in persuasion*. New Haven: Yale University Press.

Hovland, C. I., O. J. Harvey, and M. Sherif (1957). Assimilation and contrast effects in reactions to communication and attitude change. *Journal of abnormal and social psychology*, **55**, 244–252.

Hovland, C. I. and I. L. Janis (Eds.) (1959). *Personality and persuasibility*. New Haven: Yale University Press.

Hovland, C. I., A. A. Lumsdaine, and F. D. Sheffield (1949). *Experiments on mass communication*. Princeton, N.J.: Princeton University Press.

Hovland, C. I. and H. A. Pritzker (1957). Extent of opinion change as a function of amount of change advocated. *Journal of abnormal and social psychology*, **54**, 257–261.

*Hovland, C. I. and M. J. Rosenberg (Eds.) (1960). *Attitude organization and change.* New Haven: Yale University Press.

*Hovland, C. I., I. L. Janis, and H. H. Kelley (1953). *Communication and Persuasion.* New Haven: Yale University Press.

Hovland, C. I. and W. Weiss (1951). The influence of source credibility on communicator effectiveness. *Public Opinion Quarterly,* 15, 635–650.

Insko, C. A., F. Murashima, and M. Saiyadain (1966). Communicator discrepancy, stimulus ambiguity and influence. *Journal of personality,* 34 (2), 262–274.

Janis, I. L. and S. Feshback (1953). Effects of fear arousing communications. *Journal of abnormal and social psychology,* 65, 403–410.

Katz, D. (1966). The functional approach to the study of attitudes. *Public Opinions Quarterly,* 24, 163–204.

*Katz, D. and E. Stotland (1963). A preliminary statement to a theory of attitude structure and change. In S. Koch (Ed.) *Psychology: a study of a science,* Vol. 3. New York: McGraw-Hill. Pp. 423–475.

*Kelman, H. (1958). Compliance, identification and internalization: three processes of attitude change. *Journal of conflict resolution,* 2, 51–60.

*Kelman, H. (1961). Processes of opinion change. *Public Opinion Quarterly,* 25, 57–78.

Kelman, H. (1962). The induction of action and attitude change. In S. Coopersmith (Ed.) *Personality research.* Copenhagen, Denmark: Munksgaard.

Kelman, H. and C. I. Hovland (1953). Reinstatement of the communicator in delayed measurement of opinion change. *Journal of abnormal and social psychology,* 48, 327–335.

LaPiere, R. T. (1934). Attitudes versus action. *Social forces,* 13, 230–237.

Kelley, H. H. (1951). Communication in experimentally created hierarchies. *Human relations,* 4, 39–56.

*Kiesler, C., B. Collins, and N. Miller (1969). *Attitude change: a critical analysis of theoretical approaches.* New York: Wiley.

Leavitt, H. J. (1958). Some effects of certain communication patterns on group performance. In E. E. Maccoby *et al. Readings in social psychology,* 3rd ed.

Leventhal, H. and P. Niles (1965). Persistence of influence for varying durations of exposure to threat stimuli. *Psychological reports,* 16 (1), 223–233.

Leventhal, H. and R. P. Singer (1966). Affect arousal and positioning of recommendations in persuasive communications. *Journal of personality and social psychology,* 4 (2), 137–146.

*McGuire, W. J. (1964). Inducing resistance to persuasion. In L. Berkowitz (Ed.) *Advances in experimental social psychology,* Vol. 1. New York: Academic Press. Pp. 191–229.

*McGuire, W. J. (1968). Nature of attitudes and attitude change. In G. Lindsey and A. Aronson (Eds.) *Handbook of social psychology.* Reading, Mass.: Addison-Wesley.

Papageorgis, D. and W. J. McGuire (1961). The generality of immunity to persuasion produced by pre-exposure to weakened counter-arguments. *Journal of abnormal and social psychology,* 62, 475–481.

Rhine, R. J. (1958). A concept formation approach to attitude acquisition. *Psychological Review,* 65, 362–370.

Sherif, M. and C. I. Hovland (1961). *Social judgment: assimilation and contrast effects in communication and attitude change.* New Haven: Yale University Press.

*Sherif, M., C. Sherif, and R. E. Nebergall (1965). *Attitude and attitude change: the social judgment-involvement approach.* Philadelphia, Pa.: Saunders Company.

Silverman, I. (1964). In defense of dissonance theory: a reply to Chapanis and Chapanis. *Psychological Bulletin*, **62**, 205–209.
*Suedfeld, P. (1971). *Attitude change: the social judgment-involvement approach.* Philadelphia, Pa.: Saunders Company.

NORMS AND REFERENCE GROUPS (Chapter 9)

Allen, V. L. and R. S. Crutchfield (1963). Generalization of experimentally reinforced conformity. *Journal of abnormal and social psychology*, **67**, 326–333.
*Asch, S. E. (1956). Studies of independence and conformity: I. A minority of one against a unanimous majority. *Psychological monographs*, **70**, No. 9, (Whole no. 416).
Berg, I. A. and B. M. Bass (Eds.) (1961). *Conformity and deviation.* New York: Harper & Row.
Bovard, E. W. Jr. (1953). Conformity to social norms and attraction to the group. *Science*, **117**, 361–363.
*Cartwright, D. and A. Zander (1968). *Group dynamics: research and theory.* New York: Harper & Row.
Crowne, D. P. and S. Liverant (1963). Conformity under varying conditions of personal commitment. *Journal of abnormal and social psychology*, **66**, 547–555.
Cohen, B. P. (1963). *Conflict and conformity.* Cambridge, Mass.: M.I.T. Press.
Deutsch, M. and H. B. Gerard (1955). A study of normative and informational social influences upon individual judgment. *Journal of abnormal and social psychology*, **51**, 629–636.
Dittes, J. E. and H. H. Kelley (1956). Effect of different conditions of acceptance upon conformity to group norms. *Journal of abnormal and social psychology*, **53**, 100–107.
Eisenstadt, S. N. (1954). Studies in reference group behavior: I. Reference norms and the social structure. *Human Relations*, **7**, 191–216.
Festinger, L. (1942). Wish, expectation and group standards as factors influencing level of aspiration. *Journal of abnormal and social psychology*, **37**, 184–200.
*Festinger, L. (1954). A theory of social comparison processes. *Human Relations*, **7**, 117–140.
*Festinger, L., S. Schacter, and K. Back (1950). *Social pressures in informal groups: a study of human factors in housing.* New York: Harper & Row.
Fiedler, F. E. (1958). *Leader attributes and group effectiveness.* Urbana, Ill: The University of Illinois Press.
*Gamson, W. A. (1964). Experimental studies of coalition formation. In L. Berkowitz, (Ed.) *Advances in experimental social psychology*, Vol. 1. New York: Academic Press.
Gerard, H. B. (1964). Conformity and commitment to the group. *Journal of abnormal and social psychology*, **68**, 209–210.
Goldberg, S. C. (1954). Three situational determinants of conformity to social norms. *Journal of abnormal and social psychology*, **49**, 325–329.
*Hare, A. P. (1962). *Handbook of small group research.* New York: Free Press.
*Hare, A. P., E. F. Borgotta, and R. F. Bales (Eds.) (1967). *Small groups.* New York: Alfred Knopf.
*Homans, G. C. (1950). *The human group.* New York: Harcourt, Brace & World.
Homans, G. C. (1961). *Social behavior in its elementary forms.* New York: Harcourt, Brace & World.

Julian, J. W. and I. D. Steiner (1961). Perceived acceptance as a determinant of conformity behavior. *Journal of social psychology*, **55**, 191–198.

*Kelley, H. H. (1952). Two functions of reference groups. In G. E. Swanson *et al.* (Eds.) *Readings in social psychology* (rev. ed.) New York: Holt. Pp. 410–414.

*Newcomb, T. (1948). Attitude development as a function of reference groups: the Bennington study. In M. Sherif, *An outline of social psychology*. New York: Harper & Row. Pp. 139–155.

Newcomb, T. (1961). *The acquaintance process*. New York: Holt, Rinehart and Winston.

Rommetveit, R. (1955). *Social norms and roles: Explorations in the psychology of enduring social pressures*. Minneapolis: The University of Minnesota Press.

*Schacter, S. (1951). Deviation, rejection and communication. *Journal of abnormal and social psychology*, **46**, 190–207.

Schacter, S. (1959). The psychology of affiliation. Stanford, Calif.: Stanford University Press.

Sherif, M. and M. O. Wilson (Eds.) (1953). *Group relations at the crossroads*. New York: Harper.

Thibaut, J. W. (1950). An experimental study of the cohesiveness of underprivileged groups. *Human Relations*, **3**, 251–278.

Thibaut, J. W. and C. Faucheux (1965). The development of contractual norms in a bargaining situation under two types of stress. *Journal of experimental social psychology*, **1**, 89–102.

*Thibaut, J. W. and H. H. Kelley (1959). *The social psychology of groups*. New York: Wiley.

SOCIAL POWER (Chapter 10)

*Blau, P. M. (1964). *Exchange and power in social life*. New York: Wiley.

Borak, L. A. Jr. (1963). The effects of threat in bargaining: a critical and experimental analysis. *Journal of abnormal and social psychology*, **66**, 37–44.

*Cartwright, D. (Ed.) *Studies in social power*. Ann Arbor, Mich.: University of Michigan Press, 1959.

Cohen, A. R. Situational structure, self-esteem and threat oriented reactions to power. In D. Cartwright (Ed.) *Studies in social power*. Ann Arbor, Mich.: University of Michigan Press. Pp. 35–52.

Dahl, R. A. (1957). The concept of power. *Behavioral science*, **2**, 201–218.

Deutsch, M. and R. M. Krauss (1960). The effect of threat on interpersonal bargaining. *Journal of abnormal and social psychology*, **61**, 181–187.

French, J. P. R. Jr. (1956). A formal theory of social power. *Psychological Review*, **63**, 181–194.

*French, J. P. R. Jr. and B. Raven (1959). The bases of social power. In D. Cartwright (Ed.) *Studies in social power*. Ann Arbor, Mich.: University of Michigan Press. Pp. 150–167.

French, J. P. R. Jr., H. W. Morrison, and G. Levinger (1960). Coercive power and forces affecting conformity. *Journal of abnormal and social psychology*, **61**, 93–101.

Hollander, E. P. (1958). Conformity, status and idiosyncracy credit. *Psychological Review*, **65**, 117–127.

Hollander, E. P. (1961). Some effects of perceived status on responses to innovative behavior. *Journal of abnormal and social psychology*, **63**, 247–250.

Jones, E. E. (1964). *Ingratiation: a social psychological analysis.* New York: Appleton-Century-Crofts.
Raven, B. H. and J. P. R. French Jr. (1958). Group support, legitimate power and social influence. *Journal of Personality*, **26**, 400–409.
Raven, B. H. and J. P. R. French Jr. (1958). Legitimate power, coercive power, and observability in social influence. *Sociometry*, **21**, 83–97.
Rosen, S., G. Levinger, and R. Lippitt (1961). Perceived sources of social power. *Journal of abnormal and social psychology*, **62**, 439–441.
Schopler, J. and N. Bateson (1965). The power of dependence. *Journal of Personality and Social Psychology*, **2**, 247–254.
Seigel, S. and L. E. Fouraker (1960). *Bargaining and group decision making.* New York: McGraw-Hill.

GROUP DECISION MAKING (Chapter 11)

Bales, R. F. (1953). The equilibrium problem in small groups. In T. Parsons, R. F. Bales, and E. A. Shils (Eds.) *Working papers in the theory of action.* New York: Free Press. Pp. 111–161.
*Bales, R. F. and F. L. Strodbeck (1951). Phases in group problem solving. *Journal of abnormal and social psychology*, **46**, 485–495.
Bass, B. M. (1963). Amount of participation, coalescence and profitability decision making discussions. *Journal of abnormal and social psychology*, **67**, 92, 94.
Berkowitz, L. (1953). Sharing leadership in small decision making groups. *Journal of abnormal and social psychology*, **48**, 231–238.
Deutsch, M. (1949). A theory of cooperation and competition. *Human Relations*, **2**, 129–152.
Deutsch, M. (1949). An experimental study of the effects of cooperation and competition upon group processes. *Human Relations*, **2**, 199–232.
Deutsch, M. (1958). Trust and suspicion, *Journal of Conflict Resolution*, **2**, 265–279.
*Deutsch, M. (1962). Cooperation and trust: some theoretical notes. In M. R. Jones (Ed.) *Nebraska Symposium on Motivation.* Lincoln, Neb.: University of Nebraska Press. Pp. 275–318.
*Deutsch, M. and H. B. Gerard (1955). A study of normative and informational social influences upon individual judgment. *Journal of abnormal and social psychology*, **51**, 629–636.
Heise, G. A. and G. A. Miller (1951). Problem solving by small groups using various communication nets. *Journal of abnormal and social psychology*, **46**, 327–336.
Hoffman, L. R. (1961). Conditions for creative problem solving. *Journal of Psychology*, **52**, 429–444.
Hoffman, L. R. and N. R. F. Maier (1961). Quality and acceptance of problem solutions by members of homogeneous and heterogeneous groups. *Journal of abnormal and social psychology*, **62**, 401–407.
Hoffman, L. R. and C. G. Smith (1960). Some factors affecting the behaviors of members of problem solving groups. *Sociometry*, **23**, 273–291.
Large, I., D. Fox, J. Davitz, and M. Brenner (1958). A survey of studies contrasting the quality of group performance and individual performance, 1920–1957. *Psychological Bulletin*, **55**, 337–372.

Leavitt, H. J. (1951). Some effects of certain communication patterns on group performance. In E. E. Maccoby et al. Readings in social psychology, 3rd ed., 1958, pp. 546–563. Also Journal of abnormal and social psychology, 46, 38–50.

Maier, N. R. F. and L. R. Hoffman (1960). Organization and creative problem solving. Journal of applied psychology, 45, 277–280.

Mann, R. D. (1961). Dimensions of individual performance in small groups under task and social-emotional conditions. Journal of abnormal and social psychology, 62, 674–682.

Morrissette, J. O., S. A. Switzer, and C. W. Crannel (1965). Group performance as a function of sign, structure and task difficulty. Journal of personality and social psychology, 2, 451–455.

Mulder, M. (1965). Communication structure, decision structure and group performance. In I. D. Steiner and M. Fishbein (Eds.) Current studies in social psychology. New York: Holt, Rinehart and Winston. Chap. 43, pp. 424–434.

Riecken, H. W. (1958). The effect of talkativeness on ability to influence group solutions to problems. Sociometry, 21, 309–321.

Shaw, M. E. (1954). Group structure and the behavior of individuals in small groups. Journal of psychology, 38, 139–149.

*Shaw, M. E. (1964). Communication networks. In L. Berkowitz (Ed.) Advances in experimental social psychology, Vol. 1. New York: Academic Press. Pp. 111–147.

Shaw, M. E. and J. M. Blum (1963). Effects of leadership style upon group performance as a function of task structure. Journal of personality and social psychology, 3, 238–242.

Shaw, M. E., G. H. Rothschild, and J. F. Strictland (1957). Decision processes in communication nets. Journal of abnormal and social psychology, 54, 323–330.

Siegel, A. E. and S. Siegel (1953). Reference groups, membership groups and attitude change. Journal of abnormal and social psychology, 55, 360–364. Also in Cartwright, D. and Zander, A. Group Dynamics: Research and Theory. New York: Harper & Row, 1968. Pp. 74–79.

The following are recommended texts in social psychology which include expanded discussions of the material in Psych City or include additional readings appropriate to the material in this book

Brown, R. (1965). Social psychology. New York: Free Press.

Krech, D. and R. S. Crutchfield (1948). Theory and problems in social psychology. New York: McGraw-Hill.

Krech, D., R. S. Crutchfield, and E. L. Ballachy (1962). Individual in society. New York: McGraw-Hill.

Lindesmith, A. R. and A. L. Strauss (1968). Social Psychology. New York: Holt, Rinehart and Winston.

Proshansky, H. and B. Seidenberg (1965). Basic Studies in social psychology. New York: Holt, Rinehart and Winston.

Secord, P. E. and C. W. Backman (1964). Social Psychology. New York: McGraw-Hill.

Steiner, I. D. and M. Fishbein (1965). Current studies in social psychology. New York: Holt, Rinehart and Winston.

TITLES IN THE PERGAMON GENERAL PSYCHOLOGY SERIES